THE DEMISE
OF THE DEVIL

And a number of those who practiced magic arts brought their books together and burned them in the sight of all; and they counted the value of them and found it came to fifty thousand pieces of silver. So the word of the Lord grew and prevailed mightily.

Acts 19:19-20

THE DEMISE
OF THE DEVIL

Magic and the Demonic
in Luke's Writings

SUSAN R. GARRETT

Fortress Press　　Minneapolis

THE DEMISE OF THE DEVIL
Magic and the Demonic in Luke's Writings

Scripture quotations are from the Revised Standard Version of the Bible, copyright © 1946, 1952, and 1971 by the Division of Christian Education of the National Council of Churches, adapted by the author according to the original language.

Jacket illustration: The harrowing of hell, c. 1200 (M. 44 F. 11). Courtesy the Pierpont Morgan Library, New York.

Cover and text design: Publishers' WorkGroup

Library of Congress Cataloging-in-Publication Data

Garrett, Susan R., 1958—
 The demise of the Devil : magic and the demonic in Luke's writings
/ Susan R. Garrett.
     p.   cm.
 Revision of the author's thesis (Ph. D.).
 Bibliography: p.
 Includes index.
 ISBN 0-8006-2409-2
 1. Magic—Biblical teaching. 2. Devil—Biblical teaching.
3. Bible. N.T. Luke—Criticism, interpretation, etc. 4. Bible.
N.T. Acts—Criticism, interpretation, etc. I. Title.
BS2589.6.M25G37 1989
226.4'0813343—dc20   89-36046
                                                              CIP

The paper used in this publication meets the minimum requirements of American National Standard for Information Sciences—Permanence of Paper for Printed Library Materials, ANSI 7329.48-1984. (∞)™

Manufactured in the U.S.A.   AF 1-2409

93   92   91   90   89   1   2   3   4   5   6   7   8   9   10

This book is dedicated to Barney L. Jones
Duke University Professor Emeritus
in friendship and in gratitude

CONTENTS

PREFACE

For many ancient Jewish and Christian authors, to talk about magic was at one and the same time to talk about the devil. I discovered this equivalence in researching what began as a study, not of the devil, but of Luke's treatment of magic in the Gospel and Acts. Hence I have written a book that is about both topics. It is my hope that the study will contribute to the ongoing scholarly discussions of ancient Jewish and Hellenistic magic and of Luke-Acts.

Many persons helped me with this book. I would especially like to thank Wayne Meeks of Yale University, who directed the dissertation out of which the present work grew. His advice was always astute and candid, and I have benefited from his insight at many points. Abraham Malherbe, Richard Hays, and Robert Wilson, also of Yale, likewise gave me considerable assistance with the project, for which I am appreciative. John A. Hollar, Senior Editor of Fortress Press, provided invaluable help throughout the editing process. Stefanie Ormsby Cox, Associate Editor, oversaw many details and capably directed the final editing. Craig Wansink prepared the indexes for the book. The complete list of others who provided helpful suggestions and critique is too long to enumerate, but I would especially like to single out Dale Martin of Duke University; David Tiede and David Fredrickson of Luther Northwestern Theological Seminary; Beverly Gaventa of Columbia Theological Seminary; and Hendrikus Boers, Carl Holladay, and Vernon Robbins of Emory University. Finally, above all I am grateful to my husband Jim for his patience, encouragement, and enthusiasm throughout the duration of the project.

I have dedicated the book to Barney Jones, Professor of Religion Emeritus at Duke University, a friend and guide to generations of Duke students. It is he who first encouraged me to pursue a career in teaching and research, and for this I will always be grateful.

SUSAN R. GARRETT

INTRODUCTION

One seldom finds unexplored territory within the New Testament. The subject of magic in the writings of Luke, however, has remained uncharted by modern interpreters. It is a subject to which Luke gives considerable attention: in the Gospel, Luke reports that Jesus was accused of sorcery (11:14-21). Three times in Acts, the evangelist depicts "magicians" who find their best efforts foiled when they dare to operate within the potential sphere of the Christian mission: Simon, the great magician of Samaria, is cursed by Peter for trying to buy Christian "authority" (Acts 8:4-25). Bar Jesus, a Jewish magician-false prophet, is blinded by Paul for attempting to impede Paul's proclamation of the word (13:4-12). And the seven sons of Sceva, Jewish exorcists operating in Ephesus, are stripped and flogged by a demon when they attempt to perform an exorcism in Jesus' name (19:11-20). This repetition of the motif of magic's failure indicates that magic was of enormous concern to Luke. But the nature of that concern has rarely been investigated.

Perhaps embarrassment has been partly to blame for the scholarly inattention. To some readers, the magic-incidents have seemed to be relics of a bygone mentality, not easily accessible to the modern scholarly mind, and not very relevant in the face of more pressing and contemporary theological questions. Moreover, the narratives portray Christians in what some have regarded as an unflattering light. Peter curses Simon Magus, and Paul inflicts blindness on Bar Jesus. It is Paul's own "sensationalist" miracles that provoke the antics of the seven sons of Sceva. The Christians' actions seem hardly to differ from those of the "magicians" whom they oppose! Such resemblances aggravate the interpretive problem faced by those persons in the academy and church who would prefer to leave Christianity's first-century mythological framework behind.

Of course there are many Christians today who affirm the reality of the demonic realm. Among such persons, one sometimes encounters resistance of another sort: the opinion that to study magic or the

1

occult is to incur danger, to commit a sacrilege, or both. This opposition pertains to study not only of the occult in the modern era, but also of the practice of magic in biblical times. Although magic was a part of everyday life in antiquity, analysis of its forms and of the ways it functioned in society is regarded as taboo. The attitude is exemplified by several letters to the editor in a recent issue of *Biblical Archaeology Review,* in which readers expressed their dismay over the journal's earlier review of *The Greek Magical Papyri in Translation* (ed. Hans Dieter Betz [Chicago: University of Chicago Press, 1986]). One reader warned,

> The realm of the supernatural is very real. Don't be deceived. And don't offer it to your readers as something that needs to be understood and studied. The Bible states it clearly: "Rebellion is as the sin of witchcraft." They are the same.[1]

Even the effort to understand what magic is about is declared to be incongruent with biblical faith and practice. But such an attitude is not as clearly supported by the biblical witness as this writer affirms. New Testament authors were themselves aware of the prevalence and use of magic in their society; they did not shun discussion of the subject.[2]

Whether the reason be embarrassment or piety, inattention to Luke's treatment of the motif of magic has interfered with appreciation of the evangelist's larger story. Luke uses the three accounts about magicians to make the theological point that Christians wield authority over the devil in the post-resurrection era. Before the passion, Jesus had described a vision in which he "saw Satan fall like lightning from the sky" (Luke 10:18). It is a premonition of victory over the foe whom Jesus has battled from the onset of his ministry—a victory, Luke hints, that is finally to be accomplished in Jesus' resurrection and ascension. After Jesus' ascension, those who call upon Jesus' name will have "authority to tread upon serpents and scorpions, and over all the power of the Enemy, and nothing shall hurt" them (Luke 10:19). Magicians—viewed as diabolical agents—are the perfect vehicle for Luke to illustrate Satan's impotence in the period after Jesus' exaltation to glory.

ACCUSATIONS OF MAGIC?

Jesus and his followers were themselves highly vulnerable to charges of practicing magic. All four evangelists record Jesus' self-defense against accusations that he was in league with demons—in other words, that he worked his wonders by the same means that sorcerers used (Mark 3:22-27 and parallels; John 7:20; 8:48-52).[3] And, as Jesus proclaims in Matthew, "If they have called the master of the house Beelzebul, how much more will they malign those of his household" (Matt. 10:25). It was urgent that the Gospel writers and early Christian apologists show that Jesus' and the church leaders' activities were not magical in character, especially since Christians' practice of casting out demons and healing the sick "in the name of Jesus"— who had been crucified as a criminal—looked very much like the feats of conventional magicians. Jesus qualified as a *biaiothanatos* (a person who had died a violent death), and the spirits of such persons were thought to be eager to return to earth. Such spirits were regarded by many persons as readily available to do the magician's work.[4]

Later Christian apologists did offer explicit and substantial defenses against charges that Christians practiced magic,[5] but the evidence of the New Testament itself seems inconsistent. For example, in his retelling of the miracles of Jesus, Matthew eliminated the more obvious magical traits, leading John M. Hull to title this Gospel "the tradition purified of magic."[6] But Matthew also tells of "magi" following a star, healings, exorcisms, and raisings from the dead. Luke and Acts appear even more ambiguous with regard to magic than does the Gospel of Matthew. On the one hand, Luke seems to have made an intentional effort to distance Jesus and the church leaders from magical notions. For example, the people's and Herod's opinion of Jesus related in Mark 6:14-16 amounted to a charge of necromancy (in other words, a charge that Jesus worked wonders by means of the raised-up spirit of the executed Baptist);[7] in his parallel Luke rephrases the most damaging parts of the account (Mark 6:14c, 16b; cf. Luke 9:7-9). This editorial move suggests that Luke wished to avoid the implication that Jesus used suspicious methods in his performance of miracles. In Acts, on the other hand, Luke shows the Christian leaders outdoing "magicians" at their own game (Acts 13:11; 19:11-12). Luke also describes a number of miracles that to the modern observer look "magical": the sentence against Ananias and Sapphira (Acts 5:1-11), the healings "in the name of Jesus," and the healings accomplished by Peter's shadow (5:15).

Are the evangelists really being inconsistent? Rather, is it not the case that the criteria used by modern readers (and by some ancient readers as well) to identify actions as "magical" conflict with criteria applied by the evangelists themselves? The evangelists did not share modern readers' frequent assumption that identity of appearance implies actual identity. As the Beelzebul incident (Mark 3:22-27 and

parallels) demonstrates, the evangelists acknowledged that with regard to appearance miraculous deeds could be ambiguous. According
to the synoptic writers—Matthew, Mark, and Luke—Jesus does not
deny the external similarity of his deeds to those done "by the power
of Beelzebul," but argues that proper interpretation of his casting out
of demons depends on factors not apparent to the human eye.

In attempting to resolve or explain the apparently conflicting data,
several recent studies of magic and the New Testament have addressed
questions about ontological status: was Jesus a "magician" or not?
Were such deeds as Peter's action against Ananias and Sapphira and
Paul's action against Bar Jesus magic or not? Such questions assume
that it is possible to define an essence of "magical" action and belief
which transcends social, cultural, or temporal boundaries. Often this
essence is said to involve the presence of certain attitudes, such as a
"manipulative" attitude versus the "supplicative" attitude of "religion," and the use of goal-oriented techniques. Interpreters who put
the questions in these terms see their task as one of measuring the
persons, actions, and ideas depicted in the New Testament or other
early Christian literature against preestablished definitions of "magicians" or of "magic" in order to determine whether there is an ob-
jective fit between them.

But this line of questioning is not helpful, because efforts to pinpoint
the essence of magic have been futile. Anthropological studies in the
past half-century have repeatedly shown that "magic" is as much a
locative or relational category as it is a substantive one: it serves to
differentiate between the person(s) labelling and the person(s) so
labelled.[8] The effort to define an unchanging, transcultural essence of
"magic" is therefore like trying to define such an essence of "vul-
garity" or "deviance." The task is impossible, because usage of the
labels depends on the culturally governed behavioral norms of the
persons involved, on their relative social locations, and on the complex
particularities of the given situation. How the labels are applied and
received will vary as the configuration of actors, norms, and social
circumstances varies. Applying an absolute definition of magic when
analyzing such a configuration will oversimplify the complexities and
muffle the contrasting opinions of the persons involved. To avoid
these pitfalls, the interpreter must ask a different set of questions
altogether—questions that permit as many as possible of the various
actors engaged in a dispute about magic to make their voices heard.

In the Greco-Roman world, accusations of magic typically occurred
in situations of social conflict. Because the use of magic was regarded

as socially unacceptable, labelling someone a "magician" was an effective way to squelch, avenge, or discredit undesirable behavior. Thus Apuleius of Madaura, who married a certain "Pudentilla" (a wealthy widow some years his senior), found himself in court rebutting charges that he had wooed her with magic, brought against him by relatives disgruntled because they stood to lose a large inheritance.[9] In bringing such charges, the relatives were engaging in a form of social discourse; in other words, by their actions they were *saying something,* not only to each other, but also to Apuleius, Pudentilla, and the community. For the modern reader of the *Apology* the ontological question (Was Apuleius a magician?) is not likely either to find a definitive answer or to cast light on the interaction between Apuleius and his accusers. More useful will be interpretive questions. For example, what did the concerted actions of Pudentilla's relatives say about their values, rules, and expectations pertaining to such matters as courtship, inheritance, the behavior of distinguished widows, interactions between town members and intruders, and acceptable methods of recourse against various types of wrongdoers? What were the culturally governed presuppositions about magic and magicians that made the charge against Apuleius plausible to some of the persons involved? What presuppositions shaped Apuleius's own defense? Analogous interpretive questions could be fruitfully addressed to the discourses concerning magic in the Gospels and Acts.[10]

WRITTEN TEXTS AND SOCIAL "TEXTS"

Clifford Geertz compares the flow of social discourse to a text, and the role of the ethnographer to that of the literary critic. He writes, "Doing ethnography is like trying to read (in the sense of 'construct a reading of') a manuscript—foreign, faded, full of ellipses, incoherencies, suspicious emendations, and tendentious commentaries, but written not in conventionalized graphs of sound but in transient examples of shaped behavior."[11] The metaphor can be elaborated: the ethnographer, like the literary critic, must pay close attention to symbolic forms and social relationships; must interpret the whole in relationship to the parts and vice versa; must highlight recurring patterns in the text; must show how an action performed or a word spoken in one place articulates, replicates, or confirms what is depicted elsewhere.[12] The metaphor succeeds, because texts and social discourse do indeed have many points in common. But the comparison can mislead the unwary interpreter of written narratives, which possess characteristics that social "texts" do not. It will be worthwhile to explore briefly these peculiarities of written narratives.

In narratives the interaction *between characters* is not genuine "social discourse," but highly abstracted and interpreted accounts of such discourse, "stories" that are one or more times removed from (if not fictitious inventions of) the social discourse that they depict. A narrative is itself a type of social discourse *between the author and the audience:* the author's selection, arrangement, and narration of events all convey a message. What narratives depict are humans (or other characters) engaged in action, that is, meaningful behavior. Even though this action is but a portrayal of "the real thing," interpretation of it will resemble the interpretation of actions witnessed firsthand.

Both the discourse between characters in a narrative and the discourse between author and audience must be interpreted "in context," but the pertinent contexts, though interrelated, are not identical. The primary context or framework governing discourse between characters in a narrative is the "narrative world," that is, the alternate reality or "finite province of meaning" into which the author draws his or her readers, and which is marked by circumscribed meanings and modes of experience.[13] The genre of the narrative and the author's use of such literary conventions as emplotment, point of view, and closure affect the shape and depth of the narrative world. To interpret the discourse between characters in a narrative "within the context of the narrative world," one must accept its "meanings" and "modes of experience" as determinative. When reading or watching *The Wizard of Oz,* one does not argue that witches do not exist and that scarecrows do not talk; instead, one takes their existence or speech for granted and moves on to learn something about them: there are both "good witches" and "bad witches," and scarecrows (because they are filled with straw) do not have brains. On the other hand, the context or framework for interpretation of discourse between an author and her or his readers is their "culture," consisting of the beliefs, myths, values, rules, and symbols that govern perceptions, thought, and behavior. In Geertz's terms, culture consists of the "webs of significance" that humans have themselves spun, and within which they are inescapably suspended: culture determines the meanings that humans attach to all that goes on in the world around them.[14]

Authors must rely on the culturally informed knowledge and beliefs of the readers to supplement the narrative world of a text, because the authors could no more explain every detail about every person or event in a narrative than could speakers define every word of every sentence spoken. Even in Oz some things must be assumed (Dorothy, being from Kansas, already knows what a "scarecrow" is, and so, presumably, does the reader). Consequently, when interpreting discourse between characters in a narrative, familiarity not only with the narrative world but also with the cultural world of the author is essential.

Luke remarks that his readers have already been instructed in the matters that he will relate (Luke 1:4).[15] Thus he implies that they share with him the most fundamental aspects of culture (knowledge about everyday behavior and life), as well as specialized knowledge from the Christian subculture. This specialized knowledge could have consisted of information or stories about Jesus, the apostles, Satan, false prophets, the characters and events depicted in the Septuagint, and a host of other subjects relevant to Luke's narrative. Readers who participated in this Christian subculture would have entered the narrative worlds of Luke and Acts with a larger story or series of stories (from which Luke and Acts are themselves interpretive selections and arrangements) already in their heads. When writer and readers approached the telling and hearing of Luke and Acts with a shared schema already in place, they could "fit in the pieces and negotiate the text more readily."[16]

The ethnographer studying social "texts" has several advantages over the interpreter of biblical texts. First, ethnographers observing the flow of social discourse know implicitly which culture provides the relevant framework for interpretation: it is the culture of the people acting, whom they are observing firsthand. Ethnographers can observe the actors over a period of time, can ask questions and get differing perspectives, can watch perhaps dozens of performances of the ritual or other occurrence under study. They can get prompt feedback, helping to clarify the questions asked and thereby to prevent the waste of time and effort in exploring issues that are incongruent with the thinking of the people who are the subject of study. Anthropologist James L. Peacock tells that he once asked an Indonesian, "Do you believe in spirits?" The man replied, puzzled, "Are you asking, do I believe what spirits tell me when they talk to me?"[17] Clearly the question needed to be revamped.

Interpreters of biblical texts cannot interview the authors of those texts. Furthermore, because so little is known about the social setting in which some of the biblical documents were produced, interpreters often do not even know for certain which culture or cultures are relevant to a given text. With regard to Luke and Acts this problem is acute, since the place of origin of the two works and identity of their author are much debated.[18] Was Luke an inhabitant of country, town, or city, and in what part of the empire? What was his ethnic origin? Was he a Christian of the second generation, or of the third? What was the character of his and his community's relationship to Jews and to pagans in their locale? The answers to these and many other questions concerning Luke's environment would bear significantly on the interpreter's assessment of Luke's culture. Since we do not know the answers, we must "read between the lines," trying to make educated guesses.

Fortunately, even if Luke's specific social setting is unknown to us, some aspects of his culture pertinent to his understanding and portrayal of magic can be inferred (here *culture* may be defined as the beliefs, myths, values, rules, and symbols that shaped experience for Luke and for others in the same social setting). One makes such inferences by comparing Luke's discussion of magic with analogous discussions in contemporaneous, culturally related sources. Here the method is necessarily circular: one learns which sources are "culturally related" by noticing which cultural traditions Luke's writings appear most frequently to reflect, that is, by noticing where the "parallels" cluster. To anticipate the findings of chapters 2-5 below, Luke's discussion of magic most often reflects traditions exhibited also in such Jewish or Jewish-influenced documents (several with apocalyptic tendencies) as the Septuagint (LXX), the Dead Sea Scrolls, *Jubilees, Martyrdom of Isaiah, Testament of Job, Pseudo-Philo,* the Book of Revelation, and *Shepherd of Hermas;* traditions such as are found in the *Testament of Solomon* and the largely pagan magical papyri appear to have played a lesser, though not negligible, role. These findings are in accord with the recent contention of some scholars that Luke identified very strongly with the Jewish tradition, even if he was not himself a Jew by ethnic origin.[19]

The culture in terms of which the ethnographer interprets a particular instance of social discourse is never "the thing itself," but always an abstraction or interpretation, based on observation of the way a people thinks, expresses, acts.[20] No matter how many hours of observation the ethnographer has logged, or how systematically and objectively the data have been elicited, subjectivity in describing "culture" cannot be escaped. As Geertz observes, "what we call our data are really our own constructions of other people's constructions of what they and their compatriots are up to."[21] The subjectivity of the scholar of antiquity, attempting to piece together relevant bits of a long-lost culture so as to illuminate an ancient text, differs from that of the ethnographer in degree but not in kind. For both interpreters—provided that they also aim for a balancing objectivity, by allowing the categories and concerns of those who are under study to guide the research questions—a certain degree of subjectivity need not be feared. As Peacock notes, the aim is to produce an interpretation that has been filtered through the interpreter's own experience and world view, but that is nevertheless "focused sharply and precisely on the world of the native."[22]

INTERPRETING MAGIC IN LUKE'S WRITINGS

I begin my study with an introduction to ancient magic and to some of the problems faced by those who seek to understand it. In the subsequent interpretation of Luke's treatment of the motif of magic, I proceed at two levels. At the first level (comprising the main portions of chapters 2—5) I interpret the discourse between characters in the narrative by viewing it within the context of the narrative world. For example, in the effort to hear what Paul and Bar Jesus were "saying" by their respective actions and words (Acts 13:4-12), I consider such issues as the editorial treatment of false prophets elsewhere in the narrative, the placement of the Bar Jesus incident in the overall plot, the development of Paul's character prior and subsequent to this incident, and the narrative silence concerning Bar Jesus' ultimate fate. Since at every turn Luke presumes knowledge of his own cultural (or perhaps "subcultural") world, I allow this latter sphere to extend and supplement the narrative world. In practice this means that I offer parallels from contemporaneous Jewish and Christian documents to illuminate what are, to the modern reader, obscure points in the narrative.

At the second level I interpret the discourse between Luke and his readers by setting it in the context of their cultural world. In the "summary and analysis" sections of chapters 2—5, I identify Luke's emphases when talking about magic and magicians, and ask what these emphases reveal about the symbolic function of magic in Luke's culture. Here I briefly compare texts derived from persons or communities that used or perceived magic in ways that are better understood, such as the magical papyri. In the conclusion to my study, I attempt to describe the discourse that Luke carried on with his readers by means of his portrayal of magic and magicians. Were there specific problems or issues that Luke addressed through these accounts? Luke was an artist as well as a teacher and pastor, and was surely motivated as much by a desire to articulate his insights into Christian beginnings—to express himself—as by the need to deal with specific problems. His narration probably was not limited by his real readers' needs or by their ability to appreciate narrative subtleties. But phrasing the question in terms of problems or issues addressed by Luke's account should help to focus our attention on the crucial interpretive issues— on understanding what was being "said" and "heard" when Luke wrote about magic and magicians.

The topic of magic and earliest Christianity can provoke strong emotional responses, including embarrassment or indignation. How unfortunate it would be if these emotions prevented us from discerning the early Christians' own responses to the topic! Luke's particular treatment was extensive and consistent: he demonstrated that magicians have no chance of success in the new era inaugurated by Christ's resurrection. Luke suggested that the failure of human and visible magicians shows the impotence of the inhuman and invisible spiritual powers upon which they draw. Moreover, Luke's treatment of magic and magicians bears upon the interpretation of all of Luke-Acts. The trio of passages about magicians is an unexplored hillside overlooking the Lukan terrain. From this vantage point the observer confronts familiar territory from an unfamiliar angle. Some will regard the scene as startling; others will see it as beautiful—others, perhaps, as incredible. In any case, I hope that readers will find the view to be well worth the climb.

1

MAGIC AND THE
STUDY OF MAGIC

MAGIC IN THE GRECO-ROMAN WORLD

The Prevalence of Magic

Although there were widespread prohibitions against it, magic flourished in the Greco-Roman world.[1] Pliny the Elder comments that this "most fraudulent of arts has held complete sway throughout the world for many ages."[2] The attractions of magic—promises of power, protection, love, health, and knowledge—often appeared great enough to outweigh its disadvantages. The ambivalence of Lucius in Apuleius's *The Golden Ass* may have been typical: he knew that magic was wrong, but he could not resist the temptation to steal in and observe his Thessalian hostess as she plied her evil trade. He narrates, "so far from feeling inclined to be on my guard against Pamphilë I had an irresistible impulse to study magic under her, however much money it might cost me, and take a running leap into the dark abyss against which I had been warned."[3] Perhaps most people never saw a professional magician in action, but the techniques of such professionals were widely discussed, and many people used similar, homemade incantations and remedies. Ramsay MacMullen concludes that

> the total of the evidence affirms the belief of people of the time that the
> strength of their spirit could be increased by the right practices or that

another spirit could be engaged to reach out against their enemies. The ancient world was as tangled in a crisscross of invisible contracts, so it might be thought, as our modern world is entangled in radio beams.[4]

In short, everyone seemed to agree that magic was wrong, but a great many people tried to make use of it nonetheless.

The word *magos* was borrowed from Persia. In the sixth century B.C.E., if not earlier, it was an official title for the priestly Median tribe.[5] But as Arthur Darby Nock points out, already in the fifth century B.C.E. it is used to mean "quack" (as the word *goēs* often came to be used).[6] The word continued to be used in both positive and negative senses, often retaining its aura of something "Persian" and mysterious. When Apuleius is accused of being a magician in the mid-second century C.E., he can turn the tables on his accusers by exploiting the word's positive connotations. He remarks:

> Aemilianus' slander was focused on one point: that I am a sorcerer. So let me ask his most learned advocates: What is a sorcerer? I have read in many books that *magus* is the same thing in Persian as *priest* in our language. What crime is there in being a priest and in having accurate knowledge, a science, a technique of traditional ritual, sacred rites and traditional law, if magic consists of what Plato interprets as the "cult of the gods" when he talks of the disciplines taught to the crown prince in Persia? . . . Listen to this, you who rashly slander magic! It is an art acceptable to the immortal gods, an art which includes the knowledge of how to worship them and pay them homage. It is a religious tradition dealing with things divine, and it has been distinguished ever since it was founded by Zoroaster and Ormazd, the high priests of divinities. In fact, it is considered one of the chief elements of royal instruction, and in Persia no one is allowed lightly to be a "magus" any more than they would let him be king.[7]

But Apuleius depicts the case as more clear-cut than it apparently was. Pliny the Elder had expressed less charitable opinions about the magical activities of not only Plato, but also Osthanes, Pythagoras, Empedocles, and Democritus.[8] Pliny ascribes to the Magi a wide variety of potions and practices, but it is not certain that all these ascriptions are justified: the way Pliny intermingles recipes "from the Magi" with folk recipes suggests that the ultimate source of such recipes may sometimes have been a matter of speculation.[9] Since Magi-priests were thought to perform strange and incomprehensible rites, they apparently began to be credited with any and all such rites. One should not infer, however, that Greco-Roman magic was no more than a haphazard collection of folk recipes of unknown origin. By the first century C.E. there were distinct bodies of magical lore, "a kind of curriculum of occult sciences"[10] that included divination,[11] astrology, and alchemy.

The magical papyri, which are ancient "recipe books" or "instruction manuals" used by practicing magicians, provide our most valuable source of information for the sorts of ritual proceedings in which magicians actually engaged.[12] Other valuable firsthand evidence for the practice of magic are magical charms and amulets, and curse tablets *(tabellae defixionum)*.[13] Complementing the archeological finds are literary sources. Pliny's *Natural History* and Apuleius's *Apologia* are among the most valuable literary sources from the first two centuries. Also highly informative are Apuleius's *Golden Ass,* Lucian's *Menippus* and *The Lover of Lies,* and Lucan's *Pharsalia,* all of which purport to describe encounters with professional magicians. Other tales of magic and of magicians both male and female can be found in Greek and Latin literature ranging from Homer through Theocritus and Horace to Vergil.[14]

As David E. Aune suggests, ancient magic is best understood as having existed within the matrix of particular religious traditions.[15] It was a component part of Judaism and later of Christianity, as it was of other Greco-Roman cults. Jews in antiquity had a reputation for practicing magic. Moreover, Moses' role as a wonderworker and recipient of divine wisdom and the Jews' legendary knowledge of the divine name made Jewish lore attractive also to non-Jews interested in magic; such appeal may partially account for Jewish elements in the magical papyri.[16]

Magic in the Jewish Context

As P. Samain had noted,[17] discussions about magic in the Jewish and Christian world were often symbolized differently than analogous discussions in pagan circles. The picture gleaned from a variety of Jewish and Jewish-influenced texts (dating from the late second temple period through the early second century C.E.) is one in which magic, false prophecy, and satanic agency are integrally linked. I will briefly sketch the picture here, since it will bear significantly on this study of magic in Luke-Acts.

The notion of a link between false prophets and magic may date to as early as the time of the translation of the Septuagint in the third century B.C.E. J. Reiling has examined the frequency and contexts of the term "false prophet" *(pseudoprophētēs)* in the Septuagint, Philo, and Josephus.[18] Reiling points out that there is no term equivalent to *pseudoprophētēs* in the Masoretic text, and in the Septuagint the newly

coined word occurs only ten times, with all occurrences being a ren-
dering of the Hebrew *nabîʾ* and all in Jeremiah and Zechariah. But
since even in these two writings the term does not appear in every
context where one might expect it, scholars have often regarded its
use as interpretative. Reiling observes that as long as there was no
category equivalent to *pseudoprophētēs*, the problem of prophetic conflict had remained firmly situated in the heart of the Yahwistic religion.
But apparently the Septuagint translator's understanding of prophecy
could not easily encompass "two prophets in utter conflict with one
another and both claiming to proclaim the word of Jahweh." So the
translator introduced the category of the *pseudoprophētēs*, thereby pre-
judging the issue.[19] Reiling suggests that the translators tended to
resort to the easy escape when the text suggested "an association
between prophecy and pagan divination."[20] For example, in Jer. 27:9
(LXX 34:9) and 29:8 (LXX 36:8), the "false prophets" appear together
with soothsayers and dreamers, condemned throughout the Hebrew
scriptures as pagan. Even more striking is Zech. 10:2, where the
expression "unclean spirit" (referring to the inspiration of the prophets) suggests that the translator saw false prophecy as not only pagan,
but also demonic.

The association between pagan divination and false prophecy may
have been fostered in part by the structural layout of certain Deuteronomic teachings on the two subjects. Because of the physical and
conceptual proximity of passages teaching about pagan diviners on
the one hand (Deut. 18:9-14) and evil, idolatrous prophets on the
other (18:20-22; cf. 13:1-5), readers may have inferred that the diviners and the evil prophets were identical. The inference would have
been reasonable: it is explicitly stated that the evil prophets likewise
promote idolatry (18:20)[21] and perform signs and wonders (13:1-2).

The readers' own experience apparently reinforced this conceptual
fusion. Prophets and diviners were not always so very different from
one another. Their functional similarity is illustrated by a passage in
Pseudo-Philo, where the author elaborates on Saul's reasons for consulting the witch of Endor:

> And God said, "Behold Saul has not driven the wizards *(malefici)* out of
> the land for fear of me, but to make a name for himself. Behold he will
> go to those whom he has scattered, to obtain divination *(divinatio)* from
> them, because he has no prophets."
>
> (Pseudo-Philo 64:1)[22]

Since "prophets" and "wizards" often had the identical aim of pro-
viding wisdom beyond that available through everyday human chan-
nels,[23] and since there were few if any locales in the Hellenistic and

Roman periods where either Jewish or Christian prophets were entirely isolated from their pagan counterparts, reciprocal influence was always a possibility.[24] The charge that a given "prophet" utilized pagan "magic" (i.e., divinatory methods) and therefore qualified as "false" must have been valid in some cases. In Christianity, where many believers were former pagans, the likelihood of influence from pagan divinatory practice was even greater. Evidence indicates that by the early part of the second century c.e., Hellenistic revelatory traditions had influenced some Christian circles. A striking example of such influence, *Shepherd of Hermas, Mandate* 11, will be discussed subsequently, but first it will be useful to look at several texts of Jewish origin.

The *Martyrdom of Isaiah*, a document that apparently originated in the first century c.e. or earlier,[25] weaves the motifs of false prophecy, magic, and Satan (alias Sammael Malkira, Beliar, Matanbukus, and Mekembekus) into a single short narrative about a true prophet who suffered a violent death. At the opening of the narrative Isaiah prophesies how Manasseh will bring about the prophet's death at the instigation of Beliar:

> And Sammael Malkira will serve Manasseh and will do everything he wishes, and he will be a follower of Beliar rather than of me. He will cause many in Jerusalem and Judah to desert the true faith, and Beliar will dwell in Manasseh, and by his hands I will be sawed in half.
> *(Martyrdom of Isaiah* 1:8-9)

Because of Manasseh's alliance with Sammael, not only apostasy but also "sorcery and magic, augury and divination, fornication and adultery, and the persecution of the righteous" are said to have increased (2:5). Belkira, a Samaritan false prophet of the family of Zedekiah, prophesies lies in Jerusalem and causes many to join with him (3:1). He fabricates charges against Isaiah, including even the shameless accusation of false prophecy. Manasseh and his cohorts believe these charges because Beliar dwells in their hearts (3:11). Finally Beliar, acting through Manasseh and Belkira, has Isaiah sawed in half with a wood saw (5:1-14). The author views the climactic interchange between Belkira and Isaiah as a confrontation between Satan and the Holy Spirit.

An association between Satan and magic is made in other Jewish documents from the late Second Temple period. *Jubilees* attributes to Satan, called "Prince Mastema," a role in the Exodus account:

> And Prince Mastema stood up before you [Moses] and desired to make you fall into the hand of Pharaoh. And he aided the magicians of the

Egyptians, and they stood up and acted before you. Thus we let them do evil, but we did not empower them with healing so that it might be done by their hands. And the Lord smote them with evil wounds and they were unable to stand because we destroyed [their ability] to do any single sign.

(Jubilees 48:9-11)[26]

The passage is paralleled in the Damascus document (from the Qumran sectarians):

For in ancient times, Moses and Aaron arose by the hand of the Prince of Lights and Satan in his cunning raised up Jannes and his brother when Israel was first delivered.

(CD 5:17b-19)[27]

In the latter text, the example of "Jannes and his brother," the magicians of Pharaoh, is cited as a scriptural precedent for the rise of false teachers, expected to occur as part of the eschatological drama.[28] Such false teachers or false prophets were expected to lead the people astray into idolatry and perform signs and wonders. The false teachers/prophets were a frequent topic of discussion in Judaism around the turn of the millennium, as was the "Prophet like Moses." The myths surrounding the false teachers, false prophets, and the "Prophet like Moses" shared the relevant passages from Deuteronomy 13 and 18 (13:1-5; 18:18-22; discussed above) as a common point of origin, and were key components of the end-time expectations of various groups, including some groups of Christians. Mark 13:22; Matt. 24:11, 24; 2 Thess. 2:3-10; Rev. 13:11-14; 19:20; and *Didache* 16.4 all describe evil figures—"false prophets," "false Christs," "the lawless one," "the deceiver of the world"—who will use signs and wonders to lead people astray.

In general the "signs and wonders" to be performed by the false prophets or false Christs are not explicitly identified as "magic." But even if *mageia, goēteia,* or related words seldom appear, in view of the ancient propensity to label an enemy's "miracles" as "magic," such an identification may often have been presupposed. In the Book of Revelation, for example, the attribution of "magical" deeds to an eschatological false prophet seems to lie just under the surface. The "false prophet" (19:20) who exercises the authority of the beast from the sea (which in turn derives its authority from Satan, the dragon) "works great signs, even making fire come down from heaven to earth in the sight of humans, and by the signs that it is allowed to work in the presence of the beast it deceives those who dwell on earth, bidding them make an image for the beast which was wounded by the sword and yet lived" (13:13-14). David E. Aune has shown that throughout the Apocalypse, the seer John carried on a polemic against pagan magic; therefore it seems likely that John conceived of the false prophet's signs as feats of "magic."[29] Apparently John believed that, in the last days, magic and false prophecy would be Satan's primary means for compelling humans to worship him.

The notion that magic was linked to false prophecy and to Satan was familiar to the author of the *Shepherd of Hermas* (early second century). In *Mandate* 11, Hermas sees a vision of a man sitting on a chair and is told that the man is a false prophet, who corrupts the understanding of the servants of God. The revealing angel tells Hermas that by filling the false prophet with the devil's own spirit, the devil enables him to speak some true words, "to see if he can break any of the righteous" *(Mandate* 11.2-3). In an extensive analysis of *Mandate* 11, J. Reiling demonstrated that the terminology and concepts exhibited in the description of true and false prophets derive substantially from the world of pagan magical divination.[30] The author of the *Mandate* rejected such divination wholeheartedly, and was "clearly intent on bringing out how deeply this form of paganism had made its way into the Christian community."[31] It is therefore ironic that the terminology of magical divination is even reflected in the author's description of the divine spirit. Based on Reiling's analysis of the *Shepherd of Hermas, Mandate* 11, one can conclude that the association of Satan, false prophecy, and magic could survive and even intensify when Christianity took root in a predominantly pagan milieu.

Persistent Questions

Our sources for the study of ancient magic, though rich, leave many of our questions unanswered. The papyri and other artifacts inform us in detail about the techniques of practicing magicians, and literary sources describe the origin, character, and actions of mythical magicians. But the relationship between these figures remains in the dark. Did the "myth of the magus" shape the behavior of actual aspirants to the role? Or was it rather the case that the "myth" depicted accurately a social type whom many people had encountered? In a similar vein, did the seamstress who used a secret, homemade charm to gain a lover's favor imitate techniques that she supposed a professional magician would have used?[32] Or did the professionals merely adopt and embroider beliefs and practices already rife in society? Of course both sets of questions pose chicken-or-egg dilemmas: surely the myth and the reality of the magician were mutually reinforcing.

Surely magicians capitalized on folk magic as much as practitioners of folk magic borrowed from the magicians. Any effort to discover "magical influence" in ancient texts will be problematic: who or what was influencing whom?

Other questions that our sources hardly begin to answer concern the use of accusations of magic in the Greco-Roman world. What types of behavior prompted accusations? Were deeds resembling those of mythical magicians the catalyst?[33] Or were infractions of social norms more often the true provocation (as in the case of Apuleius, whose past actions were blown up by his opponents into implausible charges of magician-like behavior)? Once accusations had been leveled, what apologetic strategies would successfully refute them?[34] And how did the form of accusations and of apologetic strategies vary from one social setting to the next? The answers to such questions would help us to make more sense of the polemical and apologetic undertones of ancient texts about alleged wonderworkers.

As recent studies have shown, in polemical contexts in the Greco-Roman world there was seldom a clear-cut answer as to the significance of extraordinary deeds. Criteria according to which wondrous deeds ought to be evaluated were a source of constant dispute; even where conflicting parties ostensibly agreed about the criteria, they would subtly reinterpret these according to both their own view of the world and the polemical or apologetic needs of the moment. Alan F. Segal observes that the meaning of "magic" changed as the context in which it was used changed.[35] One can carry this argument a step further by suggesting that in the Greco-Roman world assertions about magic were useful in so many different contexts precisely because magic had no unambiguous, universally acknowledged meaning. E. Gellner has argued that

> nothing is more false than the claim that, for a given assertion, *its use is its meaning*. On the contrary, its use may depend on its lack of meaning, its ambiguity, its possession of wholly different and incompatible meanings in different contexts, *and* on the fact that, at the same time, it as it were emits the impression of possessing a consistent meaning throughout—on retaining, for instance, the aura of a justification valid only in one context when used in quite another.[36]

Gellner asserts that the very lack of a clear-cut denotation can govern the use of a particular concept. In such instances, the effort to provide such a denotation will do violence to the concept and prohibit a deep comprehension of its use. Given the broad range of its connotations in antiquity, it appears that "magic" was an irreducibly ambiguous concept. Recognition of this ambiguity in turn casts a shadow on those recent studies of magic and the New Testament that employ rigid definitions of or sets of identifying criteria for magic. Such definitions or criteria take for granted that which early Christians regarded as open to dispute.

MAGIC AND THE NEW TESTAMENT

Foundational Research

Earlier in this century, scholars demonstrated that there are intriguing points of resemblance between the miracle accounts in the canonical Gospels and ancient magical traditions. For example, Adolf Deissmann noted that the Gospels' occasional references to someone's tongue or body being "bound" may not be simply metaphorical, as had often been assumed: rather they may be analogous to the magical notion that a person could be bound by a demon or a chthonic deity.[37] As a second example, Campbell Bonner pointed out the "mystical and magical associations" of the words *stenazein* and *anastenazein* ("sigh" or "groan") in two Markan passages (Mark 7:34 and Mark 8:12). Bonner adduced instances in the magical papyri where such inhalation was meant to augment the magician's power.[38] Bonner wrote, "Deep inhalation would be regarded as an act of preparation by the prophet or wonder-worker before making an authoritative utterance or an exertion of miraculous power; the inarticulate sound produced would be interpreted as evidence of possession by a spirit."[39] He further argued that the word *embrimasthai*, which like *stenazein* and *anastenazein* was usually interpreted as a reference to strong emotion, can in two of its New Testament occurrences (Mark 1:43 and John 11:33) be better illuminated by reference to magic-related texts. Bonner claimed that when used of the behavior of a prophet, magician, or wonder-worker, *embrimasthai* signified a frenzy or raving that preceded wondrous deeds. He pointed out that such an interpretation of the word in its occurrence in John 11:33 (in the account of the raising of Lazarus) is strengthened by the technical coloring of the accompanying word *tarassein*, which probably designated the visitation of a demonic power.[40]

Bonner's contention that the Gospel miracle traditions occasionally use technical language similar to that found in the magical literature received corroboration from a work published at about the same time by Otto Bauernfeind.[41] Bauernfeind examined Mark 1:24, 3:11, and 5:7 in light of parallels in magical and other sources, and concluded that the verses depict stereotypical confrontations between the satanic

forces and the exorcist.[42] Bauernfeind believed that the exclamations
in these verses represent attempts by the demons to use magical
adjurations to defend themselves against Jesus' power; his commands
of silence are in turn meant to cut off the demons' defensive efforts.
Bauernfeind insisted that the sayings uttered by the possessed and
attributed to demons, together with Jesus' responses, were part of the
miracle traditions from the outset: these traditions accurately transmit
historical reactions of possessed persons upon encountering Jesus, the
great exorcist.[43]

Although Anton Fridrichsen approved of most of Bauernfeind's
findings, Fridrichsen argued that Bauernfeind's effort to demonstrate
the historicity of the demonic statements was ill-conceived. Fridrichsen said that the statements are better understood as apologetic ad-
ditions, making the point that Jesus could not have been in league
with Beelzebul since even the demons recognized him as the Holy
One of God.[44] Fridrichsen was not surprised to find such apologetic
motifs within the New Testament. In an earlier work,[45] Fridrichsen
had shown that the resemblances between magical jargon and practice
and the miracle traditions of the church had created a serious problem
for the early Christians, including the New Testament authors. Although the miracle accounts were a useful missionary tool, they also
caused embarrassment because they resembled accounts about char-
latans and sorcerers. Consequently, according to Fridrichsen, the miracle stories were always balanced with apology. Fridrichsen reviewed
the charges of magic against Jesus and Christian miracle workers,
leveled by outsiders ranging from the Pharisees (in the Beelzebul
account) to Celsus, and also studied the Christian responses. He noted
that even Christians who spoke approvingly of miracles often count-
ered their approval with warnings not to overvalue them.[46] Although
it is possible to quibble with specific points of Fridrichsen's exegesis,
one can hardly dispute his contention that the miracle traditions
created a problem for the earliest Christians, and that anti-magic
apology was therefore prevalent in Christian writings.[47]

The difference of opinion between Bauernfeind and Fridrichsen
about when the "magical" coloring entered the Gospel miracle traditions persists to the present day. Any simple answer to this question
runs the danger of being not only simple but simplistic, since there
is evidence to support both positions. Further, one should not assume
that apologetically motivated editors would always have removed the
so-called magical elements. As Fridrichsen noted, the Gospel portrayals of demonic cries made in response to Jesus' exorcistic efforts

may have been added for the very purpose of defending Jesus against charges that he was in league with Satan (that is, that he practiced magic). Fridrichsen's theory suggests that the editors of the miracle stories regarded the source of the power backing Jesus as more significant than the particular words used in describing exorcisms.[48] It appears that these words (and other so-called magical techniques and actions identified in the Gospels), although offensive to some early Christians, could also be interpreted in other, more positive ways.[49] The task of the modern interpreter is to determine how context and culture allowed a given incident to offend some believers while being regarded as acceptable by others.

One scholar who engaged in such contextual and cultural analysis was P. Samain, who argued that those with whom Jesus came in contact must have had to consider the possible relationship between Jesus and magic.[50] In Jewish and post–New Testament literature one can discern many traces of calumnies against Jesus that categorized him as a charlatan or sorcerer. Therefore, Samain contended, one ought to look closely to see whether such traces might also be discernible within the Gospels. Samain warned that the traces might not be obvious, since Jews and Christians translated the concept of magic into their own religious language:

> Without embracing Iranian dualism, the world is understood as the arena of the struggle between God who incarnates Good and an Adversary who incarnates Evil; two empires are in opposition, one governed by God and his Angels, the other by Satan and the demons. The battle has been fought ever since these demons, fallen angels, undertook to bring evil to the human race. Each party is represented visibly on earth by a series of human-lieutenants. Prophets are countered by false prophets, apostles by false apostles, Christ by the Antichrist. And as God gives his "saints" the power to accomplish miracles giving credence to their mission, Satan and his satellites give to their agents the power to accomplish wondrous feats which are, or at least appear to be, equivalent. These "sons of the devil" who perform wonders are the magicians.[51]

Since in such circles the magician was seen as the enemy of God, the minister of Satan, accusations of magic might be phrased as accusations of a pact with the devil.

Samain's attention to the differences between Jewish and Christian discussions of magic on the one hand, and analogous discussions in pagan circles on the other enabled him to detect and to explore neglected New Testament discussions about magic. For example, Samain demonstrated that the words *planos* (deceiver) and *planē* (deceit) in Matt. 27:63 allude to the opinion of Jesus' enemies that Jesus, who "deceived" the crowd by his speech and his illusions, was a charlatan (a magician who only created the appearance of wonders).[52] Samain supported this reading with the observations that in apocalyptic literature the verb *planan* (to deceive or lead astray) designates the actions of false prophets or false Christs, and that at least once in such a context (Matt. 24:24) the word is closely tied to a description of magical works. As a second example, Samain showed that the expression *daimonion echeis* at John 7:20 should be understood as implying that Jesus was a magician-false prophet, whose wondrous works are acccomplished by the devil. Samain noted that the same thoughts emerge even more clearly in John 8:48-52, where the Jews perceive that Jesus is presenting himself as a prophet, and reject him as false: "That is tantamount to declaring him a magician, because one cannot forget his miracles: if his speeches come from Satan, his miracles have the same origin, and he is a magician by definition."[53] A similar conclusion is drawn for the accusation at John 10:20. Samain observed that the accusations he had uncovered in the Gospel of John are quite similar to the synoptic charge that Jesus "has Beelzebul."[54] All the charges amount to Jewish or Christian versions of the accusation of magic: Jesus is believed to be a man whose power derives from Satan. In the cited cases and in others, Samain showed how important it is for the modern interpreter to recognize the wide variety of culturally conditioned expressions used in antiquity to depict magic and association with the devil. This recognition is foundational to this volume.

Recent Research

During the earlier phase of research on magic and the New Testament, little attention was given to the questions about ontological status which would come to dominate later research on the subject: Was Jesus a magician or not? Were the remarkable deeds of the church leaders as depicted in the Acts of the Apostles magic or not? Scholars who have recently addressed such questions have typically proceeded by establishing at the outset a particular definition of magic. Then they measure the actions and words depicted in the New Testament to see whether these fit the definition. Of course the results of the investigations have depended on the definitions chosen. Because these definitions are not always consistent with the authors' and their immediate audiences' own understandings of "magic" and "magicians," this approach has seldom been able to explicate what was being "said" and "heard" in the depicted social discourse. A brief overview of this approach will illustrate its shortcomings, in clarification and defense of the alternate approach that I take in this study.

In several provocative books, Morton Smith[55] has argued that the Jesus of history was indeed a magician: the Gospels portray him as doing "the things that magicians do," as known primarily from the magical papyri, ostraka, and curse tablets. Smith provides this seemingly practical definition of magician because he recognizes that abstract definitions often do not fit the evidence,[56] but the practical approach has its own problems.[57] The evangelists, Smith contends, tried to expunge or at least whitewash the blatantly magical features of Jesus' ministry, but the synoptic traditions are so thoroughly imbued with magical elements that these could never be totally eliminated or disguised. To be sure, some of these magical elements (for example, reports of the use of spittle or of touch in healing) were cut out when Matthew and Luke took over material from Mark. But other such elements (for example, the claims that Jesus was the Son of God, the miracles themselves, the Eucharist,[58] and Jesus' own magical baptism[59]) could not be excised without destroying the very heart of the tradition. Thus the evidence for Jesus' identity as a magician shines through the Gospels and Acts, despite the evangelists' best attempts to eliminate or at least hide it.[60] Furthermore, contends Smith, this identity is confirmed by the opinions of outsiders, such as the rabbis and Celsus, who insistently maintained that Jesus was a magician.[61]

Smith posits the existence in antiquity of the "social type" of the magician—called by various titles, including "divine man," "son of God," or "magician" (goēs or magos), depending on social status, success, and who was doing the calling.[62] Smith suggests that "with the difference in pretensions goes a supposed difference of technique," and probably also a difference in the experience of practitioner and customer.[63] The magical papyri, reflecting these differences, include a smorgasbord of material, ranging from simple "do-it-yourself" spells to elaborate rituals, but the differences are ones "of form, not of essential content." Smith writes,

> The difference reflects that between the do-it-yourself world of the peasants and the slave service available to the rich. Theologically (or demonologically?), however, as the magical texts show, this difference is one of form, not of essential content. And this fact is reflected by the terminology. Once the requirements of social status and decorum are met, the same man will customarily be called a *theios anēr*, or son of a god, by his admirers, a magician by his enemies. Within this area all three terms refer to a single social type, and that type is the one characterized by the actions listed above [*Clement of Alexandria*, 222–27],

which make up by far the greatest part of the Gospels' reports about Jesus.[64]

Smith's observation that ancient wonder-workers were labelled one way by their supporters and another way by their enemies is accurate. Requiring closer examination, however, is his contention that such wonder-workers, in spite of their "original diversity" and "the diversity of theological explanations and consequent titles imposed on them," all belong to a single "social type." According to Smith, differences pertaining to the status of the practitioner, the setting in which the "magical" actions were carried out, and the opinions of practitioner or audience are irrelevant in the face of the parallel actions and techniques. Thus we are left with a "social type" that has nothing "social" about it, because all social factors and characteristics have been disqualified. Assessments of the identity of the practitioner and of the significance of his or her actions depend on the actions alone; contrary opinions of wonder-worker or bystanders result from their misguided "apologetic interests" or from other factors obscuring the "essential content" of the action or technique.

As Smith contends, ancient charismatic leaders who engaged in ritual acts, such as healing and purification, were often called "magicians" by their enemies. But this understanding of events was often conditioned by the enemies' social location relative to the "suspects," and by their desire for domination and control. Therefore this evaluation should not be allowed to obscure the more positive point of view of the charismatics and their supporters. Like language, ritual acts are socially transmitted and contextually dependent. Hence, they have "meaning" only as it is attributed to them by actors and observers (enemies *and* supporters), whose various interpretations are guided by their respective social locations and by the shape of their own cultural world. Smith's "social type," abstracted "with the eye of historical faith" from the "many different patterns" of ancient holy men, is an analytic category biased in favor of the accusers. In subsuming all wonder-workers under the heading of "magician," Smith precludes any chance of understanding the point of view of the sympathizers. The only way to achieve such understanding is to look more carefully than Smith looks at what those sympathizers actually said about their leader, vis-à-vis what they said about the persons whom they themselves labelled "magicians."

In arguing that Jesus was a magician because he "did the things magicians do," Smith assumes that the direction of influence was entirely one-directional, that is, "magic" and "magicians" influenced

Jesus. But as others have pointed out, it is problematic to conclude that whatever has a parallel in the magical papyri must necessarily derive from magical practice.[65] This holds even if one accepts a first-century or earlier date for the traditions underlying the magical papyri in their present form.[66] That the beliefs and practices of the magicians were not invented *ex nihilo* and then hermetically sealed from "contamination" is patently obvious: the papyri are highly syncretistic and their contents frequently overlap with religious beliefs and practices of the wider society.[67] In other words, it appears that the papyri users themselves often adopted practices and beliefs resembling those of other segments of the population, dressing them up with elaborate procedures and "jabberwocky" (Smith's appropriate term). The existence of magical parallels for ritual acts—for example, for ritual ascent to heaven, as at Qumran; or for the symbolic consumption of a human body, as in the New Testament—do not prove direct derivation by either side. They only prove that social and cultural presuppositions made particular types of symbolic acts plausible and meaningful for various groups of people. But the "meaning" of the ritual acts will have varied from one social context to the next.

Finally, one must question the validity of Smith's assumption that magical elements of the Gospel miracle traditions are indisputable primitive indicators that Jesus was in fact a magician. The language of magic and miracle was ambiguous. As Samain observed, in the Beelzebul pericope Jesus is actually said to use "magical" language (he "binds" the strong one) to counter accusations of magic.[68] If all the "magical traits" of the Gospel accounts of Jesus' exorcisms and healings went back to the original formulators of the stories, this would prove that wonder-workers were expected to act in stylized ways and produce stylized responses from the exorcised, and that such expectations shaped Jesus' own behavior and/or his observers' perception. But it could not be further assumed that such stylized actions and responses were themselves unambiguous indicators of magic. If they had been unambiguous, then it is hard to imagine how there could ever have been any debate about Jesus' status: seeing that he "sighed" or "groaned" prior to his feats of power, observers would have had no choice but to conclude that Jesus was a magician. Instead, they wrangled about whether he did his works by means of Beelzebul or God—something much less accessible to the naked eye. Therefore, as noted earlier, it is prudent to assume that so-called magical techniques and actions could also be understood in more positive ways.

If the foregoing reasoning is sound, then there is little point in arguing that the traditions depicting Jesus as "doing the things magicians do" prove his identity as a "magician." Rather, the task is to discover how some Christians could possibly have interpreted these traditions in a positive light. As Segal observes,

> The most interesting question for scholarship, as I see it, is not whether the charge of magic against Jesus is true or not. Since he does not claim the title, there can be no possible demonstration or disproof of a charge which is a matter of interpretation in the Hellenistic world. The most interesting question for scholarship is to define the social and cultural conditions and presuppositions that allow such charges and counter-charges to be made.[69]

What were the "social and cultural conditions and presuppositions" that enabled Jesus' supporters to reject with great conviction the accusations that their Lord was a magician? Smith's approach is unable to answer this question. In conclusion, if one's interest is solely in reconstructing "through the camera's eye" the actions of the historical Jesus, Smith's learned arguments must be weighed carefully. But if one is concerned with understanding what sort of sense the New Testament discussions of magic and miracle made to their authors and to their earliest readers, then Smith's presuppositions about who qualified as a magician in antiquity render his work less than useful.

John M. Hull is the only scholar to date who specifically addresses the question as to how an awareness of magic affected the transmission and redaction of the synoptic miracle stories.[70] Hull contends that in the Greco-Roman world there were two possible backgrounds against which one could interpret miracles: the eschatological and the magical. Scholars, of course, have commonly assumed that the influence of the eschatological background on the Christian miracle traditions was strong. Hull wishes to show that the magical background could have been an equally powerful shaping factor. He contends that miracles are magical if they possess any or all of the following characteristics: they have no cause but the will of the operator; the connection between cause and effect is based on "a theory of sympathetic bonds of *mana* or something similar"; and the wonders are believed to result from the performance of rituals that are "efficacious in themselves."[71]

Applying this definition to the Synoptics, Hull finds numerous traces of magical technique and thinking in Mark's Gospel. The Gospel of Luke, Hull argues, views angels and demons as more vividly and tangibly "real" than does Matthew, attesting to Luke's "thoroughly magical world-view." Hull describes the Gospel of Matthew as "the tradition purified of magic," because it has been "purged of details which might give rise to a magical interpretation."[72] In his conclusion

Hull suggests that the synoptic traditions probably took on their magical features gradually, in the process of transmission. The transmitters of the traditions may have thought that modification along magical lines was reasonable, based on their observation that Jesus had "entered without reserve into the central conflict of the magician's art, the struggle with evil powers confronted in the persons of the possessed."[73] Was Jesus himself a magician? Hull says that probably he did not think of himself as one. "But to the early Christian the myth of the magus was helpful in various ways; it drew attention to certain aspects of the salvation of Christ in a manner which no other myth was able to do."[74]

There are many problems with Hull's exegesis, several of which Aune identifies in his astute critique.[75] But the most serious problems with Hull's work have to do with his theoretical presuppositions about what "magic" is and how it may have influenced texts. Foundational for Hull's work is his argument that in the Greco-Roman world miracles were interpreted against either an eschatological or a magical background.[76] "Magical miracles" (as opposed to "eschatological miracles") are performed and/or recounted by persons who have a "magical world-view." Hull says that it is up to the modern interpreter to determine whether such a world view was operative; the opinion of the actors are irrelevant and will indeed often be mistaken. For example, Hull writes,

> Since the ancient Hebrews had little appreciation of cause and effect, we may suppose that a prayer, the result of which was a fall of rain, was not necessarily conceived of as being magical by them. But for us, since we can fully account for the fall of rain without recourse to prayer as an explanation, such a prayer would be magical.[77]

It is necessary to "distinguish between the circumstances of one age and of another," because "growth in knowledge turns science into pseudo-science, and the divine mysteries into magic." Magic, Hull reaffirms, is "part of a world-view."

The notion of a magical world view is an anthropological one with roots going back to the works of Edward B. Tylor and James G. Frazer. Hull repeatedly refers not only to Frazer, but also to Bronislaw Malinowski and R. R. Marett. Like these early anthropologists, Hull works with an observer-oriented ("etic") definition of magic, contrasting it with modern understandings of both religion and science and discounting the subjects' opinions as irrelevant.[78] But Hull unwittingly tries to bring in subject-oriented ("emic") categories through the back door by arguing that it was the early Christians' beliefs *about* magic and magicians—their knowledge of the "myth of the magus"—that caused them to recount Jesus' miracle stories as they did. Thus the transmitters' and redactors' assumptions about magic were not irrelevant after all: such assumptions were the basis upon which these persons decided which features were consistent with Jesus' magical image. But Hull never gets around to telling us what the assumptions were, because he has already discounted them as unimportant. To describe succinctly the methodological inconsistency: according to Hull, what the Christians thought about magic does not matter, but on the other hand, they modified the synoptic traditions in accordance with what they thought about magic. Certainly both observer-oriented (etic) and subject-oriented (emic) categories can be useful in the study of ancient magic, but rather than skillfully deploying both perspectives in a complementary fashion, Hull hopscotches back and forth between them, apparently without realizing that he has contradicted himself in the process.

Especially in his treatment of Luke, Hull appears to confuse the magical world view whose features he claims to have delineated with magic itself. A comment of David Bidney (made in response to a description by anthropologists of the magical world view) is relevant:

> The so-called "magical world view" in common with what might be called "the religious world view" presupposes belief in a world of animistic and mana powers, in spiritual beings and special potencies, but neither magic nor religion is to be identified with belief or philosophy. Magic, like religion, to be practiced and institutionalized presupposes a *Weltanschauung* or "picture of the world," but magic is not essentially "a form of conceptualizing the world."[79]

Hull claims that it is precisely the general belief in a "world of animistic and mana powers, in spiritual beings and special potencies" that constitutes the essential feature of the magical world view, and whose presence is said to demonstrate the influence of magic on a given writer. But such belief was widespread in antiquity. Demons and angels, for example, were characteristic of apocalyptic literature; something like a belief in mana was widely prevalent;[80] and socially sanctioned forms of divination also presupposed a notion of sympathy.[81] Whatever magic may have influenced the transmitters and redactors of the synoptic traditions was not an abstract world view reconstructed by modern anthropologists and biblical scholars, but magic as actually experienced by first-century Christians. Scholars can gain limited access to this experience by studying the messy complex of early Christian beliefs *about* magic and magicians: beliefs nurtured by accusations both hurled and denied and by encounters or tales of encounters with people who claimed expertise. *The issue is not whether the Christians' world view was magical, but how magic functioned as an experience-ordering symbol within the Christians' world view.*

Although Howard Clark Kee rejects Hull's conclusions, he argues even more vehemently than Hull that magic springs from a particular world view, distinct from the religious world view and characterized by telltale attitudes and techniques. Kee commends Malinowski's treatment of magic as instrumental and goal-oriented, supplementing it with references to Marcel Mauss's notion of magic as efficacious ritual and Lucy Mair's contention that "magic is concerned with the manipulation of forces; religion is occupied with communication among beings."[82] Based on these assorted criteria borrowed from anthropological works on magic, Kee concludes that "as a whole," the Greek magical papyri reveal a magical world view; the New Testament, a religious one.[83] The exceptional incidents in Mark and Acts are duly noted,[84] but Kee asserts that "the occasional story within the New Testament that seems more nearly akin to magic than to miracle does not invalidate the distinction, nor does it warrant ignoring the differences between the respective world views that lie behind magic and miracle."[85] In subsequent works Kee's approach to the subject of magic and miracle has remained intact.[86]

Kee's interpretation of Mauss's position is misleading. Mauss argued consistently that the fundamental distinction between magic and religion had to do with the social circumstances in which rituals were performed. He wrote, "A magical rite is *any rite which does not play a part in organized cults*—it is private, secret, mysterious and approaches the limit of a prohibited rite" (italics his).[87] The distinctions that Kee attributes to Mauss—that magical ritual has "automatic efficacy," and that religion achieves its objectives through "differentiated spiritual intermediaries"—Mauss himself attributes to Frazer and rejects.[88] When Mauss later mentions these distinctions,[89] he explicitly qualifies them as of secondary importance. A similar complaint must be made about Kee's interpretation of Mair's work. Mair reluctantly offers the manipulation/supplication dichotomy for classifiying phenomena falling within the single sphere of the "magico-religious."[90] She notes that when anthropologists "distinguish the magico-religious from the field of everyday life" they are utilizing a modern (that is, an etic) category.[91] In her excellent introduction to the anthropological study of witchcraft, Mair takes it for granted that the ethnographer will utilize categories corresponding in some measure to those used by the subjects under study.[92] But neither Mauss nor Mair can fairly be cited in support of a distinction between "magical" and "religious" world views; both emphasize that magic and religion intermingle, and that whatever distinctions are offered depend first and foremost on the social location of the person or action in question.[93]

One of Kee's recurring emphases in *Miracle in the Early Christian World* is the need for modern interpreters to understand ancient reports of miracles in context: "not merely in literary context, but in the wider, deeper social and cultural context in which both author and audience lived, and in which the language they employed took on the connotations to which the interpreter must seek to be sensitive";[94] Kee designates this broader, deeper context the "life-world." On the subject of magic and the New Testament, however, Kee does not fully achieve this commendable goal of becoming "sensitive" to the "connotations of the language employed." The shortfall results from his effort to place the New Testament traditions into one of two artificial categories, rather than to determine through inductive exegesis how any one of the New Testament writers actually used the language pertaining to magic and magicians. Luke-Acts would have been an obvious starting point, but Kee's treatment of this material is disappointing. Kee is unable to account for apparently magical traditions that crop up in Acts. He must explain these as "traces" that ought to be subordinated to the predominantly religious world view.

In summary, despite their differences, Morton Smith, John M. Hull, and Howard Clark Kee all assume that magic is a distinct and bounded category. They insist that the distinguishing characteristics of magic have to do with action, attitude, and technique rather than with the social setting of the action or social location(s) of the actor(s). As each of the three has delimited it, magic is what an anthropologist might call an etic (or experience-distant, or observer-oriented) category: in other words, it is not necessarily the category that the original actor(s) or participant(s) would have invoked to make sense of a given situation. It is, rather, a category imposed from the outside, by the modern observer; it bears some resemblance to what sometimes was regarded as magic in antiquity, but it simultaneously obscures nuances that would have been important to the original participants. It is a category designed to give a final and definitive answer to the question "was event 'x' magic or was it not?", thereby supplanting with certainty the original ambiguity and dispute. But ambiguity is not so easily supplanted: the great variance in the conclusions of the three scholars suggests that trying to determine whether the evangelists' world view or Jesus' actions were magical is an unproductive and unsatisfying endeavor. The question can be argued endlessly, depending on which evidence one chooses to emphasize.

A somewhat different approach is taken by Aune in "Magic and Early Christianity."[95] Aune is familiar with the anthropological work on magic and has expertly used its findings in his own theoretical discussion. He rejects conceptual models that define magic (in opposition to religion) as coercive, manipulative, or utilitarian, observing that such approaches are incongruent with actual belief and practice, in which magic and religion are "so closely intertwined that it is virtually impossible to regard them as discrete socio-cultural categories." Further, he insists that magic exists within the matrix of particular religious traditions: "A particular magical system coheres within a religious structure in the sense that it shares the fundamental religious reality construction of the contextual religion."[96] Aune suggests that structural-functional studies of social deviance may be especially useful in the study of ancient magic, in view of magic's illicit character in antiquity. Accordingly, he proposes the following definition of magic:

> Magic is defined as that form of religious deviance whereby individual or social goals are sought by means alternate to those normally sanctioned by the dominant religious institution. Unless religious activities fit that definition, they will not be regarded as magical for the purposes of this study. Religious activities which fit this first and primary criterion must also fit a second criterion: goals sought within the context of religious deviance are magical when attained through the management of supernatural powers in such a way that results are virtually guaranteed [italics his].[97]

Because he has incorporated the factor of social deviance, Aune's working definition of magic is the most sensitive and flexible of those considered so far. The definition will usually identify as magical social phenomena that most ancient observers would have labeled thus, and will usually exclude from that category phenomena that most ancient observers would have labeled as religious, medicinal, or something else altogether. Consequently, for sociological analysis of historical phenomena or for social-historical taxonomy the definition will prove to be useful.

But the analytic character of the definition leaves one with nagging doubts about its adequacy for the task of interpretation. Aune finds that, inasmuch as Jesus' wonders were performed within the context of a millennial movement ("a collective form of deviant behavior"), they ought to be considered magical.[98] But one wonders whether any ground has been gained by such categorization: as exegetes we are no better able than before to construe the experience or the texts of those persons (including Jesus and the early Christians) who ostensibly met Aune's criteria but vehemently insisted and sincerely believed that they did not practice magic. Neither can we explain accusations of magic much better than without the definition, since accusations were not always made by "those within the dominant social structure to label and exert control on those in the ambiguous and unstructured areas of society."[99] Of course one can argue that hindsight, a neutral vantage point, and sociological sophistication enable modern observers to, in a sense, understand the ancients better than they understood themselves. But if one's goal is not sociological analysis or taxonomy, but nuanced interpretation of magic-related passages in the Gospels and Acts, then this stance is self-defeating. In the first century C.E., when a verdict concerning an accusation of magic had to be reached, the majority opinion (typically that of the "dominant religious institution") prevailed. But for modern exegetes the majority opinion will not do, because it is precisely the accused whose world we want to enter. By categorizing the actions of the accused in a way they themselves would not we preclude this possibility.[100]

Recently Jerome H. Neyrey has analyzed various passages in the New Testament as instances of "witchcraft accusations"—accusations of evilness and demonic control—such as anthropologists have found to arise under certain conditions in villages or small groups.[101] Neyrey does not try to measure the New Testament evidence against a prior definition of magic, as do the four scholars whose works were discussed above. But like Smith, Hull, Kee, and Aune, Neyrey categorizes the New Testament data from an etic or observer-oriented perspective. Consequently, the method Neyrey employs has the same shortcoming as do those discussed above: it is unable to assist in interpreting the New Testament passages in question within their narrative and particular cultural contexts.

In Neyrey's work, the etic categories are provided by a social scientific model designed to account for observed correlations between a group's cosmology and its social organization. According to this model, which was developed by anthropologist Mary T. Douglas and elaborated by others,[102] certain characteristics of the world view of any given social group, including attitudes toward purity, ritual (which includes magic), personal identity, body, sin, cosmology, and misfortune and punishment, are correlated in a consistent and predictable pattern with two social variables. Witchcraft societies, that is, social groups whose members are prone to make witchcraft accusations, are classified as strong on the variable known as "group" and low on the variable known as "grid." In other words, they have "a high degree of pressure to conform to societal norms" and to achieve order and control, combined with "a poor degree of fit and match between individual experiences and stated societal patterns of perception and experience."[103] Neyrey argues that the witchcraft accusations found in various strata of the New Testament indicate that the historical groups reflected in these strata, such as the community behind Matthew's form of Q, or the community in Galatia, must have taken the shape of witchcraft societies. Neyrey uses the categories of Douglas's model as the organizational template for his discussion of social and historical data culled from the New Testament documents, claiming that this approach enables the modern western reader to understand the function of witchcraft accusations in the ancient documents and to explore the conflictual, competitive social dynamics of the historical communities that are reflected therein.

By using an explicit and comprehensive model as a paradigm controlling his perception and analysis of all data, Neyrey aligns himself with an approach that has been designated by others as the "positivist" viewpoint in anthropology and the social sciences.[104] Because of their aspirations toward a "natural science of society," anthropologists in this camp have tended to stress observation and comparison of a variety of societies and the formulation of models or explicit hypotheses.[105] Having developed a model or hypothesis, the social scientist searches for data to satisfy standardized questions or correspond to standardized variables; the explicitness of the model or hypothesis and the standardization of data are thought to minimize subjectivity and to ensure that results can later be replicated or tested by others.[106]

The approach differs from the less structured one pursued by ethnographers whose perspective can be designated "interpretive" rather than positivist.[107] The interpretive ethnographer regards "culture" less as a laboratory in which the manipulation of variables produces predictable results than as a "text" which can be "read" for its meanings. Proponents of a more interpretive approach argue that the social scientists' quasi-experimental method cannot deal with the complex, multi-layered data ("thick with meanings") that are actually generated in anthropological fieldwork. Whereas the positivist proceeds by testing models or hypotheses, the interpretive ethnographer tries (as the designation implies) to "interpret" meaningful behavior by viewing it holistically within its *particular* cultural context. Thus, whereas

Neyrey explains witchcraft accusations by referring to the precon-
ceived grid/group model, an interpretive ethnographer studying accusations of evilness and demon possession would proceed inductively, observing a particular witchcraft society and trying to relate its
patterns of accusations to other patterns of action and thought characteristic of that society's culture.[108] This procedure would require
attention to detailed cultural matters such as the people's beliefs about
witchcraft, magic, the social types that engage in such activities, the
tools of the trade, the spirit world, and the proper settings and forms
for the use of magic or for the leveling of accusations of magic.[109]

Douglas's model as elaborated by Neyrey and others places in the
same category societies that share certain aspects of social and cultural
organization, and that therefore have similar values for the grid and
group variables. The model claims that such societies will also engage
in similar patterns of social discourse, including (in strong group, low
grid societies) witchcraft accusations. But in order to maintain the
existence of these cross-cultural similarities, "culture" and "patterns
of social discourse" must be defined in abstract terms.[110] Although to
most observers the "cultures" of witchcraft societies—for example,
seventeenth-century Salem, Massachusetts and a witchcraft-prone vil-
lage in Africa—look different, the model asserts that the particular
data generated in observing them can be boiled down to comparable
ideas about purity, ritual, and so forth, or to comparable accusations
of "internal corruption," "perversion," "soul-sucking," or "poison-
ing." The cultures of different societies can be reduced to the lowest
common denominator in this way because, according to the model,
it is not the specific details of a particular culture, but rather underlying
aspects of social organization that make "witchcraft accusations" a
meaningful and useful form of social discourse. In other words, culture
takes second place to social structure in the shaping of symbolization
and of its perception. The inherent tendency of the grid/group model
to efface cultural differences and to reduce social discourse to what
has been determined beforehand to be its "essence" or "core" would
be regarded by interpretive ethnographers as unacceptable. For such
ethnographers, a given society's culture in all its specificity and com-
plexity is the framework that bestows meaning on action and expression in that society.[111] Insistence on taking account of the particularity
of a people's culture is what makes cross-cultural comparison and
generalization so difficult from the interpretive viewpoint.[112]

If one grants the reliability of the grid/group model in its correlation
of social and cultural organization and cosmological attitudes, then

it would seem that Neyrey's positivist, etic approach is in some cases able to illuminate the social context in which witchcraft accusations were produced, and thereby also to shed light on the document in which those accusations are embedded. The model would appear to be especially useful where we know or suspect that the "text" in question is the product of a single person or community (as Neyrey supposes to be the case with the letters of Paul and the Q-tradition as it must have looked prior to its incorporation into Matthew). When dealing with such a text, the interpreter can, perhaps, assume that the various bits of social discourse occurring between characters in the narrative directly mirror the social discourse engaged in by the members of the community, and so can be used as a basis for inferring the organization of that community. But even if Neyrey's approach can in some cases illuminate the social organization of a group that engaged in witchcraft accusations, it does not enable us to understand the actors', authors', or redactors' understanding of the events in which such accusations played a part. To understand what was being "said" and "heard" in such interactions, one must, as Geertz notes, search out and analyze "the symbolic forms—words, images, institutions, behaviors—in terms of which . . . people actually represented themselves to themselves and one another."[113] In the case of magic in Luke-Acts, this approach will necessitate careful examination of Luke's vocabulary and imagery when talking about magicians. Further, because Luke has incorporated all accusations of magic into an interpretive narrative framework, these accusations cannot without risk of a loss of meaning be extracted and treated as raw, uninterpreted data (as is done in Neyrey's approach), but must be examined in narrative context.

Because Luke's "discussion" of magic consists of a series of stories set within a narrative framework, the primary context for interpretation must be the narrative world; hence this volume is first and foremost an exercise in literary criticism. But by attending also to aspects of Luke's cultural world relevant to his treatment of magic, I hope to be able to make inferences about the discourse that Luke carries on with his readers. Hence in some respects the questions addressed in this study are analogous to those addressed by interpretive anthropologists, who strive to "hear what is being said" in social discourse by identifying the culture-specific "vocabulary" in which it is expressed.

As discussed above (pp. 15–17, 21), in Jewish and Christian circles of the New Testament era the magician was often seen as the enemy of God and minister of Satan, and accusations of magic were often phrased as accusations of a pact with the devil. This generalization is quite applicable to Luke-Acts. Note, for example, that in Luke 11:15 observers accuse Jesus of casting out demons by the prince of demons, which Jesus interprets as a charge that he is in league with Satan. Then in Acts 13:10 the tables are turned: Luke has Paul accuse Bar Jesus, the Jewish "magician-false prophet," of being a "son of the devil" and an "enemy of all righteousness." Because Luke apparently regards Satan as the invisible authority backing all acts of magic, it will be helpful to look more closely at the evangelist's understanding of the role of the devil in the cosmic and earthly drama involving Jesus.

2

THE STRUGGLE FOR AUTHORITY: SATAN IN THE NARRATIVE WORLD OF LUKE-ACTS

INTRODUCTION

The remarks about Satan in Luke's Gospel and in Acts are, if small in quantity, mammoth in significance. When taken seriously, the traces and clues that Luke has dropped along the way suggest that one can scarcely overestimate Satan's importance in the history of salvation as told by Luke.[1] It is Satan's fierce opposition to the purposes of God that renders Jesus' battle to effect salvation so necessary and so arduous, and his victory so great. Furthermore, Jesus' success in this struggle is directly tied to his success and to the success of his followers at casting out demons and healing, because the authority that Jesus exerts and in turn delegates to his followers he gains at Satan's expense. As Jesus' authority swells, dwindles, and then swells again at his resurrection and ascension to the right hand of God, so does the authority of his followers. This chapter will trace the fall, rise, and fall of Satan's authority in the narrative world of Luke-Acts.

The "testing in the wilderness" (4:1-13)[2] is the first confrontation in Luke-Acts between Jesus and Satan. It is simultaneously a confrontation between Satan and the Holy Spirit: the evangelist emphasizes the Spirit's indwelling and leading of Jesus at the beginning of the ordeal, and when the tests are concluded, Luke alone remarks (v. 14) that Jesus returned to Galilee "in the power of the Spirit."

The passage is usually examined for the light it can shed on Christology;[3] the following selective analysis will focus instead on its implications for Luke's view of Satan and of his authority.[4]

THE TESTING IN THE WILDERNESS
(Luke 4:1-13)

Following the devil's offer to Jesus of authority *(exousia)* over the kingdoms of the world and of their glory (4:6a),[5] Luke adds the devil's clarification that this authority has been given to him, and that he may give it to whomever he will (v. 6b).[6] The statement highlights Luke's understanding of Satan as "the ruler of this world."[7] That he is ruler specifically of the human world is indicated by Luke's use of the term *oikoumenē* (inhabited world, human population) where Matthew has *kosmos* (Matt. 4:8) The parallel between Luke 4:5-7 and Rev. 13:7b-8 is striking, and not to be dismissed lightly.[8] In Revelation, the beast from the sea is allowed to make war on the saints and to conquer them:

> And *authority was given to it* over every tribe and people and tongue and nation, and *all who dwell on earth* will *worship* it, every one whose name has not been written before the foundation of the world in the book of life of the Lamb that was slain.
>
> (Rev. 13:7b-8)

The devil in Luke's account, like the beast from the sea in Revelation, "has been given authority" over the inhabited world. In both cases the exercise of this authority would have as its ultimate goal the worship of Satan (cf. Rev. 13:4). In Revelation the beast from the sea delegates his authority to a second beast, the "beast from the earth" or "false prophet," who works great signs; in Luke's account the devil *offers* to delegate authority to Jesus, and *suggests* to him that he work great signs. Had Jesus followed these instructions, he would have become something like the beast from the earth in Revelation: a false prophet, serving Satan and working magical signs that redound to Satan's glory rather than to the glory of God.[9] Having thus seduced Jesus into serving him rather than God, the devil would have foiled the divine plan for Jesus' life and retained for himself the authority and glory which are due God alone.

The issue of authority appears to be a key factor in the struggle with Satan. But what does "authority" mean for Luke, and why does it have anything to do with the devil?[10] The passage about the centurion whose slave Jesus healed (Luke 7:2-10; Matt. 8:5-13) illustrates the meaning of the word in a neutral context. Here the centurion tells Jesus that it is unnecessary to trouble himself:

> But say the word, and let my servant be healed. For I am a man set under authority, with soldiers under me: and I say to one, "Go," and he goes, and to another, "Come," and he comes, and to my slave, "Do this," and he does it.
>
> (Luke 7:8)

The centurion is "set under authority," in other words, subject to a higher power, and himself authorized by that power to command the forces under him. The soldiers "go" and "come" and "do this or that" because they recognize that their commander has been granted the authority needed to make and enforce such commands (cf. 20:2,8).

The idea that God had authorized Satan's actions characterizes two of the three reports about Satan found in the Hebrew scriptures. In the Book of Job, Satan is a member of the heavenly court who explicitly requests and receives permission to test the faithful obedience of God's servant Job (Job 1:11-12; 2:5-6).[11] In the fourth vision of Zechariah, Satan is one who stands near God's throne and accuses Joshua, the high priest of the returned exiles (Zech. 3:1). In the other Old Testament appearance of Satan (1 Chron. 21:1, in which there is no explicit or implicit indication that God has given authorization), Satan incites David to error by persuading him to carry out a census of the people. These texts illustrate three of the activities most often ascribed to Satan in subsequent literature: *he tests, he accuses,* and *he leads astray.*[12] The notion that Satan has obtained divine permission to carry out these tasks continues to appear regularly. Even though Satan often seems to be God's opponent more than a divine functionary, the devil was still supposedly exercising authority that had been divinely delegated at some previous point in time.[13]

The complementary notion that Satan in turn had forces under his own authority became increasingly popular in the Hellenistic and Roman periods.[14] Luke accepts this view, identifying Satan with Beelzebul, the ruler of demons (11:15,18). Thus Satan's "kingdom" includes the demonic realm. In a graphic expansion of his source (11:21-22; cf. Mark 3:27), Luke portrays Satan as a strong one, who is "well-armed" and who trusts in his many possessions. These "possessions" are the humans inhabited by Satan's minions, the demons. Such unfortunate humans suffer from a variety of ailments. Clearly the prevalence on every side of demon possession, sickness, and death epitomized for Luke the oppressive power of Satan in the world.[15] But Luke also shared with many of his contemporaries the belief that the advent of the Messiah and the end of the age would coincide with the demise of Satan's forces.[16] When Jesus exorcises or heals humans, he is said to be "plundering" Satan's kingdom, taking "spoil" from its lord (Luke 11:22; cf. 13:16). At Jesus' first exorcism (Luke 4:31-37) the demon cries out, "Have you come to destroy us?" The answer is certainly Yes.

Satan's statement in 4:5-6 that he has received authority over the kingdoms of "the inhabited world" refers, however, not only to his authority over demons and the scattered individuals they afflict. Luke believes that there are entire populations of humans who have long been under Satan's authority, willingly giving him glory and obeying his command. The Gentiles are one such group: according to Jesus' commission of Paul in Acts 26:18, until the Gentiles respond to the word that Paul preaches by turning to God, they exist in darkness and are subject to the authority of Satan. Implicit here is the common notion that Satan and the demons motivate idolatry, in which they themselves receive tribute.[17] Luke probably regarded the unrepentant Jews as well as the idolatrous Gentiles as subject to the Prince of Darkness: the evangelist emphasizes the Jews' habitual idolatry, acceptance of (satanic) false prophets, and rejection of (divine) true ones (Luke 6:22-23, Acts 7:39-43,51-52; 13:4-12).[18] To be sure, there are some righteous Jews, but the dwelling of David has fallen (Acts 15:16), and most of the people "resist the Holy Spirit" (Acts 7:51), as does the devil himself.[19]

Luke regarded the desire for worship by any being but God or Jesus as cause for the most severe punishment. "Because he did not give God the glory," King Herod was "immediately" smitten by an angel of the Lord, and was eaten by worms and died (Acts 12:23; see also Acts 5:36; 10:25-26; 14:12-17). Given Luke's horror at the prospect of misdirected worship, Satan's arrogation of divine glory—culminating in his brazen effort to persuade even Jesus to worship him—must have drastic consequences. Accordingly, Luke 4:6-7 ought to be paired with the remark in 10:18 about Satan's fall. There are precedents for an association between such events: in Isa. 14:4-20, a taunt song for the King of Babylon that was reinterpreted sometime in or around the first century to refer to Satan,[20] the King's desire for divine status causes him to "fall from heaven" (v. 13). The ruler had said, "I will ascend above the heights of the clouds, I will make myself like the Most High" (v. 13). But instead he is "brought down to Sheol, to the depths of the Pit," where he will be mocked by kings (v. 15).[21] In the narrative world of Luke's Gospel, Satan genuinely does possess the authority and glory of the kingdoms of the world, for many are indeed under his sway. But this intolerable situation cannot persist. By basking in undeserved glory the devil seals his own doom. His demand for worship (from all those under his jurisdiction and not only from Jesus) is a challenge to God. Since God alone is to be worshiped and served, this challenge will lead to Satan's demise.

Luke concludes his account of the testing with the remark that when Satan had finished all the tests he withdrew from Jesus for a while (4:13). The remark has generated controversy ever since Hans Conzelmann claimed that it marked the beginning of a "Satan-free" period to last for the duration of Jesus' ministry.[22] In order to make such a claim, Conzelmann took the phrase *syntelesas panta peirasmon* absolutely ("the devil had finished *every* temptation") rather than in context, that is, as referring to every temptation in the forty days just described.[23] This unbalance, combined with an equally extravagant stress on the ambiguous temporal expression that is variously translated "for a while," or "till an opportune time" *(achri kairou),* led Conzelmann to focus too much attention on what the remark says about subsequent events, and too little on its implications for the events immediately preceding. In other words, Conzelmann did not ask why Jesus' successful endurance of Satan's tests should have caused Satan to withdraw. Since the remark about this withdrawal serves primarily as a conclusion to the testing narrative, and only secondarily as an introduction to Jesus' subsequent ministry, this is a critical question.

I suggest that Luke's editorial attention to the devil's departure was prompted by the author's familiarity with a stereotyped pattern of mythical events. This hypothesis is supported by two roughly contemporaneous texts from outside the New Testament in which a righteous or Spirit-filled individual "conquers" *(nikan)* the devil by successfully enduring his onslaught, thereby causing the devil to feel shame and depart. In the *Testament of Job,* a document dating from sometime between the first century B.C.E. and first century C.E.,[24] Job's staunch endurance of Satan's attack causes the devil to concede defeat:

> And as he [Satan] stood, he wept, saying, "Look, Job, I am weary and I withdraw *(hypochōrein)* from you, even though you are flesh and I a spirit. You suffer a plague, but I am in deep distress. I became like one athlete wrestling another, and one pinned the other. The upper one silenced the lower one, by filling his mouth with sand and bruising his limbs. But because he showed endurance and did not grow weary, at

the end the upper one cried out in defeat. So you also, Job, were the one below and in a plague, but you conquered *(nikēsai)* my wrestling tactics which I brought on you." Then Satan, ashamed, left *(anachōrēsai)* me for three years.[25]

(Testament of Job 27:2-6)

In this passage a human being has conquered Satan by withstanding his terrible tests; Satan's withdrawal serves to emphasize the magnitude of the defeat. Similarly, *Hermas Mandate* 12.5.2 reports that the devil cannot oppress *(katadynasteuein)* the servants of the Lord who place all their hope in him. "The devil can wrestle with them, but he cannot throw them down. If then you 'resist him' he will be conquered *(nikēthēnai)* and 'fly from you' in shame."[26] Despite their differing provenance, both of these texts illustrate the notion that by withstanding the devil's tests the righteous person achieves victory over him. In Luke 4:13 also, the notice about the withdrawal apparently points backward, to underscore Jesus' victory.[27] Jesus has routed his foe.

But does the phrase "for a while" or "till an opportune time" also point forward, to Satan's later resumption of activity at the passion? As noted above, this was the argument of Conzelmann, who concluded that the interim between the wilderness confrontation and Satan's entry into Judas in 22:3 was therefore free from Satan's attacks. Of course one can agree with Conzelmann's premise that the phrase *achri kairou* points ahead[28] while rejecting his subsequent inference that Jesus' ministry was therefore Satan-free. It is likely that in saying that Satan withdrew "for a while" Luke was indeed hinting that the devil was not yet finished with Jesus. This does not, however, imply that Luke deliberately created the myth of a bounded interim epoch utterly free from Satan's activity and presence. Conzelmann loads more weight onto 4:13 than it can bear: the statement is primarily significant for what it says, not about the absolute quality or precise duration of Satan's resultant absence, but about Jesus' victory, of which Satan's withdrawal was both consequence and proof. Jesus is the "stronger one" who has conquered the "strong one" (11:22). He has thereby demonstrated that his own authority (4:32,36) is greater than the devil's, with the result that when accosted the demons suddenly recognize and obey Jesus (4:34,41), making exorcisms possible. To emphasize this new position of authority, Luke has Jesus immediately preach a sermon about "release to the captives" and follow this up with a series of illustrative healings and exorcisms.[29] But Satan, even if he has temporarily ceased to attack Jesus directly, is not completely absent; he has only retreated to lick his wounds and plan his next assault. Although Jesus liberates isolated persons from Satan's grip (Acts 10:38), the devil retains vast numbers firmly under his control. He is still the ruler of this world, dominating individuals and entire populations by means of his demons. Luke probably also sees Satan as making his presence felt in other ways during Jesus' ministry, for example, in the people's frequent "testing" of Jesus.[30]

In sum, Luke regards Satan as a powerful being with much of the world under his authority. He controls individuals by means of sickness and demon possession. He controls entire kingdoms, whose inhabitants live in the darkness of idolatry, worshiping Satan and giving him the glory that is due God alone. But at the testing in the wilderness, Satan's efforts to control also the Son of God fail miserably: Jesus refuses to become obedient to the devil, and so compels the Enemy to beat a retreat. Jesus then moves on with tried and proven authority to go about his work. He now initiates a series of incursions into Satan's domain, robbing him of his captives by releasing them from illness, demon possession, and sin. Satan, forced for a while to use indirect maneuvers (see, for example Luke 8:12), plots his next frontal attack. But the war is not yet over. The nature and extent of Jesus' confrontation with Satan may be assessed further by examining the Beelzebul pericope, where Luke's understanding of what occurs during Jesus' exorcisms is most clearly spelled out.

THE BEELZEBUL CONTROVERSY
(Luke 11:14-23)

In the preceding two chapters of Luke, several important incidents involving healings and the casting out of demons (9:1-5; 10:1-20) have prepared the reader for this important episode dealing with the nature of Jesus' exorcisms. Luke's version of the incident (cf. Mark 3:22-27; Matt. 12:24-29) exhibits a number of unique features, two of which will receive close attention in the following study. These are Jesus' reference in 11:20 to the "finger of God" where Matthew has "Spirit of God," and Luke's alteration and elaboration in vv. 20-22 of the statement about the strong one who must be overcome before his house can be entered.

In all three synoptic accounts of the incident, Jesus' ability to perform exorcisms is taken for granted. Further, there is no suggestion that any of the characters in these accounts considered exorcism to be inherently evil. On the contrary, Luke 11:19 implies that other exorcists in the community were accepted as such. Josephus observes that first century Jews were renowned for and proud of their exorcistic ability. To illustrate, Josephus describes the antics of a certain Eleazar, who, using the techniques handed down by Solomon, caused an evil spirit to come out through the nose of the person it had possessed and to upset a cup of water as proof of its exit.[31] In Josephus's account, as in the accounts of the synoptic evangelists, exorcism in and of itself is regarded as a good and wondrous thing.

In the synoptic accounts, the issue is not the exorcism itself but the source of power by which it was accomplished (cf. Acts 4:7). This source could be either good, in which case the wonder would be regarded by observers as a testimony that God was with the exorcist, or the source could be evil, in which case the wonder-worker would likewise be regarded as evil. One way that an "evil" exorcist could proceed was to invoke the aid of a spirit: it could be either the spirit of a dead human (typically of one who had not received a proper burial or who had been violently killed), or it could be a demon (or *daimon*).[32] This issue has already come up in Luke, in the account of Herod's reaction to the reports about Jesus. Mark reports (6:14-16) that "John the Baptist has been raised from the dead and on account of this these powers are working in him," but Luke (9:7-9) omits the incriminating latter part of the statement and tones down Mark's v. 16, apparently so as to avoid any implication that Jesus was performing necromancy by means of the power of the violently killed *(biaiothanatos)* John. But Luke does not likewise soften the accusation that Jesus performs exorcisms by the power of Beelzebul, since Jesus will refute the charge himself.[33]

The train of reasoning in vv. 17b-18 needs to be explained. Mark 3:23b (parallel Matt. 12:26) implies that Jesus understood "Beelzebul" as an alias for Satan, the ruler of demons; Luke assumes likewise although he omits this particular sentence. Jesus reasons that, in accusing him of "casting out demons by means of the power of Satan," his opponents were suggesting that Satan had turned against his very subordinates. Jesus' ensuing remarks about the divided kingdom demonstrate the illogical and unlikely nature of such an action by Satan. Luke's wording in v. 17 is more terse than in Mark's parallel verse, but makes the same point: a power, if divided, will fail. According to Jesus, it is illogical to think that Satan is casting out his own minions, for he would never willingly divide his own power in this way, lest his kingdom collapse.

The punchline comes in v. 20: "If I by the finger of God cast out demons, then the Kingdom of God has come upon you." Not only are the opponents wrong about the source of Jesus' power, but their mistake is causing them to miss the significance of Jesus' wonder-working: it heralds the Kingdom of God. The protasis of this sentence alludes to the Exodus contest between Moses and the magicians of Pharaoh (Exod. 8:19 [LXX v. 15]). On that occasion the Egyptian magicians finally were forced to conclude that the power by which Moses worked his signs was superior to the power that they themselves utilized; indeed the power tapped by Moses must be divine, "the finger of God." Whether Luke found the expression in his source or inserted it himself, he surely did not fail to grasp the significance of the allusion. Jesus was saying that his power was not like the diabolical power of magicians, Egyptian or otherwise, but was rather a triumph of God, and thus by Luke's definition a defeat of magic.[34]

Why do Jesus' exorcisms herald the Kingdom of God? Because as the Kingdom of Satan diminishes, the Kingdom of God grows proportionately. The ensuing metaphor of the stronger man wresting booty from the conquered one is apt: whenever Jesus exorcises or heals, he takes spoil from Satan's kingdom and adds it to God's own. Consequently, Luke can portray healing and the preaching of the good news as integrally related activities: the seventy(-two), for example, must "heal those who are sick and say to them 'The Kingdom of God has come near to you.' " Every healing, exorcism, or raising from the dead is a loss for Satan and a gain for God.[35]

In vv. 21-22, Luke has taken Mark's statement that "no one can enter the strong one's house" and expanded it into an allegory describing Satan's role in Jesus' exorcisms. Whenever Jesus exorcises, he as "the stronger one" (cf. Luke 3:16) is entering and plundering the domain of the conquered Satan.[36] In his careful shaping of this passage Luke has apparently been influenced by Isa. 49:25 and/or 53:12. The possible allusion to Isa. 53:12 ("On account of this he himself will inherit many and he will divide the spoil of the strong, because his soul was given up to death, and he was reckoned among the lawless") is usually overlooked or at least downplayed, probably because at this point in the narrative it seems to be irrelevant. But perhaps Luke is building on a perceived connection between Jesus' earthly control over demons and what will happen at his impending death and resurrection. Such a connection is plausible for several reasons. First, Isa. 53:12 itself tells that the reason the servant will "divide the spoil of the strong" is that his soul is given up to death, and a portion of this verse is explicitly quoted in 22:37, at just the moment when the final events of Jesus' passion are beginning to unroll. Second, Luke ties both the exorcisms and the death of Jesus to the coming of the Kingdom (11:20; 23:42-43). Third, despite the success implied by Jesus' and his followers' exorcisms (10:18 [discussed below]; 11:21-22), it is clear that Jesus has yet to win the *definitive* victory over the devil: at the passion Satan takes the offensive once again (22:3,53). An allusion to that impending and climactic confrontation would fit well into this discussion of the characters' ongoing conflict. Fourth and finally, a connection between Jesus' death and his earthly power to heal and exorcise seems to be implied by Jesus' enigmatic response to Herod in 13:32, where Jesus' acts of healing and exorcism and his "perfection" or "completion" on the third day are somehow linked.[37] Is Jesus' earthly authority over demons (and over their master, Satan) somehow to be "perfected" or "completed" in his death? The possibility must be explored.

In 11:23, Luke has Jesus conclude the incident by saying that "the one who is not with me is against me, and the one who does not gather with me scatters" (parallel Matt. 12:30). Luke is saying that there is no possibility of neutrality in the assessment of Jesus' works. One must either acknowledge that Jesus has routed Satan, thereby allying oneself with the one who has conquered and who will yet conquer, or else one allies oneself with the devil.

To summarize, in recounting the Beelzebul episode Luke has emphasized Jesus' defeat of magical-Satanic powers. By exorcising demons Jesus shows that he has conquered Satan. But Luke has hinted that the victory is not yet complete. In order to pursue this tantalizing hint, it is necessary to examine another passage, Jesus' words about the fall of Satan. The remark has no parallel in Mark or Matthew and provides a substantial opportunity to discern Satan's unfolding role in the Lukan narrative.

THE FALL OF SATAN
(Luke 10:17-20)

This passage, in which Jesus remarks that he saw Satan "fall like lightning from the sky,"[38] depicts an unabashedly apocalyptic scene in the midst of a document not usually considered to be "apocalyptic." The evangelist clearly regarded the episode as important: he places it directly before Jesus' rejoicing in the Spirit, and strengthens the temporal link between the two sections by noting that Jesus rejoiced "in that same hour" *(en autē tē hōra).*[39] Thus Jesus' remarks at the return of the seventy(-two)[40] function as the antecedent for "these things" (v. 21), that is, the divine revelations over which Jesus rejoices. But in what way? What did Luke understand by the fall of Satan and Jesus' grant of authority and protection to the seventy(-two)? Examination of specific aspects of the passage, beginning with the literary context, will help to answer these questions.

Literary placement and links with surrounding material. Since vv. 17-24 serve as the conclusion and the climax of the entire mission of the seventy(-two), Luke's purposes in relating the remarks of Jesus in vv. 17-20 may be related to the evangelist's purpose in creating the account of the mission of the seventy(-two) as a whole. Why would Luke have had Jesus appoint seventy(-two) others? The choice of such a number was probably meant to convey a symbolic message; in view of Luke's tendency to echo the scriptures wherever possible, it is safe to assume that the symbolism derived from the Septuagint.

The textual question as to whether the original number in 10:1 and 17 was seventy or seventy-two appears to be unresolvable.[41] Of course the number per se would be unimportant if it were possible in some other way to identify the Septuagint text that likely inspired the symbolism. In his study of the textual problem, Bruce M. Metzger lists the possibilities for symbolic allusions to scriptural and Jewish legendary material. Of these possible allusions, only two cohere well enough with Luke's concerns elsewhere in Luke-Acts to merit serious consideration. Curiously, both of the Septuagint passages in question involve variants between the numbers seventy and seventy-two. One of the passages is Gen. 10:2-31; if Luke were alluding to this text, the number of missionaries would apparently have symbolized the seventy(-two) gentile nations mentioned in the Genesis passage.[42] The other passage is Num. 11:16-25; if Luke were alluding to this text, then Jesus' appointment of "seventy(-two) others" would apparently have been meant to recall the action of Moses, whom the Lord had told to appoint seventy (or perhaps seventy-two) elders for help in carrying the burden of the people.[43]

The details of Luke's account do not support the suggested allusion to the nations in Genesis 10: first, the seventy(-two) are sent not "to the nations," but to the very towns that Jesus himself is to visit (10:1); and second, Acts contains no hint that Luke thought of the Gentile nations as numbering seventy(-two). By contrast, an allusion to Numbers 11 (Moses' appointment of seventy[-two] helpers at the Lord's command) is plausible for several reasons. First, it would be an obvious and straightforward case of typological imitation: Jesus appoints seventy(-two) helpers, just as Moses appointed seventy(-two) helpers.

Second, it would be consistent with Luke's concern to portray Jesus as the Prophet like Moses (Acts 3:22; 7:37). Third, and most importantly, the remarks in Numbers that God "took some of the spirit that was on Moses and put it upon the elders" (11:17,25) and that "when the spirit rested upon them, they prophesied" (v. 25) would have had attractive typological potential for Luke.[44] Realizing this potential, Luke may have conceived of the mission by "seventy(-two) others" as foreshadowing the period of the church, when not only the twelve but *many* sons and daughters would receive the Spirit of the Lord and prophesy, and would thereby be enabled to carry out Jesus' work. Because they possess the Spirit, these sons and daughters will understand the divine mysteries for which Jesus—himself possessed by the Spirit, as Luke pointedly notes—now gives praise (v. 21; contrast Matt. 11:25). Of the two possibilities considered, then, an allusion to Numbers 11 (Moses' appointment of seventy[-two] helpers) seems to be the more likely.

Other clues to Luke's purposes in describing the mission of the seventy(-two) may be gleaned from 10:21-22, the passage about Jesus' rejoicing. In Matthew's version (11:25-27), Jesus says "no one knows *(epiginōskein)* the son" and "no one knows the father"; Luke has changed this to "no one knows *(ginōskein) who is* the son," and "no one knows *who is* the father." Luke's alterations indicate that he has reinterpreted the tradition from the source he shares with Matthew so as to support his conviction that only those whom God has enlightened can know the identity of the Christ about whom the scriptures speak.[45] This conviction is illustrated also by the experience of the aged Simeon (2:25-33), who rejoices "in the Spirit" (v. 27: *en tō pneumati;* cf. 10:21a) when the Lord reveals to him that the child Jesus is the Lord's Christ. Luke believes that everything to be known about the Christ is contained in the scriptures; the only new revelation is that it is Jesus to whom these scriptural teachings apply. To give one of many examples, in Acts 18:28 Apollos, "a man well versed in the scriptures" (v. 24), confutes the Jews, "showing by the scriptures that the Christ was Jesus."[46]

But Luke regarded this insight that the scriptural teachings refer to Jesus as hard won: during Jesus' earthly life, the knowledge had been hidden from his followers (9:45; 18:34; cf. 2:50; 24:16,25,45).[47] Only when he returned to them *after* the resurrection did Jesus interpret to them "beginning from Moses and from all the prophets" the things about himself "in all the scriptures" (Luke 24:27), namely, how "it was necessary for the Christ to suffer these things and enter into his glory" (v. 26). It was also *after* the resurrection when Jesus told a group of disciples that they would be witnesses of these things, once they had received the promise of the Father (24:44-49). Only at this time were their minds finally opened to understand the scriptures (v. 45). Inasmuch as the seventy(-two) are credited with knowledge that Luke elsewhere reserves for post-resurrection followers, one can again conclude that these missionaries prefigure Jesus' followers in the days after Pentecost: then God will have put the Holy Spirit upon them, enabling them to interpret and to proclaim the scriptural teachings about Jesus the Christ for which Jesus now gives thanks.

It is possible to determine more precisely how the events of Luke 10:17-20 fit into this "schedule of concealment and disclosure," as Richard Dillon has termed it,[48] by examining the implied temporal sequence of those events.

Temporal sequence. Does the imperfect "I was watching" *(etheōroun)* indicate that Satan's fall was supposed to be occurring simultaneously with—perhaps even that it was caused by—the success reported by the seventy(-two)? Or was it rather the case that Luke thought of Jesus as reporting a prophetic vision, experienced sometime previously but perhaps yet to be fulfilled? The former hypothesis is more frequently adopted by commentators.[49] Even those scholars who agree that the statement may have originated as a report of a prophetic vision are reluctant to suppose that Luke interpreted the saying in this way.[50] The skepticism is, however, unfounded. It is quite possible, even likely, that Luke was familiar with the repeated use of the imperfect *etheōroun* to introduce the visions of the prophet Daniel (Dan. 7:2,4,6,7,9,11, 13).[51] As noted above, Luke appears to regard Jesus' response to the seventy(-two) as the content of the revelation for which he subsequently (vv. 21-22) gives thanks; a vision report analogous to those given by the earlier prophet Daniel would admirably fit this revelatory context. Hence it may be that Luke has Jesus mention Satan's fall here, not because it was simultaneous with the missionaries' casting out of demons, but because the *envisioned* fall will be related in some other way to the missionaries' exorcisms.

There are clear indications that Luke did not intend for 10:19 and the surrounding material to be understood as solely retrospective. The disciples report, not that the demons "were" subject to them, but that the demons "are" subject *(hypotassetai;* vv. 17,20). Jesus does not report that the Enemy "has in no way harmed you" but that he "will in no way harm you" *(ouden hymas ou mē adikēsē;* v. 19).[52] Both of these observations suggest that Luke saw Jesus' gift of authority and promise of protection in 10:19 as having an ongoing, even future effect. This authority and protection are, perhaps, to be used during an onslaught of "the Enemy" that is yet to come. Evidence of such an onslaught can therefore be sought—and readily found—in Acts. At the very least, Paul's stunning defeat of Bar Jesus in Acts 13 (see below, chap. 4) should be construed as an instance of Christian authority "over all the power of the Enemy." Other relevant events include the exposure and punishment of Ananias and Sapphira, who were similarly agents of Satan (Acts 5:3), the humiliation of Satan's notorious servant Simon Magus (discussed below in chap. 3), and the viper's unsuccessful attack on Paul (28:36).[53]

In sum, the implied temporal sequence appears to be something like this: the seventy(-two) return, rejoicing, and report that the demons are subject to them. What Jesus hears in this report is the news of a dramatic reduction of Satan's dominion. Jesus responds by reporting his very pertinent vision of the fall of Satan, and by announcing that the seventy(-two)—and by implication those whom they foreshadow—have authority over "snakes and scorpions" and will be invulnerable to Satan's attacks. Finally, Jesus qualifies the missionaries' present joy.

Luke's understanding of Satan's fall. The Septuagint passage after which Satan's fall has ultimately been modeled is Isa. 14:1-27. In Luke's narrative Jesus has just alluded to Isa. 14:11-15, in his woe over Capernaum (Luke 10:15). The juxtaposition can hardly be accidental: Luke, who was thoroughly familiar with the prophecies of Isaiah, appears to have recognized the allusion and used it as a cue for inclusion of the related saying about the fall of Satan.[54] The Isaiah passage tells of the fall of the mighty king of Babylon and the defeat of Assyria that are to precede the restoration of Israel, then moves to the taunt song that the Israelites will raise against the king of Babylon. The king is to be thrown down because he thought to make himself equal to the most high (v. 13). At the testing in the wilderness, Satan similarly arrogates divine glory by seeking to be worshiped (Luke 4:7). Luke—imitating the logic of the Isaiah passage, as he apparently has done in the story of Herod in Acts 12—probably supposed that Satan must likewise be thrown down from his position of control, of having "the inhabited world" at his beck and call. Also under the influence of the Isaiah passage, Luke may have reasoned that the fall would precede the restoration of the house of Jacob, when Gentiles would join themselves to the people of Israel (Isa. 14:1). Can one identify more precisely the occasion of the devil's fall in the narrative world of Luke-Acts?

One possibility is that Luke supposed the fall of Satan had *already* taken place. According to this theory, the "fall" is to be identified with the "conquering" of Satan mentioned by Jesus in Luke 11:22. But it would be unwise to accept this solution too hastily. As noted above, the account about the seventy(-two) apparently foreshadows the period of the church, and the promise of authority and protection mentioned in 10:19 will also be in effect in Acts. Hence it is possible that the vision of Satan's fall will be fulfilled between this point in Jesus' earthly ministry and the time of the birth of the church as depicted in Acts. Further, the "conquering" of Satan mentioned by Jesus in Luke 11:22 ought not to be construed as a decisive victory. Throughout Jesus' earthly ministry Satan retains potential authority over Jesus and his followers, which he exerts again at the passion. As discussed above, the affirmation in Luke 11:22 that Jesus has "conquered" Satan may (by means of an allusion to Isa. 53:12) point toward the passion as the time when the "strong one" would truly be conquered, and his spoil divided.

The last observation suggests another occasion when Luke may have supposed Satan's fall to have occurred, namely, Jesus' resurrection/ascension: the accuser of the people is to be thrown down[55] at the time when Christ is exalted to the position of judge and intercessor at God's right hand (the same position often thought to have been occupied by Satan). Identifying the fall of Satan with Jesus' resurrection and ascension helps to explain why Jesus' joy over "these things" in vv. 21-22 takes the form of a thanksgiving for Jesus' *sonship* (vv. 21-22), because it is at his resurrection that Jesus' sonship is made manifest (Acts 13:32-33).

A tie between Jesus' death/resurrection and Satan's demise had been made by members of other Christian circles by the late first or early second century. Hence it is possible that the idea of such a connection was already known to—perhaps even taken for granted by—Luke and his readers. John 12:27-33 depicts Jesus as reflecting at the conclusion of his ministry on "the hour" that lies before him:

> Now shall the ruler of this world be cast out; and I, when I am lifted up from the earth, will draw all humans to myself." He said this to show by what death he was to die.
>
> (John 12:31-33)[56]

A similar link was made by the author of the letter to the Hebrews (though without any mention of a "fall"). This author writes that Jesus partook of the nature of flesh and blood, "in order that through death he might destroy the one having the power *(to kratos)* of death, that is, the devil" (2:14; cf. 1 John 3:8; Acts 2:24; Col. 2:15). In 1 Pet. 3:21b-22, reference is made to the resurrection of Jesus and to his having ascended into heaven with angels, authorities and powers subject to him (cf. Acts 2:34-35; Eph. 1:20-22a; Phil. 2:9-11). Finally, in the Book of Revelation, the dragon's fall from heaven occurs when he and the archangel Michael do battle in heaven. But if the superior strength of Michael is said to be one cause of Satan's fall, another cause is said to be "the blood of the Lamb and the word of their testimony" (Rev. 12:11).

U. B. Müller has argued that the notion of the fall of Satan evidenced in Luke 10:18 should be understood against the backdrop of contemporaneous traditions about a heavenly battle that would usher in the eschatological age.[57] Besides Revelation 12, Müller discusses the Qumran War Scroll (esp. 1QM 15:14-17), 11QMelch 13f., and *Sibylline Oracles* 3:796-807. Müller is correct in pointing out the relevance of these texts for understanding the original meaning of the saying at Luke 10:18, but he too readily forfeits this background when he comes to interpret the meaning of the saying as it occurs within Luke's Gospel. Without adequate reason Müller denies that Luke 10:18 may be understood as in any sense proleptic (here he contrasts *1 Enoch* 83:4ff.).[58] He writes, "To be sure, within the framework of an apocalypse Luke 10:18 could be a vision of the future. But transmitted in isolation, the saying presupposes the event of which it speaks as past."[59] Unfortunately, in his effort to recover the meaning of the saying for the historical Jesus, Müller has incorrectly assessed its present literary context. Whether or not it was "transmitted in isolation," Luke has included the logion within the framework of a revelatory discourse, which is itself uttered to disciples who seem to represent Jesus' post-resurrection followers.

Of the texts that Müller cites, 11Q Melchizedek appears to be especially important for understanding Luke 10:17-24. This Qumran text describes a cosmic occurrence to take place in "the year of the Lord's favor," the final jubilee year in which release is proclaimed to the captives (Isa. 61:1; Lev. 25:10; cf. Luke 4:18-19). At God's command Melchizedek will take a throne in the heights, above the assembly of the heavenly beings, to (using Fitzmyer's reconstruction) "exact the ven[ge]ance of the jud[g]ments of God (ʾ[l]) [from the hand of Be]lial and from the hand(s) of all [the spirits of] his [lot].''[60] There are clear points of affinity to Luke's Gospel, where Jesus is similarly anointed with the Spirit to liberate the captives of Satan (Acts 10:38). It is true that in Luke 10:17-20 Luke does not explicitly mention a cosmic confrontation, nor the enthronement of a savior. But if one takes seriously the revelatory character of the passage, the picture changes, for later in the two-volume narrative Luke lays great stress on the enthronement of Jesus which takes place at his resurrection and ascension (Acts 2:22-36).[61] At that time Jesus will come into the Kingdom appointed to him (Luke 22:29; 23:42-43). Perhaps, then, in the narrative world of Luke's writings (as in that of the Melchizedek fragment), at the exaltation of the Anointed One he confronts the Prince of Darkness and emerges the definitive victor. In this case Jesus' reference to Satan's fall (Luke 10:18) anticipates an event destined to occur when Jesus is raised to God's right hand, to the place that Satan now occupies.

It may be helpful to summarize the analysis of Luke 10:17-20 up to this point. First, in an examination of the literary context of 10:17-20 I noted that Luke's purpose in relating this climax to the mission of the seventy(-two) may be related to his purposes in creating the mission account as a whole. The description of this mission apparently builds on an allusion to Numbers 11, where Moses appoints seventy(-two) Spirit-endowed elders to help him to do God's work. Luke may be suggesting that the seventy(-two) missionaries (or those whom they prefigure) are, like Moses' elders, Spirit-endowed. Hence the mission of the seventy(-two) foreshadows the time when Christians (like Jesus, who here "rejoices in the Spirit") will be enabled by the Holy Spirit to comprehend and bear witness to the mystery of Jesus' sonship. Second, examination of the temporal sequence of events mentioned in vv. 17-20 indicated that Luke could have understood the imperfect verb *etheōroun* to introduce an apocalyptic vision, as the same verb form repeatedly does in Daniel 7. Third, the missionaries' use of the present tense to describe their exorcistic success was seen to imply that Jesus' gift of authority and protection will be in effect at a future time (namely, the time of the Church as depicted in Acts). Fourth, I suggested that in order to discern Luke's understanding of Satan's fall, one must look to Isaiah 14, a passage reinterpreted in Luke's day to refer to that fall. The king in Isaiah 14 (like the devil in Luke's narrative) exalts himself in a blasphemous way; thus it would be understandable if Luke thought that Satan, like the king, must be cast down. Jesus' enthronement at the resurrection is

herein proposed as the probable occasion when Satan's fall is thought
to take place. This would parallel 11 Q Melchizedek, in which Belial
similarly confronts the Spirit-anointed redeemer in heaven when the
latter ascends to take his throne. The link between the fall and resurrection which I suggest would explain why vv. 17-20 constitute
the antecedent for the thanksgiving for Jesus' sonship in vv. 21-22,
because it is at the resurrection when Jesus' sonship is realized
(Acts 13:32-33).

Luke's account of the passion of Jesus is compatible with this reconstructed time line of events. Luke has depicted Jesus as making
substantial inroads into Satan's kingdom throughout most of Jesus'
earthly ministry. The disciples also, though sent out as "lambs" in
the midst of "wolves," had needed no purse or bag or sandals because
they enjoyed the authority and consequent protection that Jesus had
conferred.[62] But until the time when the devil is expelled from heaven,
he has the potential again to exercise authority over Jesus and his
followers and hence to work great harm. At the passion Satan exploits
this potential, once more taking the offensive and sweeping Judas
into his plot. Now, as the final dark events of the passion begin to
unfold, Jesus reverses his former directions to the disciples not to take
material supplies (Luke 22:36). Jesus' enigmatic instructions suggest
that a momentous change in the distribution of power and authority
(corresponding in some way to the distribution of material goods) is
occurring.[63] Whereas before the apostles had not "lacked anything"
(22:35), now that will alter: the authority and consequent protection
on which they could earlier rely will vanish. The necessity for a
"sword" symbolically indicates that the new situation will be one of
marked hostility, even violence.[64]

The dark and dangerous situation symbolized by the need for a
sword will not be permanent. Jesus says that this situation has come
about in order that the scripture that says "and he was reckoned with
transgressors" (Luke 22:37; alluding to Isa. 53:12) might be fulfilled,
and it is in the "hour" of "the authority of darkness" (Luke 22:53)
that this occurs: Jesus is regarded as a common thief (22:52) and is
subsequently crucified with criminals (23:32).[65] When it comes about
that Jesus is reckoned with the lawless, Satan will have taken the
position of authority; hence the apostles will no longer have divine
protection. This is when they must be on their guard, "taking up a
sword" and "praying that they not enter into testing." The devil will
sift the apostles like wheat, trying to take them captive. His authority

will be made manifest to the world in a period of oppressive darkness (23:44-45). But because of Jesus' obedience, his own ultimate rescue by God and victory over Satan at the resurrection and ascension are inevitable.[66] Then the worship that Satan wrongfully demanded (4:7) will be given to Jesus instead (24:52). And soon Jesus will send power upon the church (24:49), to complement the authority promised earlier (10:19). The period of danger will be ended.

Exactly what cosmic events Luke thought transpired while Jesus' body was in the tomb, one cannot say.[67] In his account of the three-day period Luke focuses his attention on events that occur on the human plane. But by no means does the lack of explicit statements about events in the heavenly realm imply authorial indifference about these matters. Luke believed that visible human events often have an invisible spiritual dimension. He has given many strategically placed indications that the earthly events of Jesus' suffering, death, and res-urrection had spiritual or cosmic causes and consequences (22:3,31,35-38,43-44; 23:44-45 [where Luke adds the reference to the sun's eclipse]; and esp. Acts 2:22-36). If Luke does not tell us what happened when Jesus' body was in the tomb, it is because the important thing for Theophilus and others like him to know is that Jesus rises as the son who has conquered. Satan is no longer in heaven, able to accuse, because Jesus is in his place, receiving believers who die (Acts 7:56,59) and acting as counselor to those in need (Luke 12:8-9).[68]

In light of the above explication of the salvific events in Luke-Acts, Jesus' response to the seventy(-two) when they report to Jesus that "even the demons are subject to us in your name" is appropriate, if elliptical. The implied sequence of thought may have been something like this: "What you tell me is that I have conquered Satan, and that because of my victory you can release those who are his captives. But I tell you that even greater things will soon happen: when I am raised to heaven Satan will fall from his place there, and you will have authority over all his power."[69] But what is the nature of this authority and of the protection it brings? This question remains to be answered.

The nature of the authority of the seventy(-two). Jesus promises the seventy(-two) authority to tread on serpents and scorpions and over all the power of the Enemy, and assures them that the Enemy shall in no way harm them. This promise of authority over demonic powers echoes Ps. 91:13 (LXX 90:13). Although the vocabulary in Luke 10:19 is not identical to that of the psalm, the promise of ability to trample demonic powers with immunity is very similar.[70] Luke surely recognized the allusion, because he was familiar with this Psalm: Satan had quoted the preceding two verses of it (vv. 11-12) to Jesus at the testing in the wilderness. It would thus be an ironically appropriate passage to echo when making a gift of authority over all the power of "the Enemy." This is especially so if, as evidence from Qumran suggests, the Psalm were already being used as a promise of protection from demonic powers (as was clearly the case in Rabbinic times).[71] But what does Luke understand by this gift of authority, and what connection is there between the fall of Satan on the one hand, and the gift of authority and promise of protection on the other?

A clue to the answer may be provided by the Book of Revelation, which also connects the motifs of Satan's fall and of Christians' exemption from demonic or diabolical authority. In Rev. 9:1-11, a "star" falls from heaven to earth, where it is given the key to unlock the abyss. From the abyss comes smoke, and from the smoke come locusts, to which is given authority like that of scorpions. Only those who have the seal of God upon their foreheads will escape the horrendous torture inflicted by these scorpion-like creatures. So, whereas in Luke the fall of Satan is tied to the giving of authority to Christians, that they might tread on scorpions, in Revelation 9 the fall of the "star" is tied to the granting of authority to "scorpions," that they might tread on humans. But both documents emphasize that those who belong to God are invulnerable to the evil power. The latter idea is echoed in Rev. 13:7-8, which implies that only those whose names are written in "the book of life" (cf. Luke 10:20) will be exempt from the authority of the beast and from the attendant requirement to worship it. In Rev. 12:7-12 a war in heaven results in Satan—"the great dragon, that ancient serpent, who is called the devil and Satan"— being cast down to earth. A heavenly voice cries out that this ejection of Satan, brought about "by the blood of the lamb," coincides with the arrival of the salvation, power, and authority of Christ, and of the Kingdom of God. Those who dwell in heaven are to rejoice, but those on earth should lament, "because the devil has come down to you in great wrath, because he knows that his time is short." Here, as in Luke, instructions to rejoice follow closely upon a fall of Satan to earth. Unlike Luke, the Apocalypse specifies the reason for rejoicing: the heaven-dwellers will be exempt from Satan's authority during the desperate burst of diabolical activity to precede Satan's ultimate demise at the judgment.

These ideas found in Revelation about Satan's fall, his continuing authority over humans in the period after the fall,[72] and the exemption of the faithful from this satanic authority are compatible with Luke's understanding of the fall of Satan as reconstructed above. At the resurrection Jesus will oust Satan from his position in heaven, but Satan will not yet be finished with his wicked deeds. Since resurrection has overcome death once, and since the general resurrection and judgment have thereby been guaranteed as imminent (Acts 17:31), Satan will know not only that he has been "cast down," but also that his time "is short." Soon—when God puts Christ's enemies under his feet (Acts 2:35)—the power of death will be wrested from Satan completely. Everyone will be raised, and those whose names are written in heaven will be saved from the authority of darkness (Acts 26:18,23; cf. Rev. 20:15). In the short time remaining to him, Satan will try to hold onto what authority he has had by corrupting the church (as in the incident with Ananias and Sapphira) and by interfering with the growth of the word (as in the incident with Bar Jesus). But Spirit-endowed Christians, foreshadowed in Luke by the seventy (-two), will triumph over Satan's deadly mischief. Like the humans in Revelation who "have the mark of God on their foreheads," Christians depicted in Acts are exempt from the authority of the Enemy, and he can in no way harm them. Indeed, as the analyses of the following chapters will show, the Enemy is himself subject to the authority of Christians.

Jesus' instructions to the seventy(-two) not to rejoice "that the spirits are subject to you" are not meant to denigrate or downplay miraculous power. Throughout his two-volume work, Luke regards the power to cast out demons and to heal as truly remarkable: it is an important factor in the demise of Satan's kingdom and advent of God's own, and is capable even of bringing people to faith. The reason Jesus tells the disciples not to rejoice is not that their authority over spirits is "bad," but that it pales in comparison to the wonder of their protection against post-resurrection satanic activity, and ultimately to their salvation at the judgment.

SUMMARY AND ANALYSIS

In the preceding analysis, I have argued that Satan plays a much more important role in the narrative world of Luke-Acts than is commonly supposed. Like the king of Babylon, the devil had usurped authority over the house of Jacob. He was an arrogant oppressor, who claimed for himself the worship that belonged to God alone. He even sought worship from Jesus, and when he did not obtain it he withdrew for a while, defeated. During Jesus' earthly ministry Satan was clearly the weaker, and Jesus plundered the devil's kingdom, releasing from captivity some of its oppressed and delegating authority to the disciples that they might do the same. According to Luke, Jesus saw these acts of release as a foreshadowing of the imminent day when his death and resurrection would cause Satan finally to be cast from his position of authority, to "fall like lightning from the sky." At that time God would rescue Jesus and bring him into the kingdom appointed him (Acts 2:36; 13:33). But Jesus would come as through fire: in the preceding "hour" of "the authority of darkness," Satan would use every possible weapon to try to alter the course of events. Since Jesus had temporarily lost his authority, the apostles would also temporarily lose theirs; hence the need for them to "take up a sword," in other words to be on their guard against the "well-armed strong one." Satan's efforts to sabotage God's plans would be to no avail. Jesus would take over from Satan the place of authority at the right hand of God "and reign over the house of Jacob forever" (Luke 1:33).

The struggle between Jesus (or the Holy Spirit) and Satan lies at the very heart of Luke's story. The advantage in this struggle shifts from one side to the other and back again as the plot progresses. This changing outcome in turn affects the experience of many of the characters in Luke's Gospel: of the persons whom Jesus, because of his advantage, can heal, release from demonic possession, or forgive; of the apostles who are alternately invulnerable and open to diabolical attack; of the seventy(-two), to whom the demons are subject in Jesus' name. As a result of Satan's fall from his position of authority at the time of Jesus' exaltation, the advantage shifts again, and Jesus and his followers gain the upper hand once and for all. Granted, Satan remains on the scene; he has fallen from heaven but has not yet been made a "footstool for Christ's feet." But, far from being the *ecclesia pressa* described by Conzelmann, the church in Acts is the "church triumphant." Chapters 3–5 of this work will show how time and again in Acts the church's Spirit-endowed members show that they have authority over all the power of the Enemy, and that he can in no way harm them. Satan uses every stratagem to try to maintain control over his dwindling domain, but in mighty and Spirit-filled persons like Peter and Paul, the devil more than meets his match. Christians in Acts have (as the angelic guide of Hermas puts it) power to master the works of the devil. His threats need not be feared, for to those who are faithful he proves to be as "powerless as the sinews of a dead man" *(Hermas Mandate* 12.6.2).

By expanding Jesus' explanation of the casting out of demons and reworking it so as to recall more insistently not only passages from

Isaiah commonly applied by Luke's contemporaries to Jesus, but also John the Baptist's designation of Jesus as "the one who is stronger," Luke clarifies and strengthens the anti-magic apology exhibited in the parallel versions of the Beelzebul pericope. If Matthew and Mark had hinted that Jesus' casting out of demons be seen, not as works of Beelzebul but as the scripturally predicted victory of the servant of the Lord over the "strong one" Satan, Luke virtually demands that events be interpreted in this way. Luke does not use exorcism accounts as mere "filler," that is, as a casual means of narrative transition; each and every such account conveys the earnest message of Jesus' victory over Satan. In the exorcisms, Luke insists, actions and outcome on the visible human plane point toward events on the invisible cosmic one. The specified interpretation ought to be understood as applying to all of Luke's reports of exorcisms, and probably to reports of healings as well. In other words, even passing references to exorcisms and healings included in Lukan summary reports ought to be interpreted as earthly, visible signs of victory over the invisible spiritual Enemy.

From the preceding analysis it has emerged that the earthly drama explicitly depicted in Luke's Gospel is actually a component part of an overarching but largely implicit story about conflict between God or God's Holy Spirit and Satan. The cosmic conflict began in the shadowy past; Luke suggests that its earthly manifestations could be seen already in the many instances when Jews followed false prophets and persecuted true ones. During Jesus' earthly ministry, the conflict surfaced especially in the exorcisms that he performed, and reached its climax in his death, resurrection, and ascension, when he cried out to God and was rescued from the authority of darkness. Various aspects of this overarching (and strikingly apocalyptic) story are paralleled in Jewish and Jewish-Christian documents dating from approximately 100 B.C.E. to 100 C.E. For example, the Gospel of Mark portrays Jesus as confronting Satan in the exorcisms and healings.[73] The *Martyrdom of Isaiah* tells the story of a Spirit-filled prophet who suffers at the hand of diabolically inspired rulers and false prophets. Hebrews testifies that by his death Jesus "destroyed the one who has the power of death, that is, the devil," and the author of the fourth Gospel connects the expulsion of "the ruler of this world" and Jesus' "exaltation" on the cross. The Book of Revelation tells of Satan's quest for unrighteous worship and envisions his fall, and insists that the faithful will be invulnerable to Satan's attacks after the fall. The notion of the righteous person's victory over Satan has counterparts in the Jewish *Testament of Job* and the Christian *Shepherd of Hermas*.

The conceptual analogs furnished by these documents indicate that at least the elements of Luke's story of conflict between the forces of Satan and God were conventional, perhaps even commonplace, in certain strains of first-century Jewish and Christian discourse.

As noted above, the overarching mythic story remains largely implicit in the text of Luke's Gospel. I have had to tease it out of various accounts, giving special weight to the more transparent passages, especially Luke 10:17-20 and 11:14-23. But if this story is so important for Luke, why has the evangelist nowhere made it more plain? This is a difficult question. In general, narratives may allusively presuppose their authors' fundamental convictions rather than articulating them. This is especially true if the convictions are held also by the audience; as I observed in the introduction, when writer and readers approached the telling and hearing of the story with a shared schema already in place, they could "fit in the pieces and negotiate the text more readily." The above-noted parallels to various aspects of the Lukan story point to the existence of such a schema, and the analyses in the following chapters will give reasons to believe that Luke regularly expected his readers to be able to read the story of Satan between the lines.[74]

Jesus' gift in Luke 10:19 of authority to tread on serpents and scorpions and over all the Enemy's power could easily be interpreted as a promise of "magical" prowess. Surely any pagan reading the passage would have interpreted it in this way; it is a remarkable gift, one that the users of the magical papyri would have coveted. Luke, on the other hand, interpreted the promise as an assurance that Christians would be triumphant over the evil forces that opposed the church and that made magic possible. From Luke's perspective there would be no logical contradiction in understanding Jesus' remark at 10:19 as a promise that magic could not prevail, because by Luke's definition "magic" is satanic power actualized. Therefore wherever Satan cannot utilize his power, there can be no "magic." Whenever demons are subject to Christians acting in Jesus' name, they clearly can not obey Satan, and neither can they obey "magicians." That established, it is fitting now to see how this powerlessness of Satan and of magic is illustrated in three Lukan accounts of Christian interaction with magicians. The first of these is the story of Simon Magus.

3

SIMON MAGUS

Acts 8:4-25

INTRODUCTION

Luke's account of Simon Magus is a key to any investigation of the early Christian understanding of magic. Ink spent by Luke on the "magician" in Acts 8 is substantial, and Simon, unlike the other practitioners of magic depicted in Acts, is even allowed to speak. It is true that his words are scant, and also that his magical activities are recounted with virtually no detail, but there is still much to be learned from the narrative. Simon's speech (especially 8:19) epitomizes "the trouble with magic" as Luke understands it, and Luke's silence concerning the details of Simon's thaumaturgical technique indicates merely that the author's main interest lies elsewhere, itself a useful piece of information.

From the second century onward, Simon was depicted as the original gnostic and arch heretic,[1] and these later characterizations have significantly influenced the scholarly questions most often put to the Acts account.[2] For many years, scholars commenting on this passage focused not on the question of how it may be able to illumine the early Christian view of magic, but on what information it may conceal about the possible historical connections between Simon and gnosticism. "Conceal" is the appropriate word. In an influential essay, Ernst Haenchen argued that the historical Simon was indeed a gnostic redeemer, just as depicted in later portraits; the reason his identity as such is so hard to discern in Acts 8 is that the Christian tradition had demoted him to a mere magician.[3] Thus authenticated by Haenchen as a gnostic redeemer, the figure of Simon provided the needed link between gnosticism and earliest Christianity. In other words, Simon's supposed status as a pre-Christian gnostic could be used to legitimate the interpretation of various New Testament writings in the light of gnostic ideas and concepts not actually attested until much later.

The anachronism of this approach has been discussed elsewhere.[4] Many interpreters of Luke-Acts now agree that second-and-third century gnostic ideas may not legitimately be read into Luke's pre-gnostic account. To be sure, Luke's opinion of Simon is altogether biased; by no means may one assume that Simon would have accepted the terms "magician" and "magic" as designations for himself and his work.[5] But neither may one conclude from the portrayals of Simon in post-New Testament documents that Luke concealed—even unintentionally—a more exalted and therefore more "true" identity. All efforts to gain access to the historical Simon via the Acts account will meet with obstacles, perhaps insurmountable. But even if Luke's portrayal of Simon as one who practiced "magic" is of dubious value for rediscovering the historical Simon, the portrayal may provide a different sort of historical information, concerning the way that early Christians viewed their own traditions about miracle workers vis-à-vis the analogous traditions of their competitors.

Luke's narration of the story of Simon Magus is marked by oddities. The story starts in the middle, proceeds to the beginning, takes unexpected turns, and comes to two apparent closes (vv. 8,13) before it finally skids to the actual close—which leaves the question of Simon's spiritual destiny unresolved. While there is wide agreement that at least some of these discontinuities can be attributed to Luke's use of different sources, efforts to untangle and identify these have diverged greatly.[6] In the following analysis (as elsewhere in this study) I assume that the finished narrative accurately represents Luke's own point of view, whatever sources he may have used. Nonetheless, I will pay close attention to several of the "rough spots," since these may harbor clues to Luke's intentions.

In order to discover Luke's understanding of Simon and his magic, I will first examine Acts 8:4-8, 12, Luke's description of the missionary success of Philip, one of "the Seven" (6:5). There are striking parallels between the deeds performed and response evoked by Philip on the one hand and by Simon on the other. Only after a close analysis of Philip's proclamation can Luke's conception of the enormity of Simon's failure to grasp that proclamation be discerned.

PHILIP'S MISSION IN SAMARIA
(Acts 8:4-8, 12)

Philip preached about "the Christ" (v. 5) and "the kingdom of God and the name of Jesus" (v. 12) to the Samaritans.[7] His evangelizing efforts were successful: the onlookers were closely attentive to the things that Philip said (ta legomena), "when they heard and saw the signs that he did."[8] Luke implies that the people regarded these striking signs—noisy exorcisms, and healings of the paralyzed and lame—as the corroboration of Philip's message. Because of his actions, the people attended to his words and eventually were converted (v. 12). Why did Philip's remarkable deeds draw attention to his words instead of to himself?[9] Certainly Luke knew that veneration of the wonder-worker was an ever-present possibility: it had up till that moment been the people's reaction to Simon the magician (8:10; cf. 14:11).[10] But Philip's deeds prompted belief in a message because they exemplified the content of that message. Philip's "signs" (sēmeia) were not regarded by Luke as random displays of power (as were, presumably, Simon's unspecified magic tricks, mageiai), but, rather, as virtual enactments of the word that Philip preached. Sign and proclamation were coherent, and therefore mutually reinforcing.

In order to substantiate this contention, I will try to determine what Luke understood to be the content of Philip's preaching. Such determination is feasible because the descriptions that Luke gives of Philip's message are stylized, though abbreviated. Elsewhere Luke uses similar but more fully elaborated expressions to characterize the Christian missionaries' proclamation, and from these other passages one can tentatively infer what Philip's message was imagined to have been.

Luke's note that Philip "preached to them the Christ" (v. 5) suggests that Philip preached the message that Jesus of Nazareth was the Christ about whom the scriptures spoke. God's plan concerning the Christ had been recorded in the scriptures long ago and had been waiting, dormant, for the proper person to enact it. According to Luke, the

Christian proclamation was formulated as news that the awaited person was none other than Jesus.[11] The missionaries' consistent strategy
for proving this claim was to talk about the life, death, and resurrection
and ascension of Jesus, showing how these matched up with what
was found in "the law of Moses and the prophets."[12] The passage
that for Luke identified Jesus as literally *the Christ*, (i.e. the
"anointed,") is Isa. 61:1. Luke had Jesus quote a composite of Isa.
61:1 and 58:6 in the important Nazareth sermon introducing Jesus'
ministry of liberation (Luke 4:18; cf. 7:22). Moreover, Peter alludes
to Isa. 61:1 in the speech summarizing the life of Jesus made to those
gathered around Cornelius (Acts 10:38): Jesus had been "anointed"
by God with the Holy Spirit and with power, and went about doing
good and healing those oppressed by Satan.[13]

The missionaries' message about Jesus as the Anointed One is linked
to their proclamation of the Kingdom of God (8:12). So important is
this proclamation, about which the risen Lord himself had instructed
them (Acts 1:3), that the words "the Kingdom" can be used to signify
the entire missionary message (8:12; 19:8; 20:25). This message included the news that Jesus had been taken up to heaven to occupy
"the throne of David," in accordance with the promises of Scripture
(2:22-36; cf. 13:22-23). Thus Jesus was already King, and the re-
constituted twelve apostles were already regents and judges over the
twelve tribes of Israel.[14] Nonetheless, the Kingdom was yet to be fully
implemented. Complete inauguration would coincide with the definitive subjection of all Christ's enemies—including surely the supreme
"Enemy," the devil—under his feet.[15] In the meantime, every gain
for the Kingdom of God through exorcism, healing, or conversion
was a loss for the Kingdom of Satan, who used cunning but mostly
futile tactics to try to keep people under his own authority. No one,
not even Satan, could prevent the inevitable realization of the Kingdom of God.

The last key element in Philip's proclamation is "the name of Jesus"
(Acts 8:12). Though the name of Jesus could be invoked for various
purposes,[16] what is likely in view here is its power to effect forgiveness
of (literally: "release from") sins.[17] This focus is made evident when
the people respond to Philip's proclamation by being baptized
(8:12,16), which Luke regards as the proper reaction to the message
of the forgiveness available through Jesus' name (2:38; 10:43-48;
22:16). In Luke's understanding, Christian missionaries (including,
presumably, Philip) preached that Christ was raised from the dead
and exalted to the right hand of God in order that repentance and

forgiveness might be granted to Israel and to the nations (5:31; 10:40-43; 13:37-39). The risen Christ tells Paul that hearers of the Gospel must turn from the authority of Satan to the authority of God, claiming this forgiveness and "a place [or share: *klēros*] among those sanctified by faith in me" (26:18-20). Baptism in the name of Jesus signified that the new believers had indeed repented and turned from Satan to God.

Thus Philip's message about the Christ, the Kingdom of God, and the name of Jesus was implied also to be a message about *release from Satan's authority*. Jesus, wresting spoil from "the strong one," had brought about such release during his earthly ministry, and after the resurrection his disciples continued to do so whenever they called upon his name (Luke 10:9, 17-20). Philip's dramatic exorcisms and healings of the possessed, paralyzed, and lame gave incontrovertible proof of Satan's subjugation, and hence of the certainty of the Kingdom of God with Christ as Lord. Philip's deeds were visible and audible enactments of his proclamation; consequently, the deeds were regarded by Luke as fostering belief in the things that Philip spoke. Thus it is not only because they see and hear demons being cast out that the people "rejoice" (v. 8), but also because the onlookers perceive the divine truths that those exorcisms express (cf. Luke 10:20).

SIMON MAGUS
(Acts 8:9-13)

Abruptly the time frame shifts (v. 9). In a flashback, the narrator reports on the long-standing success in the city of Simon, a certain man who had been "amazing" the city's inhabitants with his "magic" (v. 9: *mageuein;* v. 11: *mageia*). The people give the magician acclaim beyond that due any human being, calling him "the great power of God." The original form and significance of the title have long been debated, but by no means established;[18] in any case these issues lie outside the scope of this discussion. The question of the title's import within the context of Luke-Acts is much more relevant, since "the power of God" is a recurring motif throughout the two-volume work. It will be worthwhile to look in some detail at Luke's use of this motif.

In his Gospel Luke uses the term "power" *(dynamis)* more frequently than either Matthew or Mark,[19] introducing it into several accounts when it was not present in his source (Luke 4:36; 5:17; 6:19; 9:1; see also 10:19; 24:49). On occasion the evangelist's narration indicates that he conceived of "power" in material terms: it is like a substance that flows forth from someone (Luke 6:19; 8:46; cf. Acts

5:15; 19:12). But these passages are inadequate grounds for concluding that Luke thought of power as impersonal and free-floating.[20]
The evidence suggests that the deliberately acting divine agent behind
any given demonstration of power is never far from the author's view.
With regard to the miracles of Jesus and his followers, Luke frequently
takes pains to show that this agent was God or God's Holy Spirit.[21]
An especially relevant example is Acts 19:11-12: although Luke describes miracles (handkerchiefs being carried from Paul's body to heal
the sick) that would seem to betray an impersonal, "mana"-like concept of power, Luke explicitly states that God was responsible. Luke's
care in specifying God as the actor behind Jesus' and the Christians'
power is prompted by an awareness that there are other such actors
at work in the world: the Enemy also wields power (Luke 10:19; cf.
4:6), and Luke wants to preclude the suspicion that this "alternative
agent" had anything to do with the miracles of Jesus and the
Christians.

To some readers, Luke's stress on divine agency may appear to be
undercut by his remarkable conception of "the name of Jesus."[22]
Luke's notion of the great power called forth when Christians utter
"the name" looks (and looked) suspiciously like the notion, common
in magic, that spiritual beings (especially the daimons of persons who
had died young or who were killed violently) could be summoned
forth to perform a feat whenever desired. Luke must have recognized
the similarity: in portraying the Jewish officials as asking Peter "by
what power or by what name" he had healed the lame man (4:7),
Luke probably imagines that the officials supposed a demonic or
diabolical agent to be at work.[23] Similarly, in his narration of the
attempt by the seven sons of Sceva to "name the name of the Lord
Jesus over the evil spirits," Luke is probably implying that the sons
mistook Christian invocations of Jesus' name for acts of magical necromancy (see below, chap. 5). But if, as suggested here, Luke acknowledged that Christians' invocation of Jesus' name resembled
magicians' invocation of spirits or daimons, no doubt the evangelist
also insisted on the superficiality of that resemblance.[24] Luke regarded
Satan as the authority behind all acts of magic, including the sum-
moning of demonic spirits, but insisted that whenever Christians invoke the name of Jesus it is *God* who graciously "extends his hand"
(Acts 4:30). In Luke's estimation Christians doing miracles in Jesus'
name actually prove themselves to be entirely opposed and superior
to Satan, whose authority has been curtailed (Luke 10:18-19).

Luke claims that the power of God was *with, upon,* or even *in*
Jesus—but, as the occurrence of such prepositions suggests, the power

is still regarded as separate and distinct from Jesus. Luke never claims that Jesus actually *is* "the power of God."[25] For Simon to encourage such an attribution is to exalt himself in a most damning and contemptible way. Luke regards the acclaim given to Simon as analogous to that given to (and rejected by) Paul and Barnabas in Lystra (Acts 14:11-15). This honoring of Simon smacks of idolatry: it is the worship of a power that is supposedly "of God," but actually of an agent far more malevolent. That Simon does not repudiate the acclaim, but rather, cultivates it by performing magic tricks over a long period of time and "making himself out to be someone great" *(legōn einai tina heauton megan)* does not bode well for the magician. In Luke's narrative world, all others who "fail to give God the glory" meet an unhappy end.[26]

Both Simon's self-deification and his traffic in magic imply for Luke an association with the devil. In making himself out to be someone great and thereby encouraging followers to acclaim him as a god, Simon committed the same horrendous sin that the devil had once committed in the wilderness (Luke 4:6-7) and now continues to commit through his ongoing promotion of idolatry. But if Luke saw Simon as connected with both magic and Satan, does the author also regard Simon as a false prophet, despite the absence of the term "false prophet" *(pseudoprophētēs)* from the account?[27]

In trying to answer this question, it will be helpful to begin with a consideration of Luke's treatment elsewhere of false prophets. There are two references to false prophets in Luke-Acts. In Acts 13:4-12 (to be analyzed in chap. 4), Luke portrays Bar Jesus, a Jewish false prophet, as a "son of the devil" who promotes idolatry by trying to prohibit the conversion of Sergius Paulus. In Luke 6:26, Jesus proclaims, "Woe to you, when all people speak well of you, for *so their fathers did* to the false prophets." These are the only times that Luke explicitly mentions false prophets or false prophecy, but he does elsewhere include interesting complementary statements. In Luke 6:22-23 Luke has Jesus proclaim that his hearers ought to be glad when they are hated and reviled on account of the Son of Man: "Rejoice in that day, and leap for joy, for behold your reward is great in heaven; for *so their fathers did* to the prophets." In Acts 7:51-52 a similar charge is equated with "resisting the Holy Spirit," and then applied to Stephen's Jewish hearers:

> As your fathers did, so do you. Which of the prophets did not your fathers persecute? And they killed those who announced beforehand the coming of the Righteous One, whom you have now betrayed and murdered, you who received the law as delivered by angels and did not keep it.

The specific example that Stephen has given to illustrate this dark past is the people's rejection of the prophet Moses and taking up of "the tent of Moloch" and "the star of the god Rephan" (7:39-43). The culpable "deeds of the fathers," it seems, were to reject true prophets, to follow false prophets, and to commit idolatry.[28] Luke probably saw the latter two activities as interrelated; such an understanding would be consistent with the description of the false prophet given in Deut. 18:20 (cf. *Hermas Mandate* 11.4).[29] If so, then the notion of magic may also have been tied into his understanding, since pagan "magical" practices figure importantly in the idolatrous activities condemned in Deut. 18:9-14 (cf. *Didache* 3.4).

As noted in chapter 1 (pp. 16-17), these teachings from Deuteronomy figured importantly in the eschatological expectations of various groups, including some groups of Christians. Mark 13:22, for example, indicates that "false Christs" and "false prophets" will arise, doing signs and wonders to try to lead astray the elect. Luke omits this saying from Mark, but the omission does not mean that the Deuteronomic/eschatological myths were irrelevant to Luke.[30] On the contrary: Luke attempts to present Jesus as the "Prophet like Moses," and—as Luke 6:22-23,26 and Acts 7:52 indicate—is deeply concerned about what he sees as the Jewish people's history of accepting false prophets and rejecting true ones. Indeed, in Luke's understanding this history accounted for the Jews' rejection of Jesus. Though Jesus had been an anointed prophet of God, his compatriots had thrown him out of Nazareth and had tried to execute him (Luke 4:24-30); the Samaritans likewise had refused to hear him (9:52-53). Luke's portrait of Simon shares key traits with portraits given elsewhere of eschatological adversaries, including false prophets and antichrist figures.[31] Simon exalts himself as a god, and, like eschatological false prophets, draws people after himself by means of miraculous deeds.[32] The people's high acclaim for Simon can with little effort be read as a reenactment of Luke 6:26: "Woe to you when all speak well of you, for so their fathers did to the false prophets!"

In sum, Simon's practice of magic and his resemblance to the false prophets depicted in roughly contemporaneous Jewish and Christian documents suggest that Luke deliberately portrayed the magician as such a false prophet. Because here (as in Acts 5:36-37) the explicit designation "false prophet" is lacking, certainty is unattainable. But one can conclude that Luke has described Simon in such a way that readers would have regarded the designation "false prophet" as apposite. Later interpreters took the initiative and themselves supplied the label.[33]

The report of Simon's baptism in 8:13 ties off the first scene in the narrative.[34] Simon's submission to the cleansing ritual demonstrates the superiority of Christianity to magic: even a competitor recognizes something better when he sees it. But Luke's editorial postscript to the baptism, reporting that Simon "the great Power" stuck close to Philip and was "amazed" by Philip's signs and "great deeds of power" (v. 13b), leaves a bright thread dangling. The reader recalls that "amazement" was precisely the onlookers' reaction (mentioned twice, in vv. 9,11) to Simon's own deeds. Indeed, one reason Luke used the flashback arrangement—awkwardly postponing until vv. 9-11 the account of Simon's (chronologically prior) magical activities—may have been in order to bring the reports of the people's earlier amazement at Simon together with the similar report of Simon's subsequent amazement at Philip. By delaying the first reports (vv. 9,11), and molding the second (v. 13) after the first, Luke succeeds in creating the impression that Simon has interpreted the Christian signs as feats of "magic" like that which he himself performed.[35] The reader is thereby encouraged to conclude that, although Simon did believe Philip, his motives for conversion were wrong. Such an intolerable attitude cannot remain unchallenged, and Luke moves swiftly to tie up the loose end.

SIMON AND THE HOLY SPIRIT

Before turning to the climax of the narrative, namely, Simon's attempt to buy apostolic authority *(exousia)*, it is necessary to consider briefly a much-discussed problem in Acts 8:14-25: the delay between the water baptism carried out by Philip (v. 12) and the coming of the Holy Spirit when the apostles Peter and John arrive and lay hands on the believers (v. 17). In and of itself, there is nothing unusual about the coming of Jerusalem leaders to study the reception of the Gospel by a previously unevangelized population. The same thing happens later (11:22), when Barnabas is sent to investigate the conversion of Greeks in Antioch by some of the Christians who had been scattered because of the persecution over Stephen (a group which also included Philip; compare 8:4 and 11:19). But in Acts 2:38 it is presupposed that the normal sequence of events is for the gift of the Holy Spirit to follow immediately upon water baptism in the name of Jesus.[36] Why does Luke alter the normal sequence in his narration of the Samaritans' baptism? Although theological solutions have been proposed—for example, that only the apostles had the authority to confer the Spirit or that the Samaritans' faith was somehow defective—none of these is both warranted by the text in question and also consistent with Luke's views elsewhere. More plausible are explanations that attribute the delay to Luke's literary goals in combining disparate traditions: for example, Luke may have wanted to bring Simon Magus and Simon Peter into contact with each other, or to coordinate the actions of the seven and the twelve, or to demonstrate that the apostolic leaders had personally participated in (and had therefore sanctioned) the mission to Samaria.[37] It may be that Luke had more than just a single motive for constructing the narrative in this way. In any case, since Luke is himself matter-of-fact about the Spirit's delay, it is probably best not to read too much into it.

Simon's offer to buy the authority to confer the Holy Spirit (8:19) is in keeping with the ancient stereotype of the magician. As C. K. Barrett points out, it was commonly assumed that magicians "practised their art for what they could make out of it."[38] Plato, Philo, Lucian, Celsus, Juvenal, and Philostratus all assume that magicians are avaricious.[39] Hermas cited this trait as one of the characteristics distinguishing the "soothsaying" *(manteuein)* false prophet from the prophet who is divinely inspired: the former "lives in great luxury and in many other deceits, and accepts rewards for his prophecy, and if he does not receive them he does not prophesy" *(Hermas Mandate* 11.12).[40] Of course it is true that in Acts Simon does not ask for money, but rather offers it. The offer, however, betrays Simon as one who thinks that authority and the powerful deeds that follow from it can be bought for a price. Simon is thereby established as a character who, could he ever succeed in obtaining such authority, would turn right around and solicit payment for the magic that he could then perform. As Barrett observes, "If he was willing to pay money for the power of conferring the Spirit by the imposition of hands he would certainly intend to charge for the commodity when he passed it on."[41] In having Simon make such an offer to Peter, Luke reinforces his earlier hint that Simon mistakenly regarded the Christian leaders as magicians like himself. Luke then exploits Simon's apparent misconception, using it as a foil to display the apostles' utterly opposed point of view: they, unlike Simon, would never take money for what they have to offer (cf. Acts 3:6).[42] Thereby Luke demonstrates that the Christians do not share one of the most widely recognized traits of practitioners of magic.

Peter curses Simon, upbraiding him for his evil heart (8:20-21,23).[43] How one understands Peter's curse ("May your silver go with you into destruction!") depends on how one interprets the term "destruction" *(apōleia)*, which can refer either to immediate physical ruin or to eternal destruction at the judgment,[44] and which in Luke-Acts is found only here. It seems likely that Luke had the latter option in mind: at issue is the magician's failure to repent genuinely,[45] and repentance always anticipates the day on which God will judge the world by the risen Christ (Acts 17:30-31; cf. Luke 3:8-9). On that future occasion, according to Matthew, Jesus will say to the cursed, "Depart from me, cursed ones ([hoi] katēramenoi), into the eternal fire which has been prepared for the devil and his angels" (Matt. 25:41). In apparent expectation of that day, Luke now has Peter express a wish that Simon's money might accompany him in eternal damnation.[46]

A close examination of Peter's rebuke of Simon helps to clarify the magician's relationship to Satan. Peter perceives (8:23) that Simon is in the "gall of bitterness" (cholē pikrias) and the "bond of iniquity" (sundesmos adikias). Each expression is an allusion to the Septuagint, and, though brief, each appears to be significant in the present context.[47] The expression "gall of bitterness" alludes to LXX Deut. 29:17 (MT 29:18), a curse against those who disobey the covenant by committing idolatry.[48] The Lord's punishment for these wicked persons is extremely harsh:

> The Lord would not desire to be gracious to that one, but rather the anger of the Lord and his jealousy would burn against that person, and all the curses of this covenant which are written in the book of this law would cling to him, and the Lord would blot out his name from under heaven.
>
> (LXX Deut. 29:19; MT 29:20)

Not only the threat of destruction but also the stress on the impure and idolatrous heart precipitating such punishment (LXX v. 18) call to mind the description of Simon in Acts 8:21-22. By having Peter perceive that Simon is in the "gall of bitterness," Luke implies that Simon, though he has supposedly entered into the Christian community, is still an idolater, subject to punishment because still trapped (along with all idolaters) under the authority of Satan.[49] This interpretation is supported by Peter's ensuing description of Simon as in the "bond of iniquity." The expression is an allusion to Isa. 58:6—an important verse for Luke, as is made clear by his thoughtful appending of it to Isa. 61:1 in the introduction to Jesus' ministry of healing and exorcism (Luke 4:18-19). Isaiah 58:6 summarizes for Luke Jesus' task in confronting Satan (cf. Acts 10:38): Jesus was anointed with the Spirit, that he might ". . . loosen the bonds of wickedness, undo the bands of the coercing yoke, send the oppressed into freedom, and break apart every unjust contract." Now Peter tells Simon that the yoke still weighs upon his neck—in other words, Simon is himself still in bondage to Satan. Clearly Philip's visible and audible message of "release to the captives" had not been appropriated by Simon the magician, who had failed to obtain either forgiveness of sins or a share in "this word."[50] Thus Simon's offer of money to Peter is for Luke not only blasphemous but absurd: the magician wanted to purchase divine authority while himself still trapped under diabolical authority. The offer is also quintessentially satanic: Simon now, like his master during Jesus' earthly life, strives to procure and dispense authority belonging rightfully to God's chosen servant(s).[51] The punishment for such diabolical greed is destruction at the judgment.

But interspersed with Peter's words of condemnation is what appears to be a ray of hope for Simon: Peter tells him that he should repent of his wickedness and ask the Lord whether the intent of his heart might be forgiven him (v. 22). After Peter's harsh curse, the suggestion that Simon may yet be forgiven is jarring. Even more jarring, however, is Simon's humble response (v. 24): he asks Peter and John (plural: *deēthēte hymeis*) to intercede on his behalf, "that nothing of the things that you have spoken may come upon me." The import of this response is difficult to assess. Is Luke suggesting that Simon has now genuinely repented, and is to mend his evil ways? If so, then Luke has not had the magician express himself very clearly, for there is no unequivocal sign of such repentance. If original, the western text's reading that Simon "wept much" when confronted by Peter[52] could perhaps be taken as such a sign, but since elsewhere in Luke-Acts "weeping" usually accompanies personal distress or sorrow rather than repentance,[53] this interpretation is open to question. If Luke had wanted to imply that Simon would reform and be saved, the author would probably have given some less ambiguous indication that Simon regretted the actions that had led him, so to speak, to the brink of the abyss (cf. Acts 2:37; 16:29-34). But if anything, the magician resembles a cornered criminal, frightened at the prospect of punishment although not obviously remorseful over his crimes. Further, the way Simon's request for intercession echoes the requests made of Moses by Pharaoh (Exod. 8:8,28 [LXX 8:4, 24]; 9:28; 10:17)—who repeatedly "hardened his heart" once such intercession had achieved the desired result—suggests that Luke viewed Simon as insincere. Because he has not truly repented, it is not self-evident that he will be forgiven. It appears, then, that Luke has deliberately left

Simon's future unresolved. How is one to account for this lack of closure?

One explanation has been that Luke knew, and expected his readers to know, that Simon had *not* repented, but had instead gone on to do even more dastardly deeds. For Luke to have depicted such an unhappy course of events would have been to depict a mission failure; neither could he drastically refashion events to his liking by portraying Peter's victory over Simon as more definitive, since readers might have known that it was not so. So, the reasoning goes, Luke left the story hanging, and allowed the reader to fill in the gaps.[54] In a variant of this theory, Luke not only knows of Simon's later deeds but is personally acquainted with members of the Simonian sect living in Luke's own day; Peter's offer of repentance to Simon and Simon's response (understood as positive) are meant to convey a similar offer of acceptance back into the church to these Simonians.[55]

Such explanations, while not outside the realm of possibility, require something like Haenchen's concealment theory: that is, the supposition that Luke knew more than he was telling. We have no evidence to support such a theory. Preferable would be an explanation that not only respects the apparent limits of Luke's historical knowledge, but also shows how Simon's response contributes to the author's ongoing plot and character development.

In chapter 2, I argued that Jesus' promise to his missionaries that they will have the authority to "tread on snakes and scorpions, and over all the power of the Enemy, and he will in no way harm them" is to be fulfilled in the time of the church as depicted in Acts. I further suggested that in Luke's era the notion was prevalent that the devil, confronted by one who is righteous, will be reduced to shame and helplessness. For example, after his unsuccessful attack on Job in the *Testament of Job* 27, the devil "weeps" in shamed defeat and leaves— a most interesting reaction, in light of the western text's notice that Simon "wept much" when confronted by Peter. In *Hermas Mandate* 11.14, Hermas is instructed that when a false prophet, who is (by the author's definition) filled with the spirit of the devil, enters a gathering of righteous persons,

> who have a spirit of the Godhead, and intercession is made by them, that man is made empty, and the earthly spirit flees from him in fear, and that man is made dumb and is altogether broken up, being able to say nothing.[56]

The point made in Acts 8:20-24 may be the same one made in the texts cited above: Satan in the person of his servant Simon has been trampled down. Satan does still have some power, but he is handily subjugated when confronted by the vastly greater divine authority that Christians wield. Peter's righteous rebuke reduces Simon from a famous magician, impiously acclaimed by all the people of Samaria as "the great power of God," to a meek man who fears his own destruction and so asks the servant of the Lord to intercede for him (just as Pharaoh had requested of Moses).[57] Peter's words do indicate that salvation is regarded as a possibility.[58] But Luke probably does not know what eventually became of Simon, and in any case this is not what primarily interests the author. Luke's main concern is instead to show that the devil (here as later in the narrative acting through a magician; see chap. 4) has been overcome. Thus the missionaries can preach the gospel, unhindered by the devil, throughout the regions of Samaria (8:25).

SUMMARY AND ANALYSIS

Philip preached the message that Jesus of Nazareth was the Christ, anointed to bring about the Kingdom of God. A persistent if implied theme of the proclamation was "release": release to those possessed by unclean spirits, release to the lame and paralyzed, and release to those held fast by sin. Hearing Philip's message and seeing the supporting signs, the people repented of their sins and claimed "release," that is, forgiveness, for themselves, being baptized in the name of Jesus. Even Simon the magician, who had long courted personal disaster by accepting praises due God alone, submitted to baptism—though Luke hints strongly that his motives were impure. When Peter and John arrived and laid hands upon the new converts, the Holy Spirit sealed their baptism. Simon's diabolical power play, however, showed that he, unlike the other Samaritan listeners, had not experienced "release," but was still held fast in Satan's grip. The magician had never truly repented, and so his baptism was a sham. Peter exposes the fraud, and informs Simon that unless the magician repent and God be gracious, Simon is damned. Simon is immediately reduced to fear, demonstrating the feebleness of his master the devil before Christian authority. The word of the Lord moves on, sweeping the face of Samaria.

Luke's portrayal of Simon is permeated with mythological motifs. Indeed, every one of Simon's characteristics—his use of magic, his self-deification, his attraction of the people, his secretly sinful heart, his attempt to procure divine authority, and even his submission when condemned—is a stereotyped feature of contemporaneous portrayals of Satan or those who belong to Satan's lot, especially false prophets. Luke is concerned to portray Simon in such a way that readers will recognize the "magician" as a satanic figure; once such recognition is made it becomes apparent that the account is not primarily about magic, but about the downfall of a servant of the devil. Through his portrayal of Simon, Luke is demonstrating that Christians in the post-resurrection period have authority over Satan. Thus the Simon Magus-incident contributes to the overarching story, delineated above (chap. 2), about the cosmic struggle that results in Satan's fall from authority at the time of the resurrection and ascension of Christ. Simon's humble submission to Peter shows that Christ's servants have authority over Simon's master, the devil, in the period after the devil's fall. The literary function of Luke's other two accounts about magicians, the stories about Bar Jesus (Acts 13:4-12) and the seven sons of Sceva (Acts 19:8-20), will prove to be similar.

Even if the Simon Magus account is not primarily about magic, the references to magic do contribute significantly to the meaning and effect of the narrative. By labelling Simon a "magician," Luke guided his readers in their ordering of complex perceptual experience. For Luke, as for the authors of some contemporary documents (including the *Martyrdom of Isaiah* and the *Shepherd of Hermas*), the categories of "magic" and "false prophecy" implied not only duplicity or char-latanry (connotations available to a wide range of persons in the Greco-Roman world), but also idolatry, opposition to God, and in-spiration by God's opponent, Satan (connotations specific to a Jewish subculture and to the Christians who adopted its outlook and tra-ditions). Because of these culturally specific connotations, Luke and contemporaries were able to use the labels "magic" and "false proph-ecy" as symbolic bridges over which their readers could cross from the visible (or at least "imaginable") world into the invisible one where Holy Spirit and God's opponent meet. From the new perspective the reader would see that the narrated encounters are not merely skirmishes between prophets or wonder-workers, but confrontations between Satan and the spirit of God.

Thus, by describing Simon as one who does feats of magic and by portraying him as engaged also in other classically satanic patterns of behavior, Luke informs his reader that the depicted events involve more than meets the eye. Simon is no mere con artist or cheap char-latan, but someone far more sinister, endowed with the power of Satan and disguising himself as the "great power of God." Luke's double notice that Simon's magic had "amazed" the people "for a long time" suggests that this was no mere underling from the realm of darkness, but one of the most powerful servants in Satan's kingdom. Moreover, Philip's and Peter's exhibition of greater authority than Simon, and their righteous outrage at his diabolical offer of money, serve to differentiate between Christianity and magic. Christians are far above using cheap and unholy magic, for they have been granted the priceless and sanctified authority of the son of God.

The interpretation by Luke and contemporaries of false prophecy and magic as satanic was by no means the only option, even among Jewish writers. To highlight the distinctive character of this interpretation, I will briefly compare it with the way others of the era understood false prophecy and magic.

Josephus, for instance, views false prophets as frauds and deceivers who lead the people astray.[59] But if he perceived satanic agency behind the false prophets' action, he conceals this view from his (primarily pagan) readers.[60] Further, when Josephus writes about a famed Jewish exorcist, he openly uses descriptive language reminiscent of pagan ideas about magic: God granted to the ancient Solomon knowledge of the "art" or "technique" (technē) to be used against demons. This Solomon had possessed wisdom surpassing even that of the Egyptians, had investigated the properties of all things in nature, and had composed "formulas of exorcism" (tropoi exorkōseōn) and "incantations" (epōdai) by which illnesses are remedied (Antiquities 8.42-46a).[61] In Josephus' narration of Moses' encounter with the court magicians of Pharaoh, the author defends his hero against the view, attributed to the king, that Moses had "effected his return by fraud (ex apatēs) and was trying to impose on him by juggleries and magic (teratourgioi kai mageiai)." Moses responds,

> Indeed, O King, I too disdain not the cunning of the Egyptians, but I assert that the deeds wrought by me so far surpass their magic and their art (technē) as things divine are remote from what is human. And I will show that it is from no witchcraft (goēteia) or deception of true judgment (planē tēs alēthous doxēs), but from God's providence and power that my miracles proceed.[62]   (Antiquities 2.286)

Here magic is an "art" or "technique," something that deceives observers by tricking their perception.[63] The "opposition" occurring when Moses the miracle worker encounters Egyptian magicians is not between what is divine and what is satanic, but between what is divine and what is human. It appears that for Josephus neither "false prophecy" nor "magic" serves to bridge the human and spiritual realms.

The magical papyri represent the opposite extreme to Josephus. Whereas for Josephus, "magic" can be discussed without reference to its spiritual dimension, for the users of the papyri, magic is unthinkable apart from the spiritual realm. As Hans Dieter Betz has noted, for these persons "human life seems to consist of nothing but negotiation in the antechamber of death and the world of the dead."[64] The papyri users crossed over the bridge from the human realm to the spiritual one, and existed almost entirely in the latter.[65] But, for all its potential danger (to the magician as well as to any victims),[66] in one regard the spiritual world into which the reader of the papyri is drawn is more benign than the spiritual world that Luke apparently associates with magic. This is because the spiritual world implied by the magical papyri is *amoral.* The magician may lose life and limb, but it is a calculated risk, willingly taken, and always balanced by the enticing promise of life, wealth, health, and sex appeal. There is no court prepared to judge the papyri users' actions and to inflict eternal punishment on them. By contrast, in Luke-Acts and in other Jewish and Christian writings with a dualistic conception of spiritual powers, the threat of judgment hangs like Damocles' sword over the magicians' heads. At least, this is the belief of those who watch what the "magicians" do and apply the labels. For his self-aggrandizement and idolatry, Simon is threatened with nothing less than destruction at the judgment.

Luke does not describe how each wonder-worker went about his task, indicating only in summary fashion that the wonders were done (Acts 8:6-7,9-11,13). Luke's silence regarding the details of Simon's magical practice contrasts with the effort of later Christian apologists to show that the techniques or results of Christian miracle workers bear no resemblance to those of magicians.[67] Luke actually *capitalizes on the outward similarity of Christian signs and of magic,* constructing his narrative so as to suggest that Simon mistook the former for the latter. But in the case of Simon, as in that of the seven sons, Luke's concession regarding the external similarity of Christian "signs" and "magic" is a setup: it creates a pretext for the protagonists to dispel the notion that there is *any* similarity of importance between Christians and magicians. Christian authority is in no way like magical-satanic authority, for the latter can be bought but the former is solely a gift of God. The Holy Spirit can be and is used by God to confirm the word proclaimed by God's servants, but it cannot be used to bring glory to an individual. The servant of darkness may be disguised as an angel of light, but to someone like Peter, attuned to events occurring on the spiritual plane, the fraud is readily apparent. Such affirmations about the difference between Christianity and magic may in part have been Luke's reaction to accusations in his own day that Christians were false prophet-magicians, who worked wonders by means of diabolical power. Against any who would malign Christians' source of power (cf. Acts 4:7), Luke insists that believers are authorized by God. Any similarity to magic is therefore entirely superficial, for at the unseen spiritual level Christian "signs and wonders" and "magic" are worlds apart. This message will be reaffirmed in the story of Bar Jesus.

4

PAUL AND
BAR JESUS

Acts 13:4-12

INTRODUCTION

Commentators have not quite known what to do with the story of
Paul and Bar Jesus. Even Arthur Darby Nock, one of its most com-
petent interpreters, characterized the story as "lame."[1] First, the problem of the alternation and incorrect translation of the magician's
names appears to be insoluble on either source- or text-critical
grounds.[2] Second, the whole episode is historically implausible and
literarily unbalanced: if so famous a person as Sergius Paulus had
converted to Christianity (which does not seem very likely),[3] more
should have been made of it. But as Nock states, "the proconsul's
conversion . . . is just stated as though it were that of a washer-
woman."[4] Third, the significance of Paul's curse of the magician is
not readily apparent. If, as some contend, one of Luke's reasons for
relating the incident was to contrast Christianity with magic,[5] his
storytelling strategy seems to be inappropriate: to the modern reader
Paul's curse of Bar Jesus looks as "magic-like" as anything the magus

himself might have done. In short, the narrative appears to be full of unlikelihoods and inconsistencies. But Luke was not as inept a narrator as these observations would suggest. Analysis of the mythological background to the Bar Jesus account and of its literary function within the narrative of Luke-Acts will suggest that the story made a definite and important point,[6] and tied in nicely with other incidents in the two-volume account.

MISSION ON CYPRUS

The incident is the first significant event on Paul's first missionary journey. Saul and Barnabas had been consecrated by prophets in Antioch and had then departed from the port of Seleucia for Cyprus. Luke mentions whistle stops at the Jewish synagogues in Salamis (13:5),[7] and then without further delay transports the characters to the city of Paphos, on the western end of the island. Haenchen points out that for the missionaries to cross the island would have taken at least a week; Luke's silence about other mission stops along the way indicates that the Paul/Bar Jesus incident is the only one that interests the evangelist.[8] Saul (alias Paul) and Bar Jesus (alias Elymas) are the central human characters in the narrative. Paul's companions Barnabas and John play distinctly subsidiary roles, and even the character of the proconsul, Sergius Paulus, functions primarily as a foil for the confrontation between Paul and Bar Jesus.[9] Thus in 13:6 it is reported that when the Christians came to Paphos they found "a certain man, a magician, a Jewish false prophet named Bar Jesus." Sergius Paulus is mentioned almost as an afterthought, in v. 7.

The human combatants Paul and Bar Jesus in turn represent superhuman figures. On the one hand, Paul acts under the power of the Holy Spirit. In the introduction to the episode, Luke has noted that the Spirit set Barnabas and Saul aside for the entire first missionary journey (13:2) and dictated to them their itinerary (v. 4). Furthermore, just before Bar Jesus is rebuked (v. 9) Luke describes Paul as "filled with the Holy Spirit." On the other hand, Bar Jesus is closely linked with the figure of Satan. Paul calls the magician-false prophet a "son of the devil"[10] and "enemy of all righteousness."[11] Paul also accuses Bar Jesus of being "full of all deceit and all fraud" *(plērēs pantos dolou kai pasēs radiourgias)*.[12] The proximity of this vitriolic charge (v. 10a) to Luke's description of Paul as "filled with the Holy Spirit" (v. 9) serves to contrast these characters in the sharpest terms possible; Luke would have us see Bar Jesus as controlled by Satan, the very antithesis of the Holy Spirit. Thus the confrontation between Bar Jesus and Paul is also a confrontation between the Holy Spirit and the devil.[13]

Nock was surely mistaken when he suggested that Luke's description of Bar Jesus as a "magician-false prophet" *(magos pseudoprophētēs)* was "almost intentionally vague" and perhaps used merely "like *goēs*, humbug, of a practitioner of another and hostile religion."[14] First, Bar Jesus is not a member of "another and hostile religion," but a Jew, who by practicing magic commits what Luke regarded as the worst sort of idolatry. Second, Luke does not here use the designations "magician" and "false prophet" casually, but on the contrary, emphasizes both roles. The label "magician" occurs twice in close succession (vv. 7,8),[15] and although the designation "false prophet" is explicitly mentioned just once, Paul also charges Bar Jesus with "making crooked the straight paths of the Lord" (v. 10), which is the opposite of what the true prophet John the Baptist had done (Luke 3:4).[16] By making straight paths crooked—in other words, by interfering with Paul's efforts to preach to Sergius Paulus that he might believe and be saved—Bar Jesus acted according to the devil's word-obstructing designs (cf. Luke 8:11-15). Through this indirect promotion of idolatry Bar Jesus filled the classic role of the magician-false prophet as exhibited in contemporaneous Jewish and Christian literary traditions (discussed above, pp. 13-17), according to which false teachers or false prophets would arise and lead the people astray into idolatry. In light of such eschatological traditions it seems likely that Bar Jesus' composite identity as magician, false prophet and satanic stand-in was neither fortuitious nor insignificant; these three roles were thought to belong together. The designation "false prophet" *(pseudoprophētēs)*, together with Paul's accusation of deceitfulness, would have tipped off many ancient readers that Bar Jesus was something other than what he seemed. Indeed he had a *double* "double identity": he was Bar Jesus and also Elymas; he was a magus serving the esteemed Sergius Paulus and also a false prophet serving Satan. Bar Jesus' position as court magician and his diabolical effort to impede the proclamation of the word provide ample proof of the illegitimacy of any claim to prophetic status.

PAUL'S CURSE OF BAR JESUS
(Acts 13:11)

On the very first leg of Paul's very first mission to the Gentiles, he proclaims that "the hand of the Lord" is upon Bar Jesus, with the result that "mist and darkness" fall upon the false prophet. Perhaps the most striking point about this action is that it is the opposite of what Paul had been commissioned to do on his journeys to the Gentiles: namely, to "open their eyes" and to cause them "to turn from darkness to light, and from the authority of Satan to God" (Acts 26:18).[17] Why would Luke portray Paul as doing something so blatantly contrary to the directions given him?

In answering this question it will be helpful to begin by looking at Deut. 28:28-29, which has been suggested as a possible model for Luke's composition of the story of Bar Jesus' blindness.[18] In this passage, Moses tells the Israelites that the Lord shall strike those who forsake him (v. 20), so that they "shall grope at noonday, as the blind grope in darkness." This punishment is but one in a long list of curses *(katarai)* to be inflicted on those who disobey the voice of the Lord by "going after other gods and serving them" (28:14-15); Peter's rebuke of Simon had alluded to another portion of this lengthy discussion in Deuteronomy of the curses falling upon those who disobey the covenant (see above, pp. 70-71). Luke likely saw Bar Jesus as guilty of such disobedience, since magic and false prophecy were regarded as akin to idolatry. Therefore it is possible that Luke shaped his depiction of the punishment of Bar Jesus to bring it into line with the punishment of idolaters described in Deut. 28:28-29.

Evidence from the Community Rule indicates that the Qumran sectarians employed the curse language of this section of Deuteronomy in their own condemnation of idolatry. Specifically, 1QS 2:11-19 incorporates portions of Deut. 29:20-21 (LXX vv. 19-20), which is an exceptionally harsh malediction against any who commit idolatry but bless themselves in their heart, and who are therefore labelled as "a root bearing poisonous and bitter fruit" (LXX v. 17: *riza anō phyousa en cholē kai pikria;* cf. Acts 8:23). The Qumran elaboration of this Deuteronomic curse occurs within a series of imprecations to be pronounced against members of the "lot of Belial," and uses light and darkness imagery similar to that employed in the Bar Jesus account:

> And the Priests and Levites shall continue, saying: "Cursed be the man who enters this Covenant while walking among the idols of his heart, who sets up before himself his stumbling-block of sin so that he may backslide! Hearing the words of this Covenant, he blesses himself in his heart and says, 'Peace be with me, even though I walk in the stubbornness of my heart' (Deut. 29:18-19), whereas his spirit, parched (for lack of truth) and watered (with lies), shall be destroyed without pardon. God's wrath and His zeal for His precepts shall consume him in everlasting destruction. All the curses of the Covenant shall cling to him and God will set him apart for evil. He shall be cut off from the midst of all the sons of light, and because he has turned aside from God on account of his idols and his stumbling-block of sin, his lot shall be among those who are cursed for ever." And after them, all those entering the Covenant shall answer and say, "Amen, Amen!"

Thus shall they do, year by year, for as long as the dominion of Satan endures.

1QS 2:11-19[19]

The similarity to Paul's curse of Bar Jesus is notable. Those who enter the Qumran covenant community under false pretexts—feigning obedience to the law of Moses while secretly practicing idolatry—are to be cut off from the children of light and punished forever. So too in Acts, Bar Jesus the Jew—deceitfully pretending to be a prophet, but actually an idolatrous magician—is cut off from the light.[20] The Qumran curse certifies that at the judgment the idolater will be subjected to eternal punishment; Paul's curse brings instant retribution, but may also have an eschatological component.[21]

The consignment of ·Bar Jesus to "mist and darkness" is a consignment to the authority of his master, Satan (cf. Acts 26:18; Luke 22:53).[22] In Acts as in some contemporaneous writings, the punishment for being a "child of darkness" is darkness itself: Satan and his servants will be banished eternally from the light and life of the Kingdom (Matt. 8:12; 22:13; 25:30; 2 Pet. 2:17; 1QS 4:12-14; cf. Rev. 22:5,14-15; *Barnabas* 20.1). Though somewhat later than the canonical Acts, *Acts of Peter* includes a curse against the devil and his servants which illustrates this "tit-for-tat" rationale. Peter exclaims:

"Upon thee may thy blackness be turned and upon thy sons, that most wicked seed; upon thee be turned thy misdeeds, upon thee thy threats, and upon thee and thine angels be thy temptations, thou source of wickedness and abyss of darkness! May thy darkness which thou hast be with thee and with thy vessels whom thou dost possess. Depart therefore from these who shall believe in God, depart from the servants of Christ and from them who would fight for him."

Acts of Peter 4.8[23]

The last sentence vents the further conviction, shared by Luke, that the servants of Satan and the servants of Christ are as divorced from one another as east is from west, as night is from day (cf. 1 Thess. 5:5).

The blinding of Bar Jesus exposes the magician as a fraud. Bar Jesus claimed to be a prophet (or so Luke implies): as such he would have been a source of divine light and leadership, one who made paths straight so that others could follow. But Luke shows that the magician was, despite his claim, a fount of darkness and corruption (cf. 2 Cor. 11:13-15).[24] The curse of blindness communicates this true identity in terms consistent with Luke's symbolism elsewhere. The evangelist has already told his reader that the eye is the lamp of the body: "when your eye is pure [*haplous*], then your whole body has

light; but if it is bad [*ponēros*], then your body is in darkness" (Luke
11:34; parallel Matt. 6:22-23).[25] Those in the former category have
nothing whatever to do with darkness (cf. 2 Cor. 6:14-15). Bar Jesus,
on the other hand, belongs to the latter category because he is allied
with none other than the Prince of Darkness. Employing the logic of
Luke 11:34, when Bar Jesus' "eye" goes "bad," the true state of his
"whole body" is revealed. Thus Paul's curse is not only efficacious
but also expressive.

The parallels to Paul's own experience are remarkable: both Paul
and Bar Jesus had been obstructing the work of the Church when
blinded, and both must then be "led about by the hand." Bar Jesus
is a "son of the devil," and Paul—like the devil—has "authority to
bind" (9:14), tries to make Christians blaspheme (26:11),[26] and repeatedly casts them into prison.[27] The parallels suggest that Luke saw
Paul, too, as a one-time servant of the devil. But there are also differences between the experiences of Paul and of Bar Jesus: (1) Bar
Jesus is said to "make straight paths crooked" but Paul is led to "a
street called straight" (9:11); (2) Bar Jesus is blinded by mist and
darkness (13:11), but Paul had been blinded by an intensely bright
light (22:11; 26:13); (3) whereas Paul eventually made the transition
from darkness to light, Bar Jesus' blindness is not relieved within the
context of the narrative. The differences in experience signify the
diverging paths or "ways" of their lives.

The reason Luke placed the story in such a prominent position—
at the outset of the endeavor to which Paul had been called by Jesus
himself—can now be discerned. Jesus had commissioned Paul to open
the eyes of the Gentiles, that they might turn from darkness to light
and from the authority of Satan to God. But if people's eyes have
been "blinded" by Satan's control over their lives, how can Paul open
them? Or, to use Luke's other metaphor (Luke 8:11-15), if the devil
desires to snatch away the newly planted word, how can Paul stop
him? The answer is that *Paul must himself be invested with authority
that is greater than Satan's own*. In depicting Paul's successful un-
masking and punishment of Bar Jesus, Luke is saying that Paul could
do the work to which he had been called because he possessed authority over all the power of the Enemy (cf. Luke 10:19). Ironically,
this superiority of Paul to the devil is expressed by the infliction of
blindness, which Paul himself had suffered at the hand of the Lord:
thus Paul, in spite of his own "dark" past, now shows himself to be
one of the devil's staunchest foes. Paul's triumph confirms the change
that has taken place in his own life, and brings him a new external

status to match the new internal one: he departs from Paphos as the leader of the mission.[28]

Luke's apparent notion that the change in Paul's life that had occurred at his conversion was somehow perfected by his victorious confrontation with the "son of the devil" may help to explain why the evangelist chooses to mention the change of Saul's name to "Paul" at just this point: name changes in antiquity sometimes accompanied a change in status.[29] Hereafter, "Paul" will be used almost exclusively.[30] Furthermore, the seeming urgency for Luke of depicting Paul's opposition to and superiority over Satan's servant helps to account for the evangelist's failure to mention other mission stops on Cyprus, as well as his casualness regarding the conversion of Sergius Paulus. Luke's notice that the proconsul "believed" serves primarily to authenticate Paul's miracle (and thus Paul's authority), much as statements about the "marveling of the crowds" authenticate Jesus' miracles in the Synoptic Gospels. Only secondarily is the conversion a point of interest in its own right.[31]

Was Paul's curse of Bar Jesus final and irrevocable, or was there still hope for the magician? The question may be of interest to modern readers,[32] but it is slightly out of kilter with Luke's presuppositions, because (as with Simon Magus) Luke is interested in Bar Jesus as a representative or servant of Satan rather than as an individual. Thus to raise the question is like asking "Is there any hope for Satan?" Of course the answer to *that* question is a resounding No! Satan's death knell had tolled long before, in the earthly ministry of Jesus (Luke 10:18; 11:21-22). Luke does imply that the blinding is only temporary: Bar Jesus will not see the sun "for a while" (v. 11).[33] But the temporal reference is meant to underscore the decisive (i.e., not instantly fleeting) quality of Paul's victory over Satan, and so points only incidentally, if at all, to a reprieve for Bar Jesus. Satan had clearly been humbled; his once-powerful servant Bar Jesus must be "led about by the hand" like a small child. Whether or not this particular servant would eventually escape from Satan's power does not appear to be an issue for Luke. If anything, Bar Jesus' consignment to darkness may signify that this shall also be his fate at the judgment.

SUMMARY AND ANALYSIS

In Acts 13:4-12 Luke once again employs the motif of magic in the service of an overarching story. By describing Bar Jesus as a magician and a false prophet, Luke notifies his reader that this servant in the prestigious court of the proconsul is actually a servant of Satan. Should the reader miss the point, Luke has Paul let fly a long string of deeply incriminating charges: Bar Jesus is "a son of the devil," "full of all deceit and all treachery," "the enemy of all righteousness," and one who "makes crooked the straight paths of the Lord." When Paul invokes the hand of the Lord, causing mist and darkness to fall upon Bar Jesus, Paul's possession of greater authority than Satan is unmistakably confirmed. Truly this is one able to open the eyes of the Gentiles, that they might turn from darkness to light and from the authority of Satan to God. Paul's victory over Satan's servant demonstrates again the reliability of Jesus' promise that Christians will have authority to trample on "snakes and scorpions," and over all the power of the Enemy. But in this case there is an irony to the fulfillment of Jesus' promise, because Paul himself once exercised "authority to bind those who call upon the name" (Acts 9:14). Paul himself had been struck blind in the midst of an effort to hamper the growth of the word. Events have come full circle; the devil's erstwhile helper has become his foe.

In portraying Paul's curse of Bar Jesus, Luke reveals that he shared with ancient magicians (and with the authors of the other curses discussed above) the presupposition that words backed up with sufficient authority could wreak terrible damage. To borrow D. Bidney's formulation (see above, p. 28), here Luke exhibits certain elements of the "magical world view," but contends on grounds admissible within that world view (namely, on the grounds that Paul exercised divine and not demonic authority) that what Paul did was not "magic as practiced and institutionalized." Indeed, Luke viewed Paul's action as the opposite of magic: "magic" was satanic, and the authority behind Paul's words was the antithesis of satanic authority. By depicting Paul's success in cursing this "enemy of all righteousness," Luke aimed to show that Paul was *conquering* magical-satanic powers. Of course Luke's view could have been contested, even by those who inhabited essentially the same symbolic world. Ancient eyewitnesses of such a dramatic punitive action by an unknown Jewish itinerant might well have interpreted the event as magic; they (like Luke) would have been able to draw on culturally established traditions about magic and magicians to defend their point of view. The goal of the preceding analysis has been, not to identify the "right" or "wrong" point of view, but to discover how *one* of the participants in an ancient debate might have clarified and defended his assessment.

In Luke and Acts the labels "magic" and "false prophecy" help the reader to sort characters and their actions into the appropriate categories; the categories themselves are defined and delimited not only by cultural precedent but also in part by the placement of each discussion within a larger literary framework. The critic must interpret the parts in relationship to the whole and vice versa, showing how an action performed or word spoken in one place articulates, replicates, or confirms what is depicted elsewhere. Bar Jesus' behavior replicates that of the unrepentant Jews, who likewise oppose the word by refusing to allow the Gospel to be heard, who persecute true prophets, follow false prophets, practice idolatry, and do not keep the law.[34] Jesus bewails a "faithless and perverse [*diestrammenē*] generation" of Jews (Luke 9:41); Bar Jesus is a Jew who "perverts" or "makes crooked" the straight paths of the Lord *(diastrephein;* Acts 13:8,10). Bar Jesus epitomizes for Luke the tragic situation of all unrepentant Jews, and the blinding of Bar Jesus illustrates not only Christian authority over Satan, but also the sad fate of all unrepentant Jews, who, though they indeed see, do not perceive, for their eyes have closed (28:26,27). In the Bar Jesus incident one can discern a pattern of conflict between good and evil, between the purposes of God and the purposes of Satan, and between the repentant and the uncircumcised in heart which characterizes much of Christian existence as portrayed in Luke-Acts. It is a conflict that will continue in the incident involving the seven sons of Sceva.

5

THE SEVEN SONS
OF SCEVA

Acts 19:8-20

INTRODUCTION

Martin Dibelius claimed that the story of the seven sons of Sceva in Acts 19:13-20 originated as "a profane story," told to entertain.[1] The assessment was based on the seemingly humorous remark by the demon in v. 15 and on the story's apparent lack of an edifying message. Other scholars have insisted that in its present framework (19:11-20) the story serves to distinguish between Christianity and magic.[2] But even this apparently straightforward inference—"straightforward" because the outcome of the failed exorcism is the confession of magical practices and the burning of a valuable stockpile of magic books (v. 19)[3]—has been disputed. Luke had no concern to "enlighten" his readers by discounting magical notions, G. Klein contends, since Luke has himself displayed such notions in his depiction of Paul's miraculous healings (v. 11).[4] In short, there is no scholarly consensus on how best to interpret this peculiar story.

I will argue in this chapter that Luke uses the story of the seven sons of Sceva, whatever its origin and whether or not told in a humorous vein, to advance the theme of the ongoing Christian triumph over Satan, and, consequently, over magic. One reason this message has gone largely unnoticed has been a scholarly preoccupation with the passage's numerous exegetical and historical problems, which include the historical improbability that seven sons of a Jewish high priest worked as a team of itinerant exorcists in Ephesus; the fact that there was no Jewish high priest by the name of "Sceva"[5] (which, being Latin, is an unlikely name even for a fictitious Jewish high priest); the conflict between the notice in v. 14 that there were "seven" exorcists and the remark in v. 16 that the spirit overpowered (lit.) "both of them" *(amphoteros)*;[6] the elaborate textual variant at v. 14 in the western textual tradition;[7] and finally, the unexpected mention of a "house" in v. 16 when no particular setting had been mentioned before.[8] Because of their concern with these distracting historical, textual, and philological problems, commentators have failed to ask important interpretive questions, such as how the demon's vocal and physical response in vv. 15-16 relates to Luke's understanding of exorcism as exhibited in such passages as Luke 4:33-35,41; 8:28; 11:21-22; and Acts 16:16-17; and why observers could have regarded the apparent victory of a demon as a defeat of magic.[9]

The boundaries of the passage are usually taken to be v. 11 ("and God did extraordinary miracles by the hands of Paul") and v. 20 ("thus by the might of the Lord the word increased and prevailed"[10]). But the beginning of the pericope ought to be pushed back to an earlier point, because v. 11 cuts into the preceding narrative about Paul's missionary activity in Ephesus (vv. 8-11).[11] Accordingly, in the following interpretation I will consider all of Acts 19:8-20.

PAUL'S MISSION IN EPHESUS
(Acts 19:8-12)

Following his usual mission pattern as depicted in Acts, Paul initially spends his days in the city preaching about the Kingdom of God in the synagogues of the Jews (v. 8). For three months this strategy works, but then some of the Jews become stubborn and malign "the way" before the crowds, with the result that Paul is compelled to withdraw with his disciples. For the next two years he spends his time arguing daily in the hall of Tyrannus, so that "all" the residents of Asia, both Jews and Greeks, hear the Word of God. "And God did extraordinary miracles by the hands of Paul, so that kerchiefs and cloths[12] were carried away from his body to the sick, and the diseases left them, and the evil spirits went out (from them)." At this point (v. 13) the narrator's attention shifts to the disreputable activity of the Jewish exorcists.

In important respects Luke's organization of the narrative parallels his organization of the story about Philip and Simon Magus. There, too, Luke depicted a missionary who, expelled by the Jews,[13] initiates a highly successful ministry of preaching the word and healing. There, too, the picture of successful missionary activity serves as a foil for an ensuing portrayal of reprehensible deeds by a wonder-worker who is outside the Christian fold. As shown above (chap. 4). Philip's healing actions and missionary message had been regarded by Luke as mutually reinforcing: release from the grip of unclean spirits and of paralysis and lameness had visibly enacted Philip's proclamation of the release brought by "the Kingdom of God and the name of Jesus."[14] So also now, Luke likely views Paul's remarkable healings in Ephesus as consistent with the message that he preaches, indeed, as part and parcel of that message. In depicting Paul as bringing about the obedient departure of diseases and unclean spirits, Luke implies that the authority of the spirits' lord, Satan—who strives to keep the possessed and diseased under his control—has been eclipsed by the authority which is invested in Paul to heal and about which he speaks. The remarkable nature of the healings, accomplished by transported cloths, underscores the totality of this eclipse: there is no contest here between "the authority of Satan" and "the authority of God," because the latter has completely overshadowed the former.[15] The effortlessness of Paul's healings will make the seven sons' debacle all the more conspicuous.

THE SEVEN SONS
(Acts 19:13-16)

Next Luke relates that "some of the itinerant Jewish exorcists attempted to name the name of the Lord Jesus over those who had evil spirits, saying 'I adjure you by the Jesus whom Paul preaches.' Seven sons of a certain Sceva, a Jewish high priest, were doing this." By use of the partitive genitive in v. 13 ("some of the itinerant Jewish exorcists") Luke implies that there were other Jewish exorcists besides the seven operating in the area; this is historically plausible, since Jews of this period were famed for their exorcistic ability.[16] But very likely the case of the seven sons is the only one known to Luke in any detail: in order to make a general point he has treated the single event as an instance of a recurring phenomenon (cf. Acts 4:34-37).

In depicting some of the Jewish exorcists as mentioning "the Jesus whom Paul preaches," Luke indicates that the exorcists were patterning their own actions after those of Paul; we are to imagine that they had seen Paul, too, heal and cast out demons "in the name of Jesus," and so they tried to do the same.[17] Luke's designation of the seven and the others like them as "exorcists" who try to "name the name," and also his phrasing of their exorcistic formula ("I adjure you [*horkizō hymas*] by the Jesus whom Paul preaches"), are probably designed to prompt readers to make the same sort of inference about the seven sons that would earlier have been made about Simon Magus; namely, that the brothers, like the Samaritan magician, mistook the Christian wonders for feats of magic. In reporting that the seven sons tried to "name" *(onomazein)* the name of the Lord Jesus over the possessed, Luke uses a word that is for him uncustomary,[18] and that probably had magical connotations.[19] The word "exorcist" *(exorkistēs)* occurs nowhere else in the New Testament,[20] perhaps because it too had magical connotations,[21] as did the closely related verb "adjure" *(horkizein)*.[22] In the report of Jesus' healing of the Gerasene demoniac in Mark 5:7 (which includes the only other occurrence of *horkizein* in the Gospels and Acts), the demon exclaims, "I adjure you by God" *(horkizō se ton theon)*. Bauernfeind has argued plausibly that this oath represents an attempt on the part of the demon to exercise magical control over Jesus.[23] Nowhere in the Gospels is it said that Jesus "adjures" the demons. In Luke's Gospel, Jesus either addresses the demons directly with the word "command" *(paraggellein)* or else is described in third-person accounts as "rebuking" *(epitiman)* them.[24] By having the seven sons instead use the freighted word *horkizein*, Luke expresses his judgment that what they were doing was of an entirely different character than what Jesus (or the disciples) did.

It is possible that Luke's portrayal of the seven sons as mistaking Paul's wonders for magic and imitating what they inferred to have been his "magical technique" replicated actual occurrences in Paul's day and in Luke's own. When onlookers observed Christians working wonders in the name of Jesus, a man known to have been crucified, any who were familiar with the ways of exorcists might reasonably have supposed that the Christians were following standard magical procedure, invoking by name the restless daimon of one killed violently.[25] The Christians' success would have indicated to such observers that the daimon "Jesus" was available for use. Non-Christians are reported as having used Jesus' name during his own lifetime, and an invocation of Jesus' name found in the magical papyri suggests that they did so not long afterward.[26] But, in Luke's narrative world (if not in his social world), the opinion that Jesus' name is like all the other names used in magic will not be allowed to prevail for very long.

The seven sons think that because they know Jesus' name they can tap into his wondrous power, coercing him to do their bidding. But Luke has given a peculiar twist to the notion of the "knowledge" of spiritual beings: what is important is not whether the exorcist "knows" the name of Jesus, but whether the demons "know" the exorcist as one who has truly been invested with authority to call upon that holy name. Christians possessed such authority because Jesus had bestowed it upon them during his earthly ministry (Luke 10:17-19). Hence in Acts 16:16-17, although the pythonic spirit inhabiting the slave girl knows that Jesus' authorized representative Paul and his companions are "servants of the most High God," the spirit is not depicted as trying to use its knowledge of the spiritual source of their authority to hinder their actions. Quite the opposite: when Paul finally does turn to exorcise the demon, it obeys "in that hour." In Acts 19:15-16, when the demon tells the seven sons that it "knows" Jesus and Paul,[27] it appears to be saying that it acknowledges their authority.[28] The implication is that had Jesus (or Paul acting in Jesus' name) commanded the spirit, it would have obeyed. But the demon does not "know" the seven sons (i.e., it does not acknowledge their authority, and so does not obey their command). When the demon then "mastered all of them and overpowered them," the demon's amazing strength was made plain for all to see.[29] Such strength would have made its admission of willingness to acquiesce to Jesus or Paul all the more impressive.

The verbs in the foregoing statement *(katakyrieuein* and *ischyein)*[30] recall another passage in which the powerful "master" of a domain figures prominently; namely, Jesus' explanation of exorcism. In Luke 11:21-22 (as discussed in chap. 2), Luke has modified his source considerably, producing an allegory about the all-important confrontation that takes place when Jesus casts out demons. Satan, the "well-armed strong one" *(ho ischyros),* guards his palace, and his possessions are in peace (v. 21). In other words, Satan has full dominion over those whom he has bound by means of his demons.[31] "But when the one who is stronger than he has come upon him and conquered him, he takes his armor in which he trusted and divides the spoil" (v. 22). When Jesus casts out a demon, the spirit's compliant exit—the taking of Satan's "armor"—is proof that Jesus has the authority needed to overcome the "strong one" Satan. In Acts 19:15-16 when the spirit "masters" and "overpowers" the seven sons, the spirit's violent non-compliance demonstrates with equal but opposite force that the seven have no such authority. The seven sons failed to mobilize Jesus' power because they lacked the authority to invoke his holy name, and so the demon remains in control.

THE REACTION OF THE PEOPLE
(Acts 19:17-20)

Why should a demon's victory cause the residents of Ephesus, "both Jews and Greeks," to extol the name of the Lord Jesus (v. 17)? As noted above, it was a common assumption among practitioners of ancient magic that knowledge of the authentic name of a god or daimon enabled one to control it, frequently against its own will.[32] In *PGM* III. 494-611, for example, the magician seeks to establish a relationship with Helios, who will then do all things for the magician. The spell begins:

> A procedure for every [rite], for [all things]. For whatever you want, invoke in this way: "[Come,] come to me from the four winds of the world, air-transversing, great god. Hear me in every ritual which [I perform], and grant all the [petitions] of my prayer completely, because I know your signs, [symbols and] forms, who you are each hour and what your name is.
>
> (*PGM* III. 494-501)[33]

The god Helios will obey because the magician knows "his signs, symbols, and forms, who he is each hour and what his name is." These objects of knowledge are virtually a part of the god, bonded by the strongest sympathetic ties, so that when the magician recites them (following the script included in subsequent lines), the god is compelled to obey, even to "come to" the magician (line 550).[34] By having the seven "name (*onomazein*) the name of Jesus over the possessed," adjuring the demon by "the Jesus whom Paul preaches," Luke implies that they similarly thought of Jesus as a spiritual power who could be compelled to do their bidding (in this case, to evict the demon). But the demon's response shows that the sons' ill-conceived effort has failed: Jesus remains entirely absent from the scene, and so for the moment the demon maintains its position. The sons' failure, much like Peter's earlier reprimand of Simon, demonstrates that in construing Christian "miracles" as "magic," the sons had made a gross error. Their ignominious defeat by the demon shows the Ephesians that "Jesus" is a power that cannot be controlled: he will not act as lackey for anyone who calls upon his name. This name, Luke would have the reader believe, is of a wholly different character than the names that magicians invoke.[35] As the demon's defeat of the sons has shown, Jesus' name cannot be corrupted or misappropriated. Hence "the name" deserves the grandest praise.

Why do the residents of Ephesus confess their magical practices and burn their magic books (v. 18)?[36] The obvious answer is that in Luke's understanding the Ephesians perceived the defeat of the seven sons to be a defeat of magic in general: magic has become obsolete. But *why* did they interpret the sons' failure in this way?

To answer the question, one must step back and examine how Luke has laid out the events leading up to this moment. A comparison of v. 17 with v. 10 suggests that the Ephesians who confess their practices and burn their books are among the residents of Asia, "both Jews and Greeks," who had already heard "the word of the Lord," that is, Paul's preaching about the Kingdom of God and the name of Jesus. Thus they have already heard Paul proclaim the end of Satan's reign and the onset of the reign of God, and have seen this message evidenced by Paul's own casting out of demons (vv. 11-12). Now the demon admits that, in spite of its present defiance of Satan's servants the magicians, it would submit to the authority of Jesus or Paul. Those who had heard and seen Paul are thus provided with even more persuasive evidence for Paul's proclamation that Jesus has conquered Satan. If the demons no longer obey Satan's emissaries, then the devil's kingdom has been divided and will surely fall (cf. Luke 11:17-18).[37] The magic books are useless now—emblems of a defeated regime— and so must be burned.

The confession of "practices" and the burning of magic books are to be seen as acts of repentance by those who had become believers (v. 18) when they saw Paul's proclamation verified by the sons' defeat.[38] In other words, some or all of those who "extolled" or "magnified" *(megalynein)* the name also believed in it, thereby securing their own salvation (cf. 4:12) and making the only appropriate response by repenting of their sins. To be sure, Luke does not explicitly mention "belief" in v. 17, but he does remark that "fear fell upon" the residents of Ephesus, and that "the name of the Lord Jesus was being extolled." Elsewhere in Acts the verb "extol" *(megalynein)* and a report about "fearing the Lord" are closely associated with the addition of new believers to the church (9:31; 10:46).[39]

Some commentators have argued that in v. 18 the use of the perfect participle *(hoi pepisteukotes)* to refer to believers must signify that the persons had initially converted some time ago, and had continued to practice magic until the sons' defeat.[40] But several observations render that view implausible. First, since Luke viewed magic as altogether satanic and evil, the evangelist would hardly have tolerated the notion of even the briefest continuation of magical-satanic practices by the Ephesians after their profession of belief. Second, the choices of tense in Luke's other participial uses of *pisteuein* appear to have been governed by narrative and syntactical context rather than by nuances of meaning inherent in the different tenses. In Acts 19:18 the perfect participle of *pisteuein* indicates that the confessors' initial act of belief preceded their coming forward (imperfect: *ērchonto*) to confess their "practices," but does not by itself imply that their initial act of believing had occurred some time ago, or that they had continued their magical practices up until this supposed moment of awakening conscience (cf. John 8:30-31).[41] Third, as Jerome Kodell has shown, the remark in v. 20 that "the word grew" probably refers to the addition of new believers to the church.[42] Fourth and finally, to assume that the confessors had first come to believe at some earlier, undisclosed point in the narrative is to miss entirely Luke's careful structuring of vv. 8-20: "inhabitants of Asia, both Jews and Greeks" had heard Paul preach *the word of the Lord* for two years (v. 10). Subsequently some of these persons ("inhabitants of Ephesus, both Jews and Greeks"; v. 17) extol *the name of the Lord* and confess their practices. By responding this way to Paul's preaching, they cause *the word of the Lord* to grow (v. 20). In summary, despite the evangelist's compressed narration, it must be concluded that Luke supposed that the defeat of the seven had prompted a great many persons to believe in the Word. Those of the new converts who had practiced magic then *immediately* came forward to confess and repent.

In v. 19, when Luke further mentions "a number of those who practiced magic arts," we are to understand that these persons also are among those who had become "believers." The grammatical structure of the subject of v. 19 (partitive genitive: *hikanoi de tōn ta perierga praxantōn*) parallels that of v. 18 *(polloi te tōn pepisteukotōn)* and is in no way subordinate to it, so admittedly it is at least possible that in v. 19 Luke has in mind an entirely different group of persons, who perhaps are not believers at all.[43] But the statement about the burning of books is bracketed by references to the growth of the church: as argued above, vv. 17 and 20 probably imply the coming to faith of many of the residents of Ephesus. Accordingly, the report that some who practiced magic arts "burned their magic books" probably ought to be understood as a continuation or extension of the repentance of the newly converted begun in v. 18. One might paraphrase: "some of those who had become believers confessed their practices, and among these there were quite a few *(hikanoi)* who burned their magic books."[44] In any case, Luke's purpose in composing these two verses was not to give a precise tally of who confessed what, but to emphasize the sweeping victory of the Lord over the powers of darkness even in Ephesus, noted center of the magical arts. Great numbers of those who performed this highly culpable form of service to Satan have now abandoned him and come over to the camp of the Lord. The image of so many costly magic books consigned to the flames serves as a strong testimony to the Word's victorious power.

Luke concludes the incident with a reference to the "growth" of the Word. As Kodell has shown, the odd expression very likely refers to the numerical expansion of the church.[45] Luke's other summary accounts of the growth of the church follow some crisis in its life— whether internal dissension or external persecution—that had seemed to preclude all hope of growth.[46] The message conveyed by this striking literary pattern is that no opponent—internal, earthly, or cosmic— can stop the spread of God's Word. The consistency of this pattern elsewhere in Luke-Acts indicates that in Acts 19:20, also, the reference to the "growth of the word" signals that an obstacle or crisis has been overcome. What was the obstacle? It was the seemingly relentless grip that the practice of magic—the trafficking in evil spirits and concomitant loyalty to their master, the devil—had exercised on the Ephesian people. The reference to the growth of the Word in 19:20 indicates that once again a barren landscape has been transformed by the Lord *(kata kratos tou kyriou)* into a fruitful and luxuriant plain.

SUMMARY AND ANALYSIS

Despite opposition from the Jews, Paul initiated a successful ministry in Ephesus. Over a two-year period all the residents of Asia, both Jews and Greeks, heard Paul preach about the Kingdom of God, and many must also have heard of or seen the extraordinary healings that God did through Paul's hands to confirm Paul's message. Some of the itinerant Jewish exorcists, including seven sons of a high priest, witnessed these signs done (Luke implies) "in Jesus' name," and mistook them for feats of magic. They tried to imitate what they supposed to be Paul's "magical technique," uttering a formula in which Jesus' name was invoked over the possessed. Luke leads the reader to infer that the sons assumed that they would be able to control one demon by mobilizing the power of another—an assumption consistent with the methods frequently used by contemporary magicians, and similar to an earlier interpretation of Jesus' work by Herod (which Luke had minimized; see above, p. 44). But the demon's violent refusal to be cast out makes it clear that "Jesus" is not a magical power to be mobilized at will. The sons' effort to name Jesus' name fails because the demon does not acknowledge their authority to do so. They are authorized only by Satan, and Satan's authority has been eclipsed by the authority of Christ.

Paradoxically, then, the demon's apparent victory is actually a defeat of the devil. This "paradox" comes about because both the demon and the exorcists are working for Satan's side. The demon's insubordinance toward the exorcists shows that the devil is no longer in control of his realm. His kingdom has been divided and will soon collapse (cf. Luke 11:18). From now on *only Jesus or his authorized servants* will be obeyed by the demons; consequently the exorcists' magic has become entirely useless. The residents of Ephesus, both Jews and Greeks, comprehend this remarkable new development and believe the word that they had earlier heard Paul preach. They repent of their magical practices and burn their magic books.

For the first time in Acts, Luke betrays a knowledge about how magicians operate, depicting magicians (called "exorcists") in action. In his description of this action, as in the portrayal of the people's response, Luke uses vocabulary commonly associated with magical practice *(onomazein, horkizein, exorkistēs, katakyrieuein, praxis, perierga, bibloi)*. The representation of the seven sons' "technique" is not very detailed, but it does suggest that Luke knew of magicians' frequent dependence on the names of powerful spirits, which when invoked would compel their bearers to act. Luke must also have recognized that Christian invocation of the name of Jesus, preached by Paul (v. 13) as one crucified and risen, looked to outsiders like the magical invocation of the spirit of a person killed violently. In short, it appears that Luke was familiar enough with the way magicians operate to be forced to concede that what Christians do looks quite similar.

In the Beelzebul controversy (Luke 11:14-23), Jesus is accused of working wonders by means of an evil power, and in Acts 4:7, the authorities interrogate Peter concerning a miracle he had performed, asking, "By what power or by what name do you do this?" Both incidents reveal the importance to Luke of the question of *agency* in assessing miraculous deeds. In Luke's view the difference between Christian "signs and wonders" on the one hand and non-Christian "magic" on the other lay in the source of the instrumental power. Although Luke here used a distinctive vocabulary when referring to the techniques of "magicians," it is not evident that the differences in vocabulary corresponded to phenomenological differences in working methods.[47] Indeed, as noted above, Luke tacitly admits that there were enough similarities of method for observers to mistake one sort of wonder for the other. The distinctive sets of vocabulary applied by Luke reflect not so much differences in technique as Luke's logically prior assessment that the seven are authorized by the devil. The seven sons suppose that since they "know" Jesus' name they can coerce him to work for them; Luke counters by stressing that what really matters is whether the demons "know" that a wonder-worker has authority given by Christ (Luke 10:17-19). The seven sons were backed only by Satan, who has been ousted from authority. They carry currency that is not legal tender in the new economy of God.

In vv. 18-19, "practices" and "books" symbolize outwardly and visibly Satan's invisible authority over human lives. Hence the references to "magic" function here as elsewhere in Luke-Acts to help the reader to order and interpret the events of the narrative: the image of so many Jews and Greeks "renouncing their practices" and "burning their magic books" signals unmistakably the end of Satan's control. The devil's dominion continues to shrink as the Word grows.

CONCLUSION

THE DEMISE OF THE DEVIL

Darkness lies like a shroud over much of the world into which the reader of Luke-Acts is drawn. The dark regions are the realm of Satan, the ruler of this world, who for eons has sat entrenched and well-guarded, his many possessions gathered like trophies around him. The sick and possessed are held captive by his demons; the Gentiles, too, are subject to his dominion, giving him honor and glory that ought to be offered to God. Tragically, even many Jews have acquiesced to Satan's authority. For generations they have resisted the Spirit and rejected the prophets, choosing instead to follow false prophets, who themselves serve the devil as Lord. Hence the Jews are in bondage to the devil as surely as the Israelites were once in bondage to Pharaoh. But with the announcement to Zechariah by Gabriel comes the sure promise of release. Zechariah proclaims that John will go before the Lord, making known the salvation that Jesus will bring: how Jesus will give light to those who sit in darkness and in the shadow of death, guiding the people's feet into the way of peace.

Satan, like Pharaoh, will not willingly relinquish his hold on the people; hence the ministry of Jesus is from its inception a struggle with Satan for authority. At the testing in the wilderness Satan tries to divert Jesus from his God-appointed task by persuading him, too, to worship Satan as Lord. When Jesus by his obedience to God resists the devil's power, the devil departs, defeated. But Jesus' final victory is not yet won: Satan will continue to to oppose him throughout Jesus' earthly ministry, and will regain authority at the passion. For a brief period it looks as if the devil has conquered Jesus: darkness settles over the face of the earth, and Jesus dies. But then Jesus is exalted to the place at the right hand of God, and Satan falls from heaven. Henceforth (as during Jesus' ministry prior to the passion) all the faithful who call upon the name of the Lord will have authority over the Enemy's power. Their own names are written with Christ in heaven.

Satan may have fallen to earth, but his time is not yet finished. He continues to try to make crooked the straight paths of the Lord. One of his most common ploys is to seduce people into his realm by means of false prophets and magic. In acts of magic Satan and his demons perversely replicate the Word-confirming signs and wonders that Christian preachers (like the prophets of God before them) perform, thereby enabling Satan's false prophets to impersonate God's true ones. By defeating the magicians and winning away their adherents, who include the Samaritans, Sergius Paulus, and the residents of Ephesus, Christian preachers demonstrate that their authority surpasses the authority of Satan. The downfall of each of the magicians functions (as does the casting out of demons) to confirm the truth of the Christian proclamation, in which the demise of the devil's authority figures prominently (Luke 10:17-18; Acts 26:18).

This effort to view the accounts about magicians within the context of the narrative world of Luke-Acts has shown that these accounts are not exclusively or even primarily about "magic." Rather, Luke has used the incidents to drive home a message: Christ has gained authority over the devil, and consequently those in the church who faithfully call upon Jesus' name likewise have "authority to trample on snakes and scorpions, and over all the power of the Enemy." The message is interwoven with an overarching and surprisingly apocalyptic myth about Satan's struggle and fall. Luke may have assumed that his readers shared his knowledge of the basic plot of this story. At the very least, conceptual parallels furnished by contemporaneous Jewish and Christian documents indicate that the elements of the myth were conventional in the era when Luke and Acts were composed.

The symbolic use of "magic" and "magicians" in the service of a theological argument would have succeeded in part because magic was an aspect of everyday life in antiquity, and hence readily imaginable to Luke's readers. They may have seen magicians themselves, and perhaps had even used their services. If they had never observed magicians in person, they had at least heard enough stories about them to know what they were like. Furthermore, certain presumed characteristics of magicians and magic made their symbolic potential great. While "magicians" were a part of this world, they also trafficked in the world of demons; both the magicians and the demons were thought to have Satan as lord. And in the traditions on which Luke appears to have drawn (exemplified in such documents as *Jubilees*, the *Martyrdom of Isaiah*, the Dead Sea Scrolls, the Book of Revelation, and the *Shepherd of Hermas*) magic was regarded not only as satanic but also as the characteristic action of false prophets, who by means of it promote idolatry. Because of these associations with demons, idolatrous false prophets, and Satan, Luke is able to use the figure of the magician to stand for all that is hostile to the purposes of God. By depicting the defeat of magicians, he conveys the message that in the name of Jesus, the faithful shall triumph over the forces of darkness: Christians need not fear the devil, for there is no power in him against them.

But Luke expresses the message of Christian authority over the power of the devil in other ways as well. The Christians' resounding success at casting out demons and healing, the triumph of the church over the diabolical plot of Ananias and Sapphira, and the success of the Lord Jesus in overcoming the opposition of Saul appear to make the same point. In these incidents, as in the encounters with magicians, Luke has taken pains to show that behind the defeated enemies stood none other than the devil. Thus these incidents, like the ones involving magicians, point beyond the visible human arena to the invisible spiritual one, where the Holy Spirit repeatedly meets the spirit of the devil and causes it to shrink or to flee.

CONCERNS OF THE LUKAN COMMUNITY

In his depiction of Christians and magicians, Luke addressed certain issues that he may have perceived to be a concern of his anticipated readers. To begin with, by portraying the Christian leaders as staunch opponents of magicians and therefore of Satan, Luke refutes any notion that his protagonists were themselves practitioners of magic.[1] Luke believes that to the perceptive observer (epitomized by Peter, Acts 8:23; and Paul, Acts 13:9), the vast differences between magicians on the one hand and Christian leaders on the other are readily apparent: magicians exalt themselves, try to misappropriate authority (8:18-19; 19:13-14), and seek to turn people away from the Word of God. Christian miracle workers, by contrast, bring glory not to themselves but to God, thereby leading people to believe the word that they have preached and thereby to gain release from Satan's authority. Enhancing Luke's anti-magic apology is his insistence that it is ultimately God who is active in all Jesus' and the Christians' signs and wonders (Acts 4:30; 10:38; and throughout). Their authority is a gift from Jesus (Luke 10:19) and ultimately from God (Acts 8:20). Consequently even the demons testify to the difference between Christian miracle workers and magicians, acknowledging Christians' right to name Jesus' name but denying the right of magicians to do likewise (19:15).

The success of Luke's anti-magic apologetic strategy will have varied along with the cultural and social context(s) of the readers. Luke's many references and allusions to the devil, to the demonic, and to "authority" *(exousia)*—a term frequently associated with Satan's dominion in contemporaneous Jewish and Christian literature—would have arrested the attention of those ancient readers who were accustomed to thinking about Satan and his apparently intractable hold on the world. Taking for granted the diabolical origin of magical practices, such readers would have understood Luke's accounts of Christian triumphs over magicians as victories over the power of Satan, and hence as indications of Christians' complete separation from magic. Luke's apologetic strategy does not always appeal to modern readers, who are encumbered with different definitions of magic and often prefer the more aseptic treatment of the demonic by Matthew or the gleeful debunking by Lucian of Samosata. But to readers who knew that Satan regularly imitated the wonders worked by God, and who firmly believed in the power of demons and the terrible reality of their master, Luke's apologetic strategy was appropriate. Luke combats magic, not by denying it or by ridiculing it—it was much too threatening for either of those approaches—but by showing that Satan, the force behind all magic, had been bound and gagged. Luke informs his readers that Christians have never sided with magic, and therefore with Satan; to have done so would have been to ally themselves with the condemned.

Luke's anti-magic apology also has a sharp polemical edge. On two out of three occasions the magicians who concern Luke are Jewish, even though they are encountered deep in pagan territory (Acts 13:6; 19:14). On the remaining occasion (8:9-11), the magician—apparently a Samaritan—strongly resembles the false prophets who populated first-century Jewish and Christian consciousness.[2] Given Luke's highly ambivalent attitude toward the Jews, this pattern is hardly accidental. A possible clue to its significance is the observation that Simon Magus and Bar Jesus are both linked with false prophecy and hence with idolatry—diabolically controlled forms of behavior associated elsewhere in Luke-Acts with the unrepentant Jews at large.[3] Perhaps, then, for Luke the Jewish and Samaritan magicians symbolize their unrepentant compatriots. As noted earlier, Luke was probably aware of accusations that Jesus and the leaders of the early church were themselves idolatrous magicians/false prophets; it may be that instead of mentioning such accusations explicitly, Luke chose to combat them by turning the tables, accusing the unrepentant Jews of the very same evils. Like Bar Jesus, the unrepentant Jews (and Samaritans; cf. Luke 9:52-53) oppose the Word and do not see the light. The Jews had repeatedly rejected the leadership of Moses, preferring instead "the tent of Moloch, and the star of the god Rephan" (Acts 7:27,39,40-43). Their entire history had been one of following false prophets and rejecting true ones (Luke 6:22, 26; Acts 7:22). This history accounted for their rejection of Jesus: though Jesus had been an anointed prophet of God, his compatriots had thrown him out of Nazareth and had tried to execute him (Luke 4:24-30); the Samaritans likewise had refused to hear him (9:52-53). If Luke's readers had ever heard Jews accuse Jesus and his followers of magic, false prophecy, or idolatry, then Luke's cutting reversal of the charges can scarcely have been missed.

The message of Christians' present authority over Satan was not one to be taken lightly: it was not a message that all other Christian pastors proclaimed. The author of the *Epistle of Barnabas,* for example, gives the more discouraging opinion that "the worker of evil himself has authority"; he can gain authority over believers and "thrust us out from the Kingdom of the Lord" (*Barnabas* 2.1; 4.13). But neither was Luke alone in offering a message of assurance and hope. The author of 1 John claims that although the whole world lies in the grip of the Evil One, that one does not touch those who are born of God (5:18-19). The prophet John informs the members of the seven churches that despite Satan's present dominion over the dwellers of the earth, the faithful are to be exempt from Satan's authority until that day when Christ's enemies are cast into the lake of fire (see Rev. 9:4; 12:12; 13:8). And, Hermas's angelic guide in the *Shepherd of Hermas* repeatedly assures his Christian charge that the devil, though he indeed has power, shall be overcome by those who have the spirit from above (*Hermas Vision* 4.1.5-9; *Mandate* 12.6.2).

Borrowing from Frank Kermode, Paul Minear argues that if Luke and Theophilus (or those whom he represents) are pictured as members of churches "caught up in multiple perplexities which inhibited confidence and boldness," then the restoration of their confidence in the truth would have required three things:

> an imaginatively recovered past, an imaginatively prefigured future, and a sense of the concordance between the immediate predicament of the believing community and both its past and its future. To those already instructed in the Christian way the degree of confidence would also

depend on the degree of vindication of God's avowed intention; this, in turn, depended on the vindication of the "eyewitnesses and ministers of the word."[4]

By insisting that in the church's earliest days the Word of the Lord had overcome even Satan's most powerful servants, Luke offered his readers a story of their origins that could have been regarded as both realistic and reassuring. It was "realistic" because the evangelist did not shrink from describing the great variety of forces that had from the beginning opposed the Word. It was "reassuring" because he also demonstrated that the ultimate opposing force had been vanquished. Luke's several stories about Christian victories over the servants of Satan, including magicians, would indeed have invited readers to reinterpret their own present situation in light of an "imaginatively recovered past." If they themselves practiced exorcism (a reasonable possibility), then they would have been encouraged to understand this recurring event as a sign of victory accomplished and as a promise of vindication yet to come. If they believed, as Luke and others of his era apparently did, that Satan's "fall" was to be the prelude to the end time, then Luke's implication that the fall had already occurred would have made it clear to the readers that they themselves existed in the final interval.[5] They would have realized that in Luke 10:17-20 Jesus was not only speaking to missionaries from the church's earlier days, but he was also speaking to them.

LUKE AND HELLENISTIC MAGIC

Whether or not Luke writes about magic as one intimately familiar with its presuppositions and procedures is difficult to assess. The only place in his accounts of magicians where Luke shows himself to be conversant in the technical jargon of Hellenistic magic is in the story of the seven sons of Sceva.[6] But even here the "technical jargon" is not so very technical after all; it is possible that this "magical terminology" would have been familiar to most educated or even less educated persons in the Hellenistic world. Luke's apparent awareness of magicians' assumptions about the potency of names and of the spirits of those killed violently may similarly have fallen within the bounds of relatively "common knowledge," since these assumptions were quite basic to magical procedure.[7] By contrast, the depiction by Hermas of the angel of the prophetic spirit that rests upon the true prophet and of the empty, earthly spirit that fills the false prophet reveals a close working knowledge of the ideas and vocabulary of pagan magical divination (as Reiling has shown).[8]

But this apparent difference in the two authors' levels of "technical expertise," while suggestive, may also be misleading. First, any argument from silence is inherently precarious: Luke's failure to describe magical procedures in detail may simply indicate that he saw no purpose for doing so within the context of the narrative. Second, when Luke does represent magicians in action, they are not performing an act of divination but an exorcism; thus the comparison with Hermas's description of divination is problematic.[9] Third, even though Luke does not draw on pagan explanations of magic as indisputably as does Hermas, the evangelist has obviously given considerable thought to the subject of what occurs on the spiritual plane whenever Jesus or Christians exorcise. The governing paradigm is Luke's own myth of Satan as the "strong one" who sits in his palace, well-armed and trusting in his possessions, only to be conquered by "one who is stronger." Luke has creatively reinterpreted the concept of magical "knowledge" in terms of this paradigm: because the "strong one" has been vanquished, the demons no longer "know" Satan to be master; hence they do not obey his emissaries, the magicians. In the mythological paradigm of the "strong one" Luke builds on Jewish traditions about the role of Satan as lord of the demons and the role of the Messiah as one who will conquer the forces of evil at the end time. From other evidence it is clear that Luke also has been influenced by Psalm 91 (LXX Psalm 90), which may have been used at Qumran as a source of protection from demonic powers. Thus, whether Luke wrote as an outsider to magical practice or as one who, like the Ephesians in Acts 19, had practiced magic but renounced it after believing in Christ, the relationship between the demonic realm and the realm of Christ is of immense concern to the evangelist. "Magic" is not something exotic, mentioned merely to spice up his account or to "entertain" his readers. Rather, magic is the routine mode of action by the antagonists in a spiritual world that is present on all sides at all times. Magic is a gauge that indicates by its success or failure the strength or weakness of Satan and his forces.

One of my premises has been that in order to interpret the portrayal of magic and magicians in Luke-Acts, one must first understand what Luke thought about magic. Thus the driving question has not been whether Luke's world view or his characters' actions were "magical," but how "magic" and "magicians" functioned to order the events of the narrative and the perceptual experience of those who read it. Asking such a question has made it possible to discern the strong thematic coherence of the three portrayals of magicians in Acts, and also to view several other passages in Luke-Acts from a fresh and illuminating angle. Furthermore, the persistent effort to view the magic-related accounts within both their narrative and cultural contexts has made it possible to infer apologetic, polemical, and hortatory elements of the discourse that Luke apparently carried on with his readers by means of those accounts. In order to achieve these results I have tried to recover, insofar as possible, Luke's own perspective on the portrayed events. I have deliberately pushed aside the ontological questions (Were Jesus and the Christians magicians? Were their wondrous deeds acts of magic?). Such questions can never receive a definitive answer, because the answer changes as the criteria for "magic" applied by the observers—ancient and modern—change. This recognition of the relativity of any interpretation of ancient controversies over magic, including the controversies depicted in the New Testament, will perhaps be distressing to some. But to seek an Archimedean point from which to assess such controversies is to engage in an exercise in futility.

The colors and the characters in Luke's stories about Simon Magus, Bar Jesus, and the seven sons of Sceva are bolder than life—the actions and words are more channeled and intensely expressive than the actions of live persons. The "moral of the story" is never diluted as it so often is in real life. But the stories may nonetheless have opened up new possibilities for the comprehending and living of "real life" by Luke's readers. The stories furnished a vocabulary for construing the evil forces that sapped believers' resolve and caused them to desert the faith—a "vocabulary" not only of words but also of distinctive patterns of behavior and response. In one respect, this new vocabulary was not new at all: as I have shown above, Luke drew on culturally informed beliefs about magic, magicians, false prophets, demons, Satan, and the righteous person's certainty of success in confronting these evil forces. Luke's accomplishment lay not in his creation of novel forms, but in his ingenious synthesis of preexisting forms into an extended narrative. The narrative could capture the readers' imagination, and thereby persuade and uplift where straightforward exhortation could not. Luke's story showed those in need of encouragement that Christ had conquered the evil being who unlawfully claimed dominion and authority, and who had long oppressed the peoples of the world. To be sure, the final victory lay in the future. But no longer could Satan and his demonic and human servants harass and torment at will. Satan's kingdom was splintering around him, and his authority was no longer acknowledged by all. The battle

still raged but Christ's ultimate triumph was certain. Christian experience—from the earliest days to Luke's present—testified to the
demise of the devil.

ABBREVIATIONS

AB	Anchor Bible
AGJU	Arbeiten zur Geschichte des Spätjudentums und Urchristentums
AnBib	Analecta Biblica
ANRW	*Auftstieg und Niedergang der römischen Welt*
BAR	*Biblical Archaeology Review*
BHT	Beiträge zur historischen Theologie
BWANT	Beiträge zur Wissenschaft vom Alten und Neuen Testament
BZNW	Beihefte zur Zeitschrift für die neutestamentliche Wissenschaft
CBQ	*Catholic Biblical Quarterly*
CD	Cairo Geniza text of the *Damascus Covenant*
EPRO	Etudes préliminaires aus religions orientales dans l'empire Romain
ETL	*Ephemerides theologicae lovanienses*
ExpTim	*Expository Times*
GMPT	Hans Dieter Betz, ed., *The Greek Magical Papyri in Translation*
HBD	*Harper Bible Dictionary*
HDR	Harvard Dissertations in Religion
HSM	Harvard Semitic Monographs
HTKNT	Herders theologischer Kommentar zum Neuen Testament
HTR	*Harvard Theological Review*
ICC	International Critical Commentary
Interp	*Interpretation*
JBL	*Journal of Biblical Literature*
JSP	*Journal for the Study of the Pseudepigrapha*
JTS	*Journal of Theological Studies*
LCL	Loeb Classical Library
LXX	The Septuagint
MT	The Masoretic text

NorTT	*Norsk Teologisk Tidsskrift*
NovT	*Novum Testamentum*
NovTSup	Novum Testamentum, Supplements
NTD	Das Neue Testament Deutsch
NTS	*New Testament Studies*
ÖBS	Österreichische Biblische Studien
OBT	Overtures to Biblical Theology
OTP	James H. Charlesworth, ed., *The Old Testament Pseudepigrapha*
PGM	K. Preisendanz, ed., *Papyri Graecae Magicae: Die griechischen Zauberpapyri*
PW	A. Pauly, G. Wissowa, and W. Kroll, eds., *Real-Encyclopädie der klassischen Altertums Wissenschaft*
1QM	The *War Rule* from Qumran Cave 1
11QMelch	The *pesher* on Melchizedek from Qumran Cave 11
1QS	The *Rule of the Community* from Qumran Cave 1
RB	*Revue biblique*
RSR	*Religious Studies Review*
SBL	Society of Biblical Literature
SBLDS	Society of Biblical Literature Dissertation Series
SBLMS	Society of Biblical Literature Monograph Series
SBLPS	Society of Biblical Literature Pseudepigrapha Series
SBLTT	Society of Biblical Literature Texts and Translations
SBT	Studies in Biblical Theology
SNTSMS	Society for New Testament Studies Monograph Series
SO	*Symbolae osloenses*
ST	*Studia theologica*
StudNeot	Studia neotestamentica
TDNT	*Theological Dictionary of the New Testament*
WUNT	Wissenschaftliche Untersuchungen zum Neuen Testament
ZTK	*Zeitschrift für Theologie und Kirche*

NOTES

INTRODUCTION

1. *BAR* 135 (1987): 18.

2. Luke's discussion of magic is treated in the present work; see also my article, "Light on a Dark Subject and Vice Versa: Magic and Magicians in the New Testament," in *Religion, Science, and Magic: In Conflict and in Concert,* ed. Jacob Neusner et al. (New York: Oxford Univ. Press, 1989), 142-65. On anti-magic apologetic in the Book of Revelation, see David E. Aune, "The Apocalypse of John and Graeco-Roman Revelatory Magic," *NTS* 33 (1987): 481–501.

3. On Mark 3:22-27 and parallels see Anton Fridrichsen, *The Problem of Miracle in Early Christianity* (Minneapolis: Augsburg Publishing House, 1972), 102–10; P. Samain, "L'Accusation de magie contre le Christ dans les Évangiles," *ETL* 15 (1938): 449–90, esp. 464–72. The Lukan account of this incident (Luke 11:14-23) will be discussed in chap. 2.

4. See T. Hopfner, "*Mageia,*" PW 14/1 (1928): col. 330. David E. Aune writes, "In considering the early use of the name of Jesus in the performance of healings and exorcisms in 'Acts', it must surely have appeared to Jewish and pagan observers that early Christian wonder-workers were practising necromancy" ("Magic in Early Christianity," *ANRW* 2.23.2 [1980]: 1545). Several observations suggest that Luke knew of accusations that Jesus and the church leaders were magicians or false prophets. An explicit accusation that Jesus practiced sorcery is found at Luke 11:14-23. Moreover, in Luke 23:2, Luke reports that Jews had accused Jesus of "perverting" the nation *(diastrephein);* the same word is used to describe the actions of the magician/ false prophet Bar Jesus in Acts 13:8,10. After his resurrection the Jewish leaders classed Jesus with Theudas and Judas the Galilean, who like false prophets had exalted themselves and drawn the people after them (Acts 5:35- 39; cf. 21:38). The Jewish leaders also tried to restrain the Christian prophets who were continuing Jesus' work, asking them "in what power or in what name" they did their remarkable deeds (Acts 4:7; cf. Luke 11:15); the question implies that the authorities suspected an illicit (demonic) power to be at work.

5. Ignatius argued that with Christ's birth, all magic had been abolished (*Ephesians* 19.3; cf. Origen *Against Celsus* 1.60; Justin *1 Apology* 14; Tertullian *On Idolatry* 9; *Barnabas* 20.1; *Didache* 2.2; 5.1). For discussion of these and other anti-magic apologetic passages in early Christian writers, see Fridrichsen, *The Problem of Miracle,* 85–102; Harold Remus, *Pagan-Christian Conflict Over Miracle in the Second Century,* Patristic Monograph Series 10 (Cambridge, Mass.: Philadelphia Patristic Foundation, 1983), 56, 59, and passim; Eugene V. Gallagher, *Divine Man or Magician? Celsus and Origen on Jesus,* SBLDS 64 (Chico, Calif.: Scholars Press, 1982). For a thorough review of the outsiders'

charges, see Morton Smith, *Jesus the Magician* (San Francisco: Harper & Row, 1978), 21–67.

6. John M. Hull, *Hellenistic Magic and the Synoptic Tradition*, SBT, 2d series, 28 (London: SCM Press, 1974), 116. For example, Matthew (and Luke also) omitted the stories of the healings of the deaf mute (Mark 7:31-37) and of the blind man near Bethsaida (Mark 8:22-26), both of which might lend themselves to magical interpretation. See the discussion in Aune, "Magic in Early Christianity," 1537–38.

7. Carl H. Kraeling, "Was Jesus Accused of Necromancy?" *JBL* 59 (1940): 147–57. Kraeling recognizes (p. 147) that "necromancy" in the strict sense of the term refers to the obtaining of information about the future by consulting the dead, but he further observes that the term had "a wider connotation by virtue of which it describes the practice of accomplishing through the instrumentality of the spirits of the dead any or all of the deeds belonging to the sphere of 'black magic.' "

8. For a review of anthropological research on magic, see my dissertation, *Magic and Miracle in Luke-Acts* (Ann Arbor, Mich.: Univ. Microfilms, 1989), 41–53. On the use of "devil worship" and the "demonic" (both notions that were often associated with "magic") as locative categories in the ancient world, see the excellent article by Jonathan Z. Smith, "Towards Interpreting Demonic Powers in Hellenistic and Roman Antiquity," *ANRW* 2.16.1 (1978): 425–39.

9. The incident is known from Apuleius's *Apologia* (or *Pro se de Magia*), which is a transcription of his courtroom defense (possibly revised). For the Latin text (with German translation), see Apuleius Madaurensis, *Verteidigungsrede; Blutenlese*, ed. and trans. R. W. O. Helm (Berlin: Akademie Verlag, 1977). For an English translation see H. E. Butler, trans., *The Apologia and Florida of Apuleius of Madaura* (1909; reprint, Westport, Conn.: Greenwood Press, 1970).

10. Years ago others asked "interpretive" questions about the understanding of magic exhibited in the Gospels and Acts. Anton Fridrichsen and S. Eitrem, for example, attempted to rediscover the "mythical view of the universe" (the expression was Fridrichsen's) in light of which magic-related passages in the New Testament made sense (Anton Fridrichsen, "The Conflict of Jesus with the Unclean Spirits," *Theology* 22 [1931]: 122–35; Samain, "L'Accusation de magie"). More recently Alan F. Segal, David E. Aune, Eugene V. Gallagher, and Harold Remus have successfully addressed interpretive questions, but primarily in reference to ancient literature other than Luke and Acts. See Alan F. Segal, "Hellenistic Magic: Some Questions of Definition," in *Studies in Gnosticism and Hellenistic Religions*, eds. R. van den Broek and M. J. Vermaseren, EPRO 91 (Leiden: Brill, 1981), 349–75 (the article is reprinted in *The Other Judaisms of Late Antiquity*, [Brown Judaica Series 127; Atlanta: Scholars Press, 1987], 79–108; citations below are from *Studies in Gnosticism*); Aune, "Apocalypse of John"; Gallagher, *Divine Man or Magician?*; Remus, *Pagan-Christian Conflict*.

11. Clifford Geertz, *The Interpretation of Cultures* (New York: Basic Books, 1973), 10, cf. 448–50.

12. In anthropology, the effort to see the whole in terms of the parts and vice versa—in other words, to perceive how many different aspects of group life interrelate, rather than isolating artificially abstracted aspects—is called "holism," or "thinking holistically." Anthropologist James L. Peacock calls the effort to understand societies holistically the most distinctive feature of the ethnographic method (*The Anthropological Lens: Harsh Light, Soft Focus* [Cambridge: Cambridge Univ. Press, 1986], 18–19).

13. The definition of "narrative world" is based on the discussion of "finite provinces of meaning" by Peter L. Berger and Thomas Luckmann, *The Social Construction of Reality: A Treatise in the Sociology of Knowledge* (Garden City, New York: Doubleday & Co., 1966–67), 25. For a helpful discussion of the relationship between "narrative worlds" and "social worlds," see Norman R. Petersen, *Rediscovering Paul: Philemon and the Sociology of Paul's Narrative World* (Philadelphia: Fortress Press, 1985), 17–30.

14. Geertz, *Interpretation of Cultures*, 5.

15. Luke mentions only one reader by name ("most excellent Theophilus"). But the dedication, which may be intended to ensure publication, probably does not imply that Luke genuinely had only a single reader in view. More likely "Theophilus" (whether or not a historical person) represents many "friends of God" who had been instructed in all matters (v. 3), but who, Luke believed, needed "assurance" or "truth" *(asphaleia)* concerning them. See Paul S. Minear, "Dear Theo: The Kerygmatic Intention and Claim of the Book of Acts," *Interp* 27 (1973): 132; Henry J. Cadbury, *The Making of Luke-Acts* (New York: Macmillan, 1927), 194–204. Even this wider group need not have corresponded precisely to a specific body of individuals personally known by Luke; by addressing the discourse to "Theophilus"—i.e., to an eminent individual who has been instructed about Christianity and yet needs "assurance"—Luke implicitly casts all his readers into this role.

16. Emil M. Bruner, "Ethnography as Narrative," in *The Anthropology of Experience*, ed. Victor W. Turner and Emil M. Bruner (Urbana: Univ. of Illinois Press, 1986), 151. Bruner uses the phrase in reference to the "story" that ethnographers and their subjects share.

17. Peacock, *Anthropological Lens*, 18.

18. For convenience, throughout this study the author of Luke and Acts (hereafter Luke-Acts) will be referred to as "Luke." On the effort to determine the authorship and place of origin of Luke-Acts, see, e.g., Robert J. Karris, "Windows and Mirrors: Literary Criticism and Luke's Sitz im Leben," in *SBL 1979 Seminar Papers*, ed. Paul J. Achtemeier, 2 vols. (Missoula, Mont.: Scholars Press, 1979), 1:47–58; and Luke T. Johnson, "On Finding the Lukan Community: A Cautious Cautionary Essay," ibid., 1:87–100. It is clear that Luke's environment was a thoroughly Hellenized one (see David L. Tiede, *Prophecy and History in Luke-Acts* [Philadelphia: Fortress Press, 1980], 8), but of course many specific locales would fit this criterion.

19. See Tiede, *Prophecy and History*, 7–16; Donald Juel, *Luke-Acts: The Promise of History* (Atlanta: John Knox Press, 1983), 7, 113–23.

20. Cf. Peacock, *Anthropological Lens*, 20.

21. Geertz, *Interpretation of Cultures*, 9; cf. Peacock, *Anthropological Lens*, 86–89. The vexing problem of how to represent cultures fairly has in recent

years spawned diverse and creative "experimental" ethnographies; for a review of some of these and a discussion of the present state of the ethnographic enterprise, see G. E. Marcus and M. M. J. Fischer, *Anthropology as Cultural Critique: An Experimental Moment in the Human Sciences* (Chicago: Univ. of Chicago Press, 1986).

22. Peacock, *Anthropological Lens,* 90.

CHAPTER 1
MAGIC AND THE STUDY OF MAGIC

1. Ramsay MacMullen notes "that the foundation of antimagic legislation was laid by Sulla, and that it could support a broad structure of prohibition and punishments because of the very looseness of thought on the whole subject. . . . There was thus no period in the history of the empire in which the magician was not considered an enemy of society, subject at the least to exile, more often to death in its least pleasant forms" (*Enemies of the Roman Order: Treason, Unrest, and Alienation in the Empire* [Cambridge: Harvard Univ. Press, 1966], 125 26; see also Hopfner, *"Mageia,"* cols. 384 87; Arthur Darby Nock, "Paul and the Magus," in *The Beginnings of Christianity. Part 1. The Acts of the Apostles,* ed. F. J. Foakes Jackson and Kirsopp Lake, 5 vols. [London: Macmillan, 1920–33], vol. 5: *Additional Notes to the Commentary* [ed. Kirsopp Lake and Henry J. Cadbury, 1933], 164–88, esp. 172–74 [repr. in *Essays on Religion and the Ancient World,* ed. Z. Stewart, 2 vols. [Cambridge: Harvard Univ. Press, 1972], 1:316–17; citations here and subsequently are from *Beginnings*). Less official prohibitions of magic were also widely prevalent in the ancient world; see, e.g., Plato *Laws* 10.909B; Exod. 22:18; Gal. 5:20 *(pharmakeia);* Rev. 22:15 *(hoi pharmakoi); Didache* 2.2 *(ou mageuseis, ou pharmakeuseis;* cf. *Barnabas* 20.1); *Pseudo-Phocylides* 149 *(pharmaka mē teuchein, magikōn biblōn apechesthai); Mishnah Sanhedrin* 10:1 (discussed in Judah Goldin's superb article on Rabbinic attitudes toward magic, entitled "The Magic of Magic and Superstition," in *Aspects of Religious Propaganda in Judaism and Early Christianity,* ed. Elizabeth Schüssler Fiorenza [Notre Dame, Ind.: Univ. of Notre Dame Press, 1976], 115–47).

2. *Natural History* 30.1 (LCL, Pliny, vol. 8). Pliny reflects on the origins of magic in *Natural History* 30.1–4. The standard reference work on ancient magic is still T. Hopfner's encyclopedic *Griechisch-Ägyptischer Offenbarungszauber,* 2 vols. (Leipzig: H. Haessel, 1921–24); see also his more accessible condensed treatment, *"Mageia,"* cols. 301–93. Aune ("Magic in Early Christianity") presents a concise and informed discussion of a variety of issues pertaining to Greco-Roman magic and early Christianity; his article, which is a gold mine of bibliographic information, should be the first resource consulted by scholars interested in this subject. Other useful scholarly discussions include *GMPT* (Chicago: Univ. of Chicago Press, 1986), xli–liii; Nock, "Paul and the Magus"; and Georg Luck, *Arcana Mundi: Magic and the Occult in the Greek and Roman Worlds* (Baltimore, Md.: Johns Hopkins Univ. Press, 1985), 3–60.

3. Apuleius, *The Golden Ass* 2.6, trans. Robert Graves (New York: Farrar, Straus & Giroux, 1951), 29.

4. MacMullen, *Enemies*, 103. MacMullen refers primarily to the second to fourth centuries, but the evidence suggests that "magic fever" had been heating up since considerably earlier. Cf. the comment by Betz that "magical beliefs and practices can hardly be overestimated in their importance for the daily life of the people" (*GMPT*, xli).

5. Nock, "Paul and the Magus," 164–65.

6. Ibid., 165. Nock cites Sophocles *Oedipus Tyrannus* 387, and Hippocrates *On the Sacred Disease* 2.1–5.

7. *Apologia* 25–26. The translation is from Luck, *Arcana Mundi*, 110–111; regarding the Latin text, see the introduction, n. 9. In *Life of Apollonius*, Philostratus is troubled by the negative connotation of *magos* (1.2), but can similarly capitalize on its more positive sense (1.32). Philo (*Special Laws* 3.100–101) also comments on the difference between "the true magic" (*hē alēthēs magikē*) practiced by the Persians and that of reprehensible counterfeits.

8. Pliny, *Natural History* 28.2.6; 30.2.8–11.

9. Nock ("Paul and the Magus," 178–79) thinks that in discussing the Magi Pliny referred to a definite body of doctrine, citing from a doxographic source. Nock writes, "In xxi.62 he gives Pseudo-Democritus as an intermediary source, and it may be that this was commonly his source."

10. Luck, *Arcana Mundi*, 25.

11. Not all divination was considered illicit. Private, secret divination was the most likely to be labeled "magic." It was greatly feared by political leaders, since it could lead to the discovery of potentially disastrous information, such as the name of the next emperor. *Ammianus Marcellinus* 29.1.25–32 tells how a party of diviners trying to discover just this fact were caught in the act, tried, and put to death (the story is recounted in Luck, *Arcana Mundi*, 256; Luck's work also contains useful introductions to the various types of divination, as well as to alchemy, astrology, and demonology).

12. The Greek edition of the papyri is *PGM*, 2d ed. of vols. 1–2 ed. A. Henrichs (Stuttgart: B. G. Teubner, 1973–74), 1st ed. of vol. 3 (incl. indexes) ed. K. Preisendanz (Leipzig: B. G. Teubner, 1941). The recent English translation of the papyri edited by Betz *(GMPT)* includes a number of texts not in Preisendanz and is a great boon to scholarship in this field. Citations of other published texts of magical papyri are given in Aune, "Magic in Early Christianity," 1516 n. 32. Secondary studies of the papyri are also listed in Aune's article (ibid.); see in addition Segal, "Hellenistic Magic"; and Morton Smith, "The Jewish Elements in the Magical Papyri," in *SBL 1986 Seminar Papers*, ed. Kent H. Richards (Atlanta: Scholars Press, 1986), 455–62. There are reasons to be cautious when generalizing about the figure of the magician on the basis of the magical papyri. Although these papyri were discovered in Egypt, their preservation there is due to the country's dry climate; collections of magical recipes from elsewhere may have looked somewhat different. Further, the late date of most of the surviving papyri necessitates caution when making inferences about magical practice in the first century; in most cases the manuscripts date from the third to fifth centuries C.E. There are, however, strong indications that many of the texts have been copied one or more times, so that it is reasonable to assume that the majority of traditions

therein date back to a much earlier period. On the age of the traditions preserved in the papyri, see the discussions in Betz, *GMPT*, xlv; and Arthur Darby Nock, "Greek Magical Papyri," in his *Essays on Religion and the Ancient World*, ed. Z. Stewart, 2 vols. (Cambridge: Harvard Univ. Press; 1972), 1:176–94.

13. The curse tablets were called *tabellae defixionum* because they were often pierced with a nail before being cast into a grave, a well, or spot associated with a violent death (Hull, *Hellenistic Magic*, 9). For bibliography on charms, amulets, and curse tablets, see Aune, "Magic in Early Christianity," 1517, nn. 33–34.

14. English translations of a wide range of literary selections relevant to the study of magic are conveniently collected in Luck, *Arcana Mundi;* each entry includes a brief introduction. In addition to the secondary literature cited in Aune, "Magic in Early Christianity," 1517 n. 35, see S. Eitrem, "La magie comme motif littéraire chez les Grecs et les Romains," *SO* 21 (1941): 39–83; J. de Romilly, *Magic and Rhetoric in Ancient Greece* (Cambridge: Harvard Univ. Press, 1975).

15. "Magic and Early Christianity," 1519. Hence, argues Aune, the syncretism of ancient magic is to be attributed to the syncretistic character of Greco-Roman religious cults in general. For further discussions of the syncretistic nature of the papyri, see Betz, *GMPT*, xlv–xlvi; Segal, "Hellenistic Magic," 351–55; Hopfner, "*Mageia,*" col. 307; M. Smith, "Jewish Elements."

16. On the Jews' reputation for magic, see John G. Gager, *Moses in Greco-Roman Paganism*, SBLMS 16 (Nashville: Abingdon Press, 1972), 142–43. The date at which a distinctive form of Jewish magic actually developed is open to debate. Aune (reacting against J. Trachtenberg, *Jewish Magic and Superstition: A Study in Folk-Religion* [New York: Behrman, 1939]) suggests that a distinctive Jewish form of magic had emerged well before the post-Talmudic era ("Magic in Early Christianity," 1520). For general bibliography on Jewish magic see ibid., 1520 n. 52; additional sources include *Sepher Ha-Razim: The Book of the Mysteries*, trans. M. A. Morgan, SBLTT 25 and SBLPS 11 (Chico, Calif.: Scholars Press, 1983); P. S. Alexander, "Incantations and Books of Magic," in E. Schürer, *The History of the Jewish People in the Age of Jesus Christ (175 B.C.-A.D. 135)*, 3 vols., rev. and ed. Matthew Black et al. (Edinburgh: T. & T. Clark, 1973–86), 3/1: 342–79; I. Gruenwald, *Apocalyptic and Merkavah Mysticism* (Leiden: Brill, 1980); Dennis C. Duling, "The Eleazar Miracle and Solomon's Magical Wisdom in Flavius Josephus's *Antiquitates Judaicae* 8.42–49," *HTR* 78 (1985): 1–25; M. Smith, "Jewish Elements."

17. Samain, "L'Accusation de magie," 449–90.

18. J. Reiling, "The use of PSEUDOPROPHĒTĒS in the Septuagint, Philo and Josephus," *NovT* 13 (1971): 147–56.

19. Ibid., 152–53. Reiling shows that the translators of Jeremiah did not introduce the term where it would have been less appropriate: e.g., where the invective was directed mainly at the prophets' moral life rather than at their prophecies (as in 23:9–32), or where the introduction of the term *pseudoprophētēs* would have "spoiled the pointed contrast between the man and what he had to say, in Greek between *prophētēs* and *pseudos* (e.g., 23:26 [ibid., 149]).

NOTES

119

20. Ibid., 154. Reiling plausibly suggests (p. 151) that a similar association lay behind Philo's use of the term in *Special Laws* 4.8. In Josephus the term seems to have lost the connotations of pagan divination.

21. False prophets continued to be associated with idolatry throughout Luke's era: see, e.g., Rev. 2:20; 13:11-15 (cf. 19:20); and *Hermas Mandate* 11.4; cf. *Didache* 3:4; *Pseudo-Philo* 34:1–5.

22. Trans. from Latin by D. J. Harrington, in *OTP*, 2 vols. (Garden City, N.Y.: Doubleday & Co., 1983–85), 2:376.

23. On the ever-increasing role of the predictive element in Israelite-Jewish and early Christian prophecy, see J. Reiling, *Hermas and Christian Prophecy: A Study of the Eleventh Mandate*, NovTSup 37 (Leiden: E. J. Brill, 1973), 73–79; also (regarding specifically the Essenes) Martin Hengel, *Judaism and Hellenism* (Philadelphia: Fortress Press, 1974), 1:239–41.

24. David E. Aune *(Prophecy in Early Christianity and the Ancient Mediterranean World* [Grand Rapids: Wm. B. Eerdmans, 1983], 230) writes, "Although Israelite Jewish and Greco-Roman revelatory traditions have many mutually distinct features, the interpenetration of east and west during the Hellenistic and Roman period makes it very difficult if not impossible to untangle the blended elements (even if such an untangling were desirable)."

25. Translations cited here (from the Ethiopic text) are by M. A. Knibb *(OTP* 2:143–76). The *Martyrdom of Isaiah* comprises 1:1—3:12 and 5:1–16 of the composite *Ascension of Isaiah*. Scattered bits are to be attributed to later Christian writers, as is 3:13—4:22, but Knibb dates the basic material in the *Martyrdom of Isaiah* (on which the discussion here is based) to the first century c.e., and suggests that in substance this material may date to the time of Antiochus Epiphanes, 167–164 b.c.e.

26. Trans. from the Ethiopic text by O. S. Wintermute, *OTP* 2:139.

27. *The Dead Sea Scrolls in English,* 3d ed., Trans. Geza Vermes (Sheffield, Eng.: JSOT, 1987), 102. Regarding the devil's role in the legends about the magicians of Pharaoh, see A. Pietersma and R. T. Lutz, "Introduction to *Jannes and Jambres,*" *OTP,* 2:429. The translators point out that although this fragmentary pseudepigraphon (1st–3rd c. c.e.) does not make any explicit reference to the devil's role, the last lines of the Chester Beatty fragment (26ar) suggest that such may have been presupposed. Here Jannes, who has been struck with a fatal illness as a result of his contest with Moses, "sent word to the king [saying, 'This] active [power] is of God.' Therefore I deliberately *(thelōn)* op[posed Moses]" (ibid.; cf. Exod. 8:19 [LXX v. 15]). See also *Testament of Solomon* 25:3-4, where it is not Satan but the demon Amelouth who was called to the aid of Jannes and Jambres in their opposition to Moses.

28. See the discussion of the false prophet motif at Qumran and elsewhere in Wayne A. Meeks, *The Prophet-King: Moses Traditions and the Johannine Christology* (Leiden: Brill, 1967), 47–57.

29. Aune, "Apocalypse of John," esp. 494.

30. Reiling, *Hermas and Christian Prophecy.* Most instructive in this regard are Reiling's analyses of the "empty spirit" which fills the false prophet *(kenon pneuma: Hermas Mandate* 11.3, 11, 13, 15, 17; discussed in ibid., 38–43, 55),

of the characterization of the false prophet as "shameless," "reckless," and "talkative" (anaidēs, itamos, polylalos; Mandate 11.12; discussed in ibid., 91–95), and of the "angel of the prophetic spirit" which "rests upon the prophet" (ho keimenos pros auton) when he prophesies (Mandate 11.9; discussed in ibid., 86, 104–11). Reiling demonstrates that the "angel of the prophetic spirit" is related to the divinatory notion of an "assistant daimon" (daimōn paredros; see, e.g., PGM I.1ff.; such "assistant daimons" are discussed in Reiling, Hermas and Christian Prophecy, 88–90; for additional PGM citations and bibliography, see GMPT, 332–33, s.v. "Assistant Daimon [paredros]"). The notion of the "assistant daimon" may also have influenced Hermas's depiction of the inspiration of the false prophet in Mandate 11.5–6 (see Reiling, Hermas and Christian Prophecy, 86–91). In his analysis of the magic-related terminology and imagery in Mandate 11, Reiling presupposes the important work of E. Peterson on the Visions in Shepherd of Hermas ("Beiträge zur Interpretation der Visionen im 'Pastor Hermae,' " in Frühkirche, Judentum und Gnosis: Studien und Untersuchungen [Darmstadt: Wissenschaftliche Buchgesellschaft, 1982], 254–70; and "Kritische Analyse der fünften Vision des Hermas," in ibid., 271–84).

31. Reiling, Hermas and Christian Prophecy, 95.

32. For an example and interpretation (relevant to this question) of such a love charm, see G. Adolf Deissmann, Bible Studies (1923; reprint, Winona Lake, Indiana: Alpha, 1979), 273–300.

33. It has often been argued that one group of persons frequently required to defend themselves against accusations of mageia or goēteia were the candidates for "divine man" status (see Jonathan Z. Smith, "Good News is No News: Aretalogy and Gospel," in Christianity, Judaism, and Other Greco-Roman Cults, ed. Jacob Neusner, 4 vols. [Leiden: Brill, 1975], 1:21–38; Morton Smith, "Prolegomena to a Discussion of Aretalogies, Divine Men, the Gospels and Jesus," JBL 90 [1971]: 174–99; idem, Clement of Alexandria and a Secret Gospel of Mark [Cambridge, Mass.: Harvard Univ. Press, 1973], 227–29; idem, Jesus the Magician, 74–75; Hans Dieter Betz, Der Apostel Paulus und die sokratische Tradition, BHT 45 [Tübingen: Mohr (Siebeck), 1972], 13–42). In more recent years the heuristic category of the "divine man" has received telling critique; see esp. David L. Tiede, The Charismatic Figure as Miracle Worker, SBLDS 1 (Missoula, Mont.: Scholars Press, 1972); Carl H. Holladay, THEIOS ANER in Hellenistic-Judaism: A Critique of the Use of This Category in New Testament Christology, SBLDS 40 (Missoula, Mont.: Scholars Press, 1977). In Divine Man or Magician? Gallagher contends that although the divine man (theios anēr) construct has fallen under attack, it can be useful if one keeps its status as an "ideal type" in mind. After reviewing the treatment of divine men in Origen, Lucian, Philostratus, and Eusebius, Gallagher concludes that "there was considerable interest in the world of Late Antiquity in answering the question of who was a theos and who was magos, especially since both epithets were likely to be applied to the same individual" (ibid., 174). But the criteria brought to bear when answering the question were shifting and flexible, and the "native Hellenistic" conception of the divine man (if there was such a thing at all) was "a more fluid conception than is portrayed in much contemporary scholarship" (ibid., 177).

34. On this question see A. B. Kolenkow, "A Problem of Power: How Miracle Doers Counter Charges of Magic in the Hellenistic World," in *SBL 1976 Seminar Papers*, ed. George MacRae (Missoula, Mont.: Scholars Press, 1976), 105–10; also relevant are Segal, "Hellenistic Magic"; Remus, *Pagan-Christian Conflict*; and Gallagher, *Divine Man or Magician?*.

35. Segal, "Hellenistic Magic," 350–51; cf. Nock, "Paul and the Magus," 170–71.

36. "Concepts and Society," in *Rationality*, ed. Bryan Wilson (Oxford: Basil Blackwell, 1979), 45; italics his.

37. G. Adolf Deissmann, *Light from the Ancient East*, 2d ed. (London: Hodder & Stoughton, 1910), 306–10.

38. Campbell Bonner, "Traces of Thaumaturgic Technique in the Miracles," *HTR* 20 (1927): 171–74. See also Bonner's later article, "The Technique of Exorcism," *HTR* 36 (1943): 39–49.

39. Bonner, "Traces of Thaumaturgic Technique," 174.

40. Ibid., 176–80. With regard to Mark 1:41-43, Bonner suggested that the original text may have had *embrimēsamenos* in v. 41 (in place of *splagchnistheis*), in connection with the dismissal of the leper in v. 43 (ibid., 179–80).

41. Otto Bauernfeind, *Die Worte der Dämonen im Markusevangelium*, BWANT series 3, no. 8, (= no. 44) (Stuttgart: W. Kohlhammer, 1927).

42. Ibid., 34.

43. Ibid., 93–99.

44. Fridrichsen, "Conflict of Jesus with Unclean Spirits." Regarding Bauernfeind's work Fridrichsen wrote, "Bauernfeind's demonstration that the demoniacal utterances take their form from the conjuration formulas retains its value also from this apologetic point of view" (ibid., 125).

45. Fridrichsen, *The Problem of Miracle*. The work was first published in French, in 1925.

46. Ibid., 146–47 (with regard to Paul).

47. Fridrichsen was not the first to notice the dilemma and the consequent apologetic tendencies (see, e.g., G. P. von Wetter, *"Der Sohn Gottes." Eine Untersuchung über den Charakter und die Tendenz des Johannes-Evangeliums* [Göttingen: Vandenhoeck & Ruprecht, 1916]), but Fridrichsen's treatment of the Christian materials was especially wide-ranging. Regarding accusations that Jesus practiced necromancy, see also Kraeling's article, "Was Jesus Accused of Necromancy?"

48. Cf. Samain's statement ("L'Accusation de magie," 471) that "the distinction between an authentic miraculous work and a magic work is found less in the procedures or in the result of the operation itself than in the supernatural powers that intervene in it." This point is made especially clear by the Beelzebul pericope (Luke 11:14-23 and parallels), discussed in chap. 2.

49. In "Paul and the Magus" Nock demonstrated that the various words used to designate magicians, or magical acts or materials (e.g., *magos, mageia, goēs, philtron, pharmakon, epōdē*), do not always possess a precise and technical meaning, but can have positive as well as negative connotations, depending on the context.

50. "L'Accusation de magie."

51. Ibid., 454–55. See also Samain's n. 37.

52. Ibid., 456–64.

53. Ibid., 475–76. Samain was aware of von Wetter's work on the accusations of demon possession in John (see n. 47 above), but rejected von Wetter's thesis that the title "Son of God" meant the same thing in the Gospels as in Hellenistic literature, objecting that to arrive at this thesis Wetter had to rely on documents originating later than the Gospel ("L'Accusation de magie," 478 n. 152).

54. Or, that "Beelzebul has Jesus." On the meanings of each of these translations, see Kraeling, "Was Jesus Accused of Necromancy?" 153–55 (discussed below, in chap. 2 n. 33).

55. Morton Smith, *Clement of Alexandria;* idem, *The Secret Gospel: The Discovery and Interpretation of the Secret Gospel According to Mark* (New York: Harper & Row, 1973); idem, *Jesus the Magician;* cf. idem, "Prolegomena."

56. Smith, *Jesus the Magician,* 69.

57. A full evaluation of Smith's reconstruction of Jesus' career as one of a magician would have to consider several distinct issues, including the authenticity of the letter of Clement and the fragment of the "Secret Gospel of Mark" which were discovered and analyzed by Smith (see *Clement of Alexandria;* also, *Secret Gospel*), and the reliability of Smith's historical inferences from the New Testament and extrabiblical materials. These issues are tangential to the present study. Smith himself reviews the reactions to his work in "Clement of Alexandria and Secret Mark: The Score at the End of the First Decade," *HTR* 75 (1982): 449–61. On the opinions of the scholarly community, see also H. M. Schenke, "The Mystery of the Gospel of Mark," *Second Century* 4 (1984): 65–82.

58. The Eucharist is "a simple report of a familiar magical operation" (Smith, *Jesus the Magician,* 122; cf. *Secret Gospel,* 102–3).

59. Smith, *Jesus the Magician,* 104.

60. Ibid., 92–93; Smith, *Clement of Alexandria,* 224.

61. Smith, *Jesus the Magician,* 21–80.

62. Smith, *Clement of Alexandria,* 227–29; *Jesus the Magician,* 68–80; "Prolegomena," 181. Smith writes (ibid.) that "though one can discern (with the eye of historical faith) a common social pattern behind a number of the figures . . . Graeco-Roman antiquity knew many holy men of many different patterns."

63. Smith, *Clement of Alexandria,* 228–29.

64. Ibid., 229; also *Jesus the Magician,* 68–93.

65. E. V. Gallagher, review of *Jesus the Magician,* in *Horizons* 6 (1979): 126–27; cf. Segal, "Hellenistic Magic," 355 n. 20.

66. See n. 12.

67. On the highly syncretistic character of the papyri, see the works cited in n. 15. Smith certainly recognizes this syncretistic character ("Jewish Elements"), but seems unwilling to acknowledge its implications: that magicians may have been as influenced by the practices of Christians as vice versa, or that the practices of both groups may derive from a common cultural milieu.

68. "L'Accusation de magie," 471. On the ambiguity of magical terminology, see also n. 49.

69. Segal, "Hellenistic Magic," 369–70.

70. Hull, *Hellenistic Magic.*

71. Ibid., 54.

72. Ibid., 116.

73. Ibid., 143.

74. Ibid., 145.

75. Aune, "Magic in Early Christianity," 1543.

76. The distinction between the magical and eschatological backgrounds is artificial. Why should eschatologically oriented groups have been immune from interest in magic? Apocalyptic literature is often replete with allusions to magic, as Hull recognizes in his discussion of Revelation (*Hellenistic Magic,* 144; cf. Matt. 24:24; 2 Thess. 2:9).

77. Ibid., 59.

78. Hull writes, "The criteria by which the magical miracle was detected in the Hellenistic world were rather different from the ones suggested here, and much confusion in the discussion of magic would be avoided if the two sets of criteria were kept clearly in mind" (ibid., 60). Hull has not heeded his own advice. On the difference between "emic" and "etic" categories in the social sciences, see R. Feleppa, "Emics, Etics, and Social Objectivity," *Current Anthropology* 27 (1986): 243–55.

79. Response to M. and R. Wax, "The Notion of Magic," in *Current Anthropology* 4, no. 5 (1963): 505–6.

80. This was the point of F. Preisigke's *Die Gotteskraft der frühchristlichen Zeit,* Papyrusinstitut Heidelberg 6 (Berlin and Leipzig: Walter de Gruyter, 1922).

81. Aune, "Magic in Early Christianity," 1513.

82. Howard Clark Kee, *Christian Origins in Sociological Perspective* (Philadelphia: Westminster Press, 1980), 64; cf. idem, *Medicine, Miracle and Magic in New Testament Times,* SNTSMS 55 (Cambridge: Cambridge Univ. Press, 1986), 3; on the questionable validity of the "manipulation/supplication" dichotomy, see Aune, "Magic in Early Christianity," 1513. The cited works are Marcel Mauss, *A General Theory of Magic* (New York: W. W. Norton & Co., 1972; originally published in French, in 1902–3); and Lucy Mair, *An Introduction to Social Anthropology,* 2d ed. (Oxford: Clarendon Press, 1972).

83. Kee, *Christian Origins,* 65–67.

84. Ibid., 66. See also Kee's discussion of the "traces of magic" in Acts, in *Medicine, Miracle and Magic,* 115–16. Kee concludes (115), "Although these stories border on magic, Luke seems to be telling them to demonstrate that God is in control of history and of human life, rather than as a self-contained demonstration of magical technique."

85. Kee, *Christian Origins,* 66. In *Medicine, Miracle and Magic,* 114–16, Kee seems to contend that these "respective world views" held sway at different times: the religious world view was predominant in the first century, whereas the magical world view took firm hold in the second century and beyond. This periodization is why, Kee presumes, one can begin to see magical tendencies in a later book like Acts (ibid., 115). To defend this argument about

the periodization of world views, Kee must firmly reject any suggestion that the magical papyri contain traditions going back to the first century (ibid., 114; cf. idem, *Miracle in the Early Christian World: A Study in Sociohistorical Method* [New Haven, Conn.: Yale Univ. Press, 1983], 211 n. 69, 214). But such insistence on the later origin of the papyri is untenable: granting that there is evidence for post-Christian influence, it is nonetheless likely that the bulk of the traditions preserved in the magical papyri date back to a much earlier period (see above, n. 12). Furthermore, other evidence (e.g., the writings of Pliny the Elder) indicate that the practice of magic was in full swing by the time the evangelists wrote.

86. Kee, *Miracle in the Early Christian World,* 63 n. 47 (see pp. 62–64, 211–18); *Medicine, Miracle, and Magic,* 2–4, 8, 95–121 passim.

87. Mauss, *A General Theory of Magic,* 24.

88. Ibid., 21.

89. Ibid., 136; cited by Kee in *Miracle in the Early Christian World,* 63.

90. Kee acknowledges Mair's reluctance, but still implies that the dichotomy of magical and religious world views is consistent with her thought. Cf. Mair's *Introduction to Social Anthropology,* 224–25, where she writes, "Most anthropologists have thought it was an advance to see magic and religion as belonging to a single complex of phenomena, where earlier writers, each for a different reason, had treated magic as something of an inferior order. But it has never proved possible to sort out the ritual activities of a society into Malinowski's two categories [of magic and religion]." She goes on to give examples of activities that would defy description as either "magic" or "religion."

91. Ibid., 229; cf. Lucy Mair, *Witchcraft* (New York: McGraw-Hill, 1969), 24.

92. Mair, *Witchcraft;* esp. 19–24.

93. Even Malinowski can hardly be cited in support of a distinction between a magical world view and a religious one: he differentiated between magic and religion, but assumed that the same people (who, presumably, had only a single "world view") regularly practiced both.

94. Kee, *Miracle in the Early Christian World,* 3.

95. Aune, "Magic in Early Christianity," 1507–57. The topics covered in the article include: "The Nature and Function of Magic," "Magic in Graeco-Roman Religions," "Jesus and Magic," "Gospel and Aretalogy," "The Magical Use of the Name of Jesus," "Glossolalia and *Voces Magicae,*" "Magical Prayer," and "Magical Motifs in Early Christian Literature." In this study, only Aune's definition of magic and its utility for the study of the Gospels will be discussed.

96. Ibid., 1516.

97. Ibid., 1515.

98. Ibid., 1527, 1538.

99. Ibid., 1523; cf. Segal, "Hellenistic Magic," 370. Consider Luke's accusation against Bar Jesus and against the seven sons of a high priest, or the accusations by disgruntled residents of Oea against Apuleius, or the accusations of rhetors against one another in the fourth century (discussed by

Peter Brown in "Sorcery, Demons, and the Rise of Christianity from Late Antiquity into the Middle Ages," in *Witchcraft: Confessions and Accusations,* ed. Mary T. Douglas [London: Tavistock, 1970], 17–45). In each of these cases, the question as to who was a member of "the dominant social structure" and who was "socially deviant" is something of a judgment call, if it can be decided at all.

100. To Aune's great credit, when he actually turns to interpret a magic-related text he is not stymied by his own definition. In "Apocalypse of John," Aune argues that the seer John engaged in anti-magic polemic designed to counter the threat posed by pagan competitors of Christian prophets. Focusing on first-century assumptions about magic and holding in abeyance the taxonomic questions, Aune is able to illuminate otherwise obscure passages.

101. Jerome H. Neyrey, and Bruce J. Malina, "Jesus the Witch: Witchcraft Accusations in Matthew 12," in Bruce J. Malina and Jerome H. Neyrey, *Calling Jesus Names: The Social Value of Labels in Matthew* (Sonoma, Calif.: Polebridge Press, 1988), 3–32; Jerome H. Neyrey, "Witchcraft Accusations in 2 Cor. 10–13: Paul in Social Science Perspective," *Listening* 21 (1986): 160–70; idem, "Bewitched in Galatia: Paul and Cultural Anthropology," *CBQ* 50 (1988): 72–100. The numerous witchcraft accusations identified by Neyrey and Malina in the Q tradition in the Gospel of Matthew include not only charges as obvious as that Jesus "casts out demons by the prince of demons" (Matt. 9:34), but also the Christian community's own accusations against the unbelieving Pharisees (e.g., 10:28: "they destroy both soul and body in Gehenna"). In Paul's letters, Neyrey identifies 2 Cor. 11:3, 13–15 and Gal. 1:8; 3:1 as witchcraft accusations.

102. Douglas, *Natural Symbols* (New York: Pantheon Books, 1982); for discussion and use of the model by New Testament scholars see esp. Bruce J. Malina, *Christian Origins and Cultural Anthropology: Practical Models for Biblical Interpretation* (Atlanta: John Knox Press, 1986; see also my review in *JBL* 107 [1988]: 532–34); Leland J. White, "Grid and Group in Matthew's Community: The Righteousness/Honor Code in the Sermon on the Mount," in *Semeia* 35 (1986): 61–90; Jerome H. Neyrey, "The Idea of Purity in Mark's Gospel," *Semeia* 35 (1986): 91–128; idem, "Body Language in 1 Corinthians: The Use of Anthropological Models for Understanding Paul and His Opponents," *Semeia* 35 (1986): 129–70. In general on Douglas's work see S. R. Isenberg and D. E. Owen, "Bodies, Natural and Contrived: The Work of Mary Douglas," *RSR* 3 (1977): 1–17.

103. Neyrey and Malina, "Jesus the Witch," 8. Douglas discusses witchcraft in *Natural Symbols,* 107–24. She defines "grid" as "the rules which relate one person to others on an ego centered basis," and "group" as "the experience of a bounded social unit" (ibid., viii).

104. Marcus and Fischer (*Anthropology as Cultural Critique,* 179 n. 3) note that although the term "positivism" has philosophical roots, it has come to be used to refer loosely to the recent dominant style of social science which "relies on theoretical formulation and quantitative measurement and holds the methods of the natural sciences as an ideal." Peacock uses the term in

this way in *Anthropological Lens,* 68–72. (Peacock's explication of the differences between "positivism" and "interpretation" [ibid.] is very helpful; the following discussion is much indebted to it.)

105. Ibid., 68–69.

106. See, however, Peacock's restrictions on the social-scientific claims to objectivity, ibid.

107. Recognizing that there are many points in between, Peacock (ibid., 69) writes, "Simplifying, however, we can identify the dominant viewpoint in the social sciences—psychology, sociology, economics—as positivist and an influential viewpoint in ethnography as interpretive." For a description of the interpretive approach see ibid., 65–72; and Marcus and Fischer, *Anthropology as Cultural Critique,* vii–xiii, 1–44. Clifford Geertz is perhaps the best known practitioner of "interpretive anthropology"; the roots of the approach go back to Max Weber.

108. The trend among proponents of the hypothetico-deductive approach to the New Testament (exemplified in the volume *Social-Scientific Criticism of the New Testament and its Social World, Semeia* 35, ed. John H. Elliott [Atlanta: Scholars Press, 1986]) is to label all efforts by New Testament scholars to proceed inductively as "intuitive" or "ethnocentric." Such criticisms parallel the criticisms raised by positivist social scientists against proponents of interpretive anthropology (see esp. Peacock, *Anthropological Lens,* 69–72, and the criticisms by P. Shankman [and the reactions to them by other social scientists] in Shankman, "The Thick and the Thin: On the Interpretive Theoretical Program of Clifford Geertz," in *Cultural Anthropology* 25 [1984]: 261–80). On the place of subjectivity (a less derogatory term than "intuition" and "ethnocentrism") in the work of interpretive anthropologists, see above, pp. 8-9; see also Geertz, *Local Knowledge: Further Essays in Interpretive Anthropology* (New York: Basic Books, 1983), 55–70, esp. 57–58, 69–70.

109. An example of a recent interpretive approach to the study of witchcraft accusations is J. Favret-Saada's *Deadly Words: Witchcraft in the Bocage* (Cambridge: Cambridge Univ. Press, 1980).

110. Malina (*Christian Origins,* 16) writes, "It is important to realize that, since the traits of each cultural script are chunks or abstractions, they will not be found in any society in the terms listed in the diagram or the following explanation."

111. Cf. Peacock, *Anthropological Lens,* 72.

112. Cf. Geertz, *Interpretation of Cultures,* 25–26. See also the important discussion of the problem of "commensurability" between societies, in Stanley K. Stowers, "The Social Sciences and the Study of Early Christianity," in *Approaches to Ancient Judaism,* vol. 5: *Studies in Judaism and Its Greco-Roman Context,* ed. William S. Green, Brown Judaic Studies 32 (Atlanta: Scholars Press, 1985), 149–81.

113. Geertz, *Local Knowledge,* 58.

CHAPTER 2
THE STRUGGLE FOR AUTHORITY

1. Contrast Hans Conzelmann's assessment in *The Theology of St. Luke* (Philadelphia: Fortress Press, 1982), 156, that "Satan does not enter as a

factor in the saving events. In fact the only part he plays is the negative one of being excluded from the period of Jesus' ministry." Conzelmann has been criticized for this view; see e.g., Schuyler Brown, *Apostasy and Perseverance in the Theology of Luke*, AnBib 36 (Rome: Pontifical Biblical Institute Press, 1969), 6–19; G. Baumbach, *Das Verständnis des Bösen in den synoptischen Evangelien* (Berlin: Evangelische Verlagsanstalt, 1963), 122–207. The case for Mark's view of Jesus' ministry as a struggle with Satan was made strongly by James M. Robinson, *The Problem of History in Mark*, SBT 21 (London: SCM Press, 1957).

2. In this context the verb *peirazō* is best translated "test" rather than "tempt." Despite important differences, the story of Satan's testing of Jesus stands in the tradition of the tests of faith and obedience undergone by other righteous individuals, especially Abraham (and note that according to *Jubilees* 17:16, it is "Mastema" [= Satan] who prompts God to test Abram by commanding him to sacrifice Isaac) and Job; see also Wis. 2:17-20. Furthermore, the three passages that Jesus quotes from Deuteronomy (8:3; 6:13,16) recall the testing of the Israelites in the wilderness and their own sinful testing of God, which Jesus refused to repeat.

3. Exceptions are E. Fascher, *Jesus und der Satan*, Hallische Monographien 11 (Halle: Max Niemeyer, 1949), which contains an overview of German research on the testing narrative and scattered exegetical insights (but still relatively little about Satan); S. Eitrem, "Die Versuchung Christi," *NorTT* 24 (1923–24): 1–37; and B. Noack, *Satanás und Sotería: Untersuchungen zur neutestamentlichen Dämonologie* (Copenhagen: G. E. C. Gads, 1948), 83–86.

4. Satan *(Satanas)* is a transliteration from the Hebrew *śāṭān* meaning, literally, "adversary"; in the LXX it is often translated as *ho diabolos*. In the New Testament *Satanas* and *ho diabolos* are used interchangeably, along with a variety of other designations and proper names. Luke generally prefers *ho diabolos*, but sometimes *Satanas* appears. On the Old Testament occurrences of Satan, see Peggy L. Day, *An Adversary in Heaven: śāṭān in the Hebrew Bible*, HSM 43 (Atlanta: Scholars Press, 1988). For a more general discussion of the evolving ideas about Satan from the pre-exilic period through the Rabbinic era, see esp. Noack, *Satanás und Sotería;* N. Forsyth, *The Old Enemy: Satan and the Combat Myth* (Princeton: Princeton Univ. Press, 1987); and Jeffrey Burton Russell, *The Devil: Perceptions of Evil from Antiquity to Primitive Christianity* (Ithaca, N.Y.: Cornell Univ. Press, 1977). Also useful are W. Foerster and G. von Rad, "diaballō, diabolos," *TDNT* 2 (1964): 71–81; and James M. Efird's entry on "Satan," *HBD*, ed. Paul J. Achtemeier et al. (San Francisco: Harper & Row, 1985), 908–9. There are numerous studies of the Lukan "temptation narrative" more general than the one here; especially good is J. Dupont, *Les Tentations des Jésus au désert*, StudNeot 4 (Bruges: Desclée De Brouwer, 1968), 43–72.

5. Matthew mentions the kingdoms and their glory, but says nothing about "authority." In Luke 4:6a the plural pronoun (*their* glory; *tēn doxan autōn*) must refer back to "kingdoms" (cf. Matt. 4:8), suggesting that Luke has himself inserted the noun *exousia* and its modifiers, but without adjusting the possessive pronoun to match its new antecedent.

6. Luke has apparently added the statement, since it seems unlikely that Matthew would have omitted so significant a saying by the devil. Cf. Dupont, *Les Tentations,* 57; and Joseph A. Fitzmyer, *The Gospel According to Luke,* 2 vols., AB 28 and 28A (Garden City, N.Y.: Doubleday & Co., 1981–85), 1:507.

7. Cf. John 12:31 (commented on by Noack, *Satanás und Soteria,* 77–78); 2 Cor. 4:4; *Martyrdom of Isaiah* 1:3.

8. M.-M. Boismard ("Rapprochements littéraires entre l'évangile de Luc et l'Apocalypse," in *Synoptische Studien: Alfred Wikenhauser zum siebzigster Geburstag,* ed. J. Schmid and A. Vögtle [Munich: Karl Zink, 1953], 53–63) argues that Revelation and the Gospel of Luke must have shared a common written source, but familiarity with Dan. 7:6 (cf. vv. 14,27) and/or with oral traditions (probably also drawing upon Daniel) about Satan and his activities could account for this and other parallels. Even if Boismard goes too far, he rightly calls attention to apocalyptic turns of phrase in Luke's Gospel that commentators often brush aside, if they mention them at all. Eitrem ("Die Versuchung Christi," 16–19) sees the origin of these motifs in legends about Seth Typhon, who also sought dominion over the world; for discussion of the various ancient myths featuring the struggle of rival divinities for power, see Forsyth, *The Old Enemy;* also Adela Yarbro Collins, *The Combat Myth in the Book of Revelation,* HDR 9 (Missoula, Mont.: Scholars Press, 1976), esp. 79–82.

9. Noack (*Satanás und Soteria,* 83–86) has reached a similar conclusion, but without reference to Revelation; cf. J. M. Creed, *The Gospel According to St. Luke* (London: Macmillan, 1957), 63; Fascher, *Jesus und der Satan,* 20–21; Eitrem, "Die Versuchung Christi," 10; also *Martyrdom of Isaiah* 5:8–16.

10. Besides Luke 4:6, see 4:36; 10:19; 22:53; Acts 26:18; Col. 1:13; Rev. 12:10; 13:2,4,5,7,12. For a general treatment of Luke's view of authority, see Paul S. Minear, *To Heal and to Reveal: The Prophetic Vocation According to Luke* (New York: Seabury Press, 1976), 3–30. Hull (*Hellenistic Magic,* 114) clarifies the distinction between "authority" and "power" in Lukan thought: "'Authority' is the control or freedom which makes it possible for a side to make effective use of its power." Luke 10:19 illustrates the point well: here "Jesus does not give his disciples power against the power of the enemy, which would mean a prolonged struggle to see which power had authority; he gives them authority over the enemy's power, i.e., the power to restrict the effectiveness of the power of the other side." See also C. K. Barrett, *The Holy Spirit and the Gospel Tradition* (London: SPCK, 1958), 78.

11. H. Seesemann ("peira ktl.," *TDNT* 6 [1968]: 25) points out that although the technical terms for "test" do not occur in the Masoretic text of Job, they do appear in the LXX (*peiraterion:* 7:1; 10:17; 19:12; *peirates:* 16:9; 25:3).

12. TESTING: See, e.g., *Testament of Job* 4:4-9 (and passim in chaps. 1–27), where the concept of testing is clearly present, even if the technical terms are not; see also *Jubilees* 17:16; 1 Cor. 7:5. For secondary treatments, see Seesemann, "peira ktl.," esp. 25–27; Noack, *Satanás und Soteria,* 20–22, 62–65; K. G. Kuhn, "New Light on Temptation, Sin, and Flesh in the New Testament," in *The Scrolls and the New Testament,* ed. Krister Stendahl (New

York: Harper & Bros., 1957), 94–113. ACCUSING: See e.g., *Jubilees* 1:20;
48:15; *Martyrdom of Isaiah* 3:6 (through the person of a false prophet); 5:2–
3. See also Noack, *Satanás und Sotería*, 22, 36, 114. LEADING ASTRAY: Most
often Satan "leads astray" by promoting idolatry (e.g. *Jubilees* 11:4-5; 22:16-
17; *Martyrdom of Isaiah* 1:9; 2:4; *Testament of Job* 2:2—3:5; CD 12:2b-3); but
this is not always the case. For other types of "leading astray," see, e.g., *Life
of Adam and Eve (Vita)* 9:1—11:3; *Testament of Job* 23:11; 26:6.

13. See, e.g., *Apocalypse of Abraham* 13:9-13; 23:11-13 (Abraham asks
God, "Why then did you adjudge him [Azazel] such dominion that through
his works he could ruin humankind on earth?" [trans. R. Rubinkiewicz,
OTP, 1:701]); *Testament of Job* 8:1-3; 16:2, 4; 20:1-3; *Jubilees* 10:7-9 (Mastema
asks God for permission to retain one-tenth of the spirits, by which Mastema
exercises the authority of his will and corrupts and leads astray the evil
humans). Luke 22:31 is also relevant: Satan "demanded to have" the apostles.
Von Rad and Foerster ("diaballō, diabolos," 73—75) point out that the writings
of the post–Old Testament period exhibit a shift from the nondualistic view
represented in, e.g., Job, in which Satan was integrated into the heavenly
court, toward "the complete absolutizing of Satan over against God." For a
discussion of the theological tension produced during this shift in, e.g., *Jubilees*, see: Noack, *Satanás und Sotería*, 41-42, 47; or in the Dead Sea Scrolls:
Kuhn, "New Light," 99; also James H. Charlesworth, "A Critical Comparison
of the Dualism in 1QS 3:13—4:26 and the 'Dualism' in the Gospel of John,"
NTS 15 (1968–69): 389–418 (repr. in *John and Qumran* [London: Geoffrey
Chapman, 1972], 76–106).

14. The notion that Satan is lord of the demons probably arose in the
intertestamental era (Noack, *Satanás und Sotería*, 14, 23, 33, 44, 72). See
Luke 11:14-23 (discussed below); 13:10-17; *Jubilees* 10:7-13. Regarding
belief in demons at the time of Jesus, see W. Kirchschläger, *Jesu exorzistisches
Wirken aus der Sicht des Lukas: Ein Beitrag zur lukanischen Redaktion*, ÖBS 3
(Klosterneuburg: Österreichisches Katholisches Bibelwerk, 1981), 45–54;
also Everett Ferguson, *Demonology of the Early Christian World*, Symposium
Series 12 (New York: Edwin Mellen Press, 1984).

15. Luke uses the term *daimonion* more often than Matthew or Mark
(Matthew, 10x; Mark, 11x; Luke, 21x). Luke's similar terminology for demon
possession and illness suggests that he viewed them as closely related; see,
e.g., 4:40-41 (cf. Mark 1:32-34); 7:21; 9:1; and Acts 10:38. Also notable
are Jesus' healings of Peter's mother-in-law, who had been "gripped" by a
fever which must be "rebuked" (4:38-39; see Kirchschläger's analysis in *Jesu
exorzistisches Wirken*, 55–69), and the woman with a bent back, said to result
from Satan's control (13:16). In general on Luke's "demonization" of his
narrative, see M. H. Miller, *The Character of Miracles in Luke-Acts* (Ann Arbor,
Mich.: University Microfilms, 1971), 158–60; and U. Busse, *Die Wunder des
Propheten Jesus: Die Rezeption, Komposition und Interpretation der Wundertra-
dition im Evangelium des Lukas*, Forschung zur Bibel 24 (Stuttgart: Katholisches
Bibelwerk, 1977), 23–24, 79–80, 90, 114, 181–82, 185, 219, 285, 288, 297,
302. Hull (*Hellenistic Magic*, 96–105) rightly observes that Luke thought of

demons in a very "literal" manner and regarded them with great "serious-ness," but Hull's development of this thesis is problematic. Especially trou-blesome is his habit of reading the more elaborate (and often Christian-influenced) demonology of the *Testament of Solomon* into Luke's account.

16. See, e.g., John 12:31; Rom. 16:20; Rev. 20:1-3; *Jubilees* 23:29; 50:5; *1 Enoch* 69:27-29; *Testament of Moses* 10:1; 1QM 1:1; 4:1b-2a; 11:8; 13:11-16; 15:2-3,15–18; 17:5b-6; 18:1, 3, 11. In the *Testaments of the Twelve Pa-triarchs*, see *TSimeon* 6:6; *TLevi* 18:12-13; *TZebulon* 9:8-9; *TDan* 5:11; *TAsher* 7:3. See also the discussions in Noack, *Satanás und Sotería*, 72; Von Rad and Foerster, "diaballō, diabolos," 79–81; Barrett, *The Holy Spirit and the Gospel Tradition*, 57–59.

17. In *Testament of Job* 2:2—3:3 Job (alias Jobab) asks God who it is that is venerated in a nearby idol's temple, and is informed that "this one whose whole-burnt offerings they bring and whose drink offerings they pour is not God. Rather, it is the power *(hē dynamis)* of the devil, by whom human nature is deceived" (3:3; trans. R. P. Spittler, *OTP*, 1:840). Satan's vested interest in idolatry accounts for his opposition to mission efforts (see *Testament of Job* 4:3-5; Luke 8:12; 10:19; Acts 13:6-12; 26:18; and below, chap. 4; see also Noack, *Satanás und Sotería*, 82, 109–11).

18. In Jewish and Christian thought of this era it was frequently assumed that false prophets, who led the people astray into idolatry, acted as agents of Satan and practiced magic. See the discussion above, pp. 13–17.

19. The notion that God's people has gone astray was nothing extraordinary in the theological cauldron of Judaism around the turn of the millennium, and ultimately goes back to the Old Testament (see Nils A. Dahl, *Jesus in the Memory of the Early Church* [Minneapolis: Augsburg Publishing House, 1976], 77 n. 35; see also Tiede, *Prophecy and History*, 42, 58–59, 110). The idea is attested, for example, in the Dead Sea Scrolls, the *Martyrdom of Isaiah*, and the Gospel of John.

20. See *Life of Adam and Eve (Vita)* 12:1—16:3, and n. 12a in M. D. Johnson's translation of the same (*OTP* 2:262); see also n. 54 below. It is possible that Isaiah 14 has influenced Luke's recounting of Herod's demise (Acts 12:20-23): Herod was "eaten by worms" *(skōlēkobrōtos;* on this word, attested in the papyri, see Lake and Cadbury, *Beginnings*, vol. 4: *English Translation and Commentary* [1933], 140 n. 23) and died, whereas the King of Babylon lay in putrefaction and had worms *(skōlēx)* as his covering. Cf. 2 Macc. 9:5–12; Josephus *Antiquities* 17.169; 19.343–52; and *War* 1.656. The passages are discussed in my article, "Exodus from Bondage: Luke 9:31 and Acts 12:1-24," *CBQ* (forthcoming).

21. A similar oracle, directed against the prince of Tyre, occurs in Ezek. 28:1-21. The Ezekiel passage (like Isaiah 14) draws on ancient Near Eastern combat myth traditions; see Forsyth, *The Old Enemy*, 139–42.

22. Conzelmann, *Theology*, 16, 80–81, 132, 156–57, 200.

23. Ibid., 28.

24. R. P. Spittler (*OTP* 1:833) observes that the document was "almost certainly written in Greek, probably during the first century B.C. or A.D.," and that "although Christian editing is possible, the work is essentially Jewish in character."

25. Trans. R. P. Spittler, *OTP* 1:851. Cf. Justin *Dialogue with Trypho* 125.41: "After Jesus had become human, the devil (that power [*dynamis*] which is also called Serpent and Satan) came to him to tempt him, and he struggled to overcome him by demanding that he worship him. But he [i.e., Jesus] destroyed *(katalysai)* and overcame *(katabalein)* him, convicting him of his wickedness when, contrary to the scripture, he asked to be worshiped as God. . . . Then the devil, defeated and convicted *(hēttēmenos kai elēlegmenos)*, departed." Justin ties this interpretation to the tradition about Jacob's wrestling with the angel, regarding which see Jonathan Z. Smith's introduction and translation of the *Prayer of Joseph, OTP* 2:700–14.

26. The words in single quotes may allude to Jas. 4:7 (itself relevant to this discussion). Cf. *Hermas Mandate* 12.5.4: when the devil comes to those who are full of faith he tries to test *(ekpeirazein)* them, but they withstand him and he departs because there is no room by which to enter. But when the devil comes to those who are half empty he can enter them and do what he wills, and "they become his servants" *(ginontai autō hypodouloi)*. In *Hermas Vision* 4.1.5–9, Hermas sees a terrible beast, but when he takes courage and confronts it, the beast stretches itself out harmlessly on the ground until Hermas has passed.

27. R. Leivestad (*Christ the Conqueror: Ideas of Conflict and Victory in the New Testament* [New York: Macmillan, 1954], 53 n. "*"*) is familiar with Justin's interpretation of the temptation narrative as a battle won by Christ (*Dialogue with Trypho* 125.41; see n. 25 above), but Leivestad concludes that "this aspect is not present in the gospels' story of the event." It is true that Luke does not explicitly refer to the testing as a battle or use the word "conquer" in 4:13, but cf. 11:22, where Luke changes Mark's *dēsai* to *nikēsai*. The reasonable assumption that Luke did know of such traditions explains simply and plausibly his editorial attention to the devil's withdrawal.

28. Note that when Paul tells Bar Jesus that he will not see the sun "for a while," the phrase *achri kairou* points forward, but only in a general way, since Bar Jesus is never mentioned again.

29. Cf. Otto Betz, "The Kerygma of Luke," *Interp* 22 (1968): 136. Robinson (*Problem of History*, 30, 35) contends that in Mark's Gospel the exorcisms are integrally related to the struggle with Satan at the temptation. Miller (*Character of the Miracles*, 155–66) argues persuasively that Luke understood the prophecy about "release to the captives" (Isa. 61:1 and 58:6) to be fulfilled in the exorcisms; cf. Dahl, *Jesus in the Memory of the Early Church*, 90. Busse (*Wunder*, 184) cites fourteen scholars who hold that Acts 10:38 alludes back to Luke 4:18 (itself a quotation of Isa. 61:1); the point is significant since Acts 10:38 explicitly describes Jesus' lifework as one of "healing those oppressed by Satan."

30. Conzelmann (*Theology*, 188 n. 4) decides *a priori* that 4:13 implies a Satan-free ministry for Jesus, and concludes solely on this basis that such passages as Luke 11:17-23 "do not mean that there is a constant conflict with Satan during Jesus' ministry; they have a symbolic meaning and are meant primarily to be a comfort to the church of Luke's time, which knows that since the Passion of Jesus it is again subject to the attacks of Satan."

Brown (*Apostasy and Perseverance,* 6–19) argues that 4:13 signals an end to temptation or testing *(peirasmos)* during not only Jesus' earthly ministry but also the time of the church (though Brown says that Satan does pursue other forms of attack). Brown's interpretation of Luke 8:13 and refusal to see any hint of Satanic complicity in the people's testing of Jesus (Luke 22:28) are problematic, as is his contention (82–86) that Judas Iscariot was not tested: it is true that Luke says Satan "entered" rather than "tested" Judas (22:3), but cf. *Hermas Mandate* 12.5.4. Satan's "sifting" *(siniasai;* mentioned in 22:31) may well encompass testing; the verb is too obscure simply to rule out the possibility as does Brown (p. 85). Finally, Jesus' two exhortations to the apostles (22:40,46; only once in Mark) that they "pray not to enter into testing" show that Luke wants to portray the possibility of such "entry" as real; otherwise Jesus' instructions are superfluous.

31. Josephus *Antiquities* 8.45–49 (cf. *Jewish War* 7.185). See Duling, "The Eleazar Miracle," 1–25; also above, p. 13. See also 1QapGen 20 (discussed in Joseph A. Fitzmyer, "Some Observations on the *Genesis Apocryphon,*" *CBQ* 22 [1960]: 283–84); W. Kirchschläger, "Exorzismus in Qumran?" *Kairos* 18 (1976): 135–53; Howard Clark Kee, "The Terminology of Mark's Exorcism Stories," *NTS* 14 (1967–68): 232–46.

32. Kraeling writes, "Between demons as the servants of magicians, and spirits of the dead used in a similar way there is no basic distinction. Both are beings of the spiritual order, not limited by time or space, and endowed with supernatural powers" ("Was Jesus Accused of Necromancy?" 154; cf. Hopfner, "*Mageia,*" cols. 301–2, 330–32). In the magical papyri, the clearest exorcistic formulas (*PGM* IV.1227–64, 3007–86) have been influenced to some extent by Christian practice (both invoke Jesus); in *GMPT* see also the translation of *PGM* LXXXV.1–6 and the accompanying note (p. 301). The magical papyri also include spells of a more general nature, enabling the magician to obtain an assistant daimon (*daimōn paredros;* see chap. 1 n. 30). Such "assistants" could perform numerous tasks, including, presumably, exorcism (see, e.g., *PGM* I:115). On the paucity of demonstrably early (first century C.E. or prior) exorcistic texts, see Kirchschläger, *Jesu exorzistisches Wirken,* 51.

33. In 11:15 Luke does, however, omit Mark's *hoti Beelzeboul echei* (Mark 3:22; Matthew likewise omits the clause). Kraeling ("Was Jesus Accused of Necromancy?" 153–54) argues that in the Synoptics, only in Luke 8:27 (regarding the Gerasene demoniac) is the expression *echein daimonion* applied to someone possessed *by* a demon (although in John 7:20; 8:48,49,52; and 10:20 the expression does indicate that Jesus is thought to be possessed); elsewhere in the Synoptics (incl. Mark 3:22) the phrase means "to have a demon under one's control and to make it do one's bidding."

34. It is commonly argued that Luke's version must be original, since Luke would hardly have changed "Spirit of God" (cf. Matt. 12:28) to the anthropomorphic "finger of God" (e.g., Vincent Taylor, *The Teachings of Jesus* [London: SCM Press, 1949], 82; Norman Perrin, *Rediscovering the Teachings of Jesus* [New York: Harper & Row, 1976], 63; Fitzmyer, *Luke* 2:918; I. Howard Marshall, *The Gospel of Luke: A Commentary on the Greek Text* [Grand Rapids: Wm. B. Eerdmans, 1978], 476); but cf. the opposing arguments by C. S.

Rodd, "Spirit or Finger," *ExpTim* 72 (1960–61): 157–58; also Kirchschläger, *Jesu exorzistisches Wirken,* 234. Another factor supporting the theory that Luke changed the verse to its present form is his penchant for alluding to the LXX; an allusion to the Egyptian magicians' acknowledgment of God's wholly "other" power would be quite apt in this Lukan context of anti-magic apologetic. Compare Josephus's rewriting of the contest between Moses and the magicians of Pharaoh (*Antiquities* 2.284–87).

35. For the association of healing and preaching, see Luke 6:18; 9:2,11; 10:9; Acts 4:29-30; 8:6-7; also G. W. H. Lampe, "The Holy Spirit in the Writings of St. Luke," in *Studies in the Gospels: Essays in Memory of R. H. Lightfoot,* ed. D. E. Nineham (Oxford: Basil Blackwell, 1967), 184–85.

36. In v. 21, *hotan* + the pres. subj. *phylassē* denotes a general condition: "whenever" or "as long as" the well-armed strong one guards his palace, his possessions are in peace. In v. 22, *epan* + the aor. subj. *nikēsē* should indicate that the action of the dependent temporal clause was completed prior to that of the main clause: "But when the one who is stronger than he has come upon him and conquered him, he takes his armor. . . ." According to this reading the "conquering" could feasibly be taken to refer to a single past event, perhaps to Jesus' victory over Satan at the testing in the wilderness (cf. W. Grundmann, "ischyō," *TDNT* 3 [1965]: 399–40; on the grammatical structure, cf. Demosthenes 9.69, cited in H. W. Smyth, *Greek Grammar* [Cambridge: Harvard Univ. Press, 1956], §2410). But Luke's omission of the phrase *ean mē prōton* (Mark 3:27) may indicate a reluctance to portray the "conquering" as a decisively completed event. Satan's seizure of authority at the passion seems to indicate that Jesus' "conquering," accomplished (or attested) by the exorcisms, has still been only provisional: the decisive victory is yet to come.

37. M. Miyoshi (*Der Anfang des Reiseberichts: Lk 9,51—10,24,* AnBib 60 [Rome: Biblical Institute Press, 1974], 23) concludes that Luke 13:32b ought to be understood in light of early Christian beliefs about the exaltation of Christ (e.g., Acts 2:34, quoting Ps. 110:1 [LXX 109:1]; Heb. 1:13; Phil. 2:10; 1 Pet. 3:22), according to which the exalted Christ subjects all powers and authorities to himself. Miyoshi writes, "Through his exaltation he completes the driving out of demons that he began on earth" (ibid.). The argument to be developed below is consistent with Miyoshi's interpretation of this verse.

38. It is not evident whether *ek tou ouranou* should be taken with the preceding noun *astrapē* ("lightning-from-the-sky") or the following participle *pesonta* ("falling-from-the-sky"). Comparison with apocalyptic parallels (esp. Rev. 12:9) supports the latter option. Cf. Miyoshi, *Anfang,* 99.

39. Cf. Matt. 11:25: *en ekeinō tō kairō.* Luke also uses the expression *(en) autē tē hōra* at 2:38; 12:12; 13:31; 20:19; 24:33; see Fitzmyer, *Luke* 1:117.

40. There is a textual variant with regard to the number of missionaries (seventy or seventy-two), both here and at the initial commissioning in 10:1. Manuscript support is about evenly divided; both readings are attested at a very early date. The problem will receive further discussion below.

41. See n. 40. After a careful review of the evidence, Bruce M. Metzger concludes that the textual problem cannot be resolved ("Seventy or Seventy-two Disciples?" *NTS* 5 [1958–59]: 299–306). Metzger notes that although

P[45] is frequently cited as support for the reading "seventy-two" at Luke 10:17 (so still in Nestle-Aland, *Novum Testamentum Graece*, 26th ed.), this is based on an inaccurate reading of the manuscript: the correct reading is actually "seventy." Metzger was unable to take account of P[75], which supports the reading "seventy-two."

42. The MT of the Genesis passage has seventy nations, whereas the LXX has seventy-two. Though Luke would have used the LXX, a later scribe may have tried to "correct" the reading.

43. The variant between seventy and seventy-two depends on whether one takes Eldad and Modad into account (Num. 11:26). A scribe may have altered the original Lukan number to make it more consistent with that scribe's own reading of the Numbers passage.

44. Robert C. Tannehill (*The Narrative Unity of Luke Acts: A Literary Interpretation*, vol. 1: *The Gospel According to Luke* [Philadelphia: Fortress Press, 1986], 233) notes that an allusion to the Numbers passage "makes good sense in Luke's context," but still argues in favor of an allusion to Genesis 10, based on his judgment that "seventy-two" is the more difficult reading (and therefore the more likely to be authentic). But as Tannehill recognizes, Luke or a later scribe could have written "seventy-two" *even if* alluding to the Numbers passage. Miyoshi (*Anfang*, 110–11; cf. 60–61) suggests that Luke's recognition in 9:49-50 of an allusion to the Eldad and Modad incident may be what prompted him to describe the mission of the seventy(-two).

45. In favor of Lukan (rather than Matthean) alterations, see Fitzmyer, *Luke* 2:867; Marshall, *Luke*, 436. Concerning Luke's purposes in making these alterations, cf. Tannehill, *Narrative Unity*, 237; Miyoshi, *Anfang*, 137–41.

46. See also Luke 24:27, 44–45; Acts 8:34-35; 9:20, 22; 10:42-43; 13:27 *(touton agnoēsantes)*, 33–39 ; cf. Acts 9:5, 20; 22:8; 26:15; 28:23, 31. On this subject see Jacob Jervell, *The Unknown Paul: Essays on Luke-Acts and Early Christian History* (Minneapolis: Augsburg Publishing House, 1984), 96–121, esp. 108–9; and ibid., 122–37, esp. 129–30, 135. See also Paul Schubert, "The structure and significance of Luke 24," in *Neutestamentliche Studien für Rudolf Bultmann*, ed. W. Eltester, BZNW 21 (Berlin: Alfred Töpelmann, 1954), 165–86, esp. 173–77; and G. Delling, " '. . . als er uns die Schrift aufschloss'. Zur Lukanischen Terminologie der Auslegung des Alten Testaments," in *Das Wort und die Wörter: Festschrift Gerhard Friedrich zum 65. Geburtstag*, ed. H. Balz and S. Schulz (Stuttgart: Kohlhammer, 1973), 75–84.

47. Peter recognizes Jesus as the Christ (9:18-22), but does not understand the necessity for Jesus "to suffer and die and on the third day be raised," as taught in the scriptures.

48. R. J. Dillon, "Easter Revelation and Mission Program in Luke 24:46-48," in *Sin, Salvation, and the Spirit*, ed. D. Durken (Collegeville, Minn.: Liturgical Press, 1979), 244–45. On pp. 262–63 n. 33, Dillon cites secondary literature on Luke's treatment of the messianic secret.

49. Marshall, *Luke*, 428–29; Fitzmyer, *Luke* 2:860; Eduard Schweizer, *The Good News According to Luke* (Atlanta: John Knox Press, 1984), 180; A. Plummer, *A Critical and Exegetical Commentary on the Gospel According to S. Luke*,

ICC, 5th ed. (Edinburgh: T. & T. Clark, n.d.), 278; H. Flender, *St. Luke: Theologian of Redemptive History* (Philadelphia: Fortress Press, 1967), 103: "The imperfect *etheōroun* leaves no doubt that the victory has already been won."

50. Such reluctance is exhibited by, e.g., U. B. Müller, "Vision und Botschaft: Erwägungen zur prophetischen Struktur der Verkündigung Jesu," *ZTK* 74 (1977): 419. Barrett (*The Holy Spirit and the Gospel Tradition*, 64) thinks Luke portrays Jesus as recounting a vision, but one regarded as fulfilled during his (foregoing) messianic work; cf. Creed, *St. Luke*, 147. E. E. Ellis *The Gospel of Luke* (London: Oliphants, Marshall, Morgan, Scott, 1974), 157, suggests that v. 18 may be an (apocalyptic) vision, but doesn't pursue the matter. J. M. Nützel (*Jesus als Offenbarer Gottes nach den lukanischen Scriften*, Forschung zur Bibel 39 [Echter Verlag, 1980], 145–46, 149–51) thinks that Luke *had* to interpret 10:18 as a vision of something not yet fully accomplished, because otherwise Satan's activity at the passion makes no sense; Nützel argues further that the vision is not to be fulfilled by a single event, but rather by the ongoing process of Satan's demise that is being effected by Jesus and then by the Church. G. B. Caird's position, compatible with my own, appears to be a minority one: "The vision is prophetic: the exorcisms of Jesus and his disciples were not themselves the decisive victory over Satan, but only tokens of a victory yet to be won through the cross" (*Saint Luke* [Harmondsworth, Eng.: Penguin Books, 1963], 143).

51. Verbs in the imperfect are also used to introduce visions in Acts 11:6 (*katenooun kai eidon*) and Josephus *Antiquities* 2.83, where the king tells Joseph, "I saw seven ears of corn. . ." (*stachuas hepta heōrōn). Theōreō* in the present tense occurs in Stephen's vision (7:56). Marshall (*Luke*, 428) and others have noted that the aorist of *theōreō* was not in common use.

52. Note that some MSS (א, A, D, L, W, Γ, Θ, 1, 28, 1241, et al.; *Didache*) have the future indicative *(adikēsei)* here. Along these same lines, note the strongly attested textual variant with regard to the verb "I have given" *(dedōka)* in v. 19: in its place, several important witnesses have the present tense *(didōmi)*. MSS reading *didōmi* include P⁴⁵, A, C³, D, Θ, Ψ, f¹³, 𝔐, c, sy, Ir^lat; cf. Justin *Dialogue with Trypho* 76.68.

53. Cf. Miller, *Character of the Miracles*, 207 n. 1. In general on Luke's use of prophecy as a narrative ordering device, see C. H. Talbert, "Promise and Fulfillment in Lucan Theology," in *Luke-Acts: New Perspectives from the Society of Biblical Literature Seminar*, ed. Charles H. Talbert (New York: Crossroad, 1984) 91–103 (includes a discussion of earlier literature).

54. Cf. Boismard, "Rapprochements," 56; Marshall, *Luke*, 428–29; and Nützel, *Offenbarer Gottes*, 147. Fitzmyer (*Luke* 2.862) denies the allusion since "there is no mention of Satan in that text—a later tradition prone to identify Satan and Lucifer notwithstanding." Such caution is unwarranted. The Isaiah passage itself incorporated motifs from ancient Near Eastern myths about rivalry between heavenly figures (see Yarbro Collins, *Combat Myth*, esp. 79–85; also Forsyth, *The Old Enemy*, 134–39). It is likely that the *interpretation* of the laments from Isaiah and Ezekiel as refererences to the devil was conventional in some circles by the time Luke wrote his Gospel. Luke 10:18 (Jesus saw Satan *ek tou ouranou pesonta*), which looks like an allusion to Isa.

14:12 *(exepesen ek tou ouranou)*, is itself sound evidence for this contention; the fall of the stars to earth in Rev. 8:10 and 9:1, and the fall in chap. 12 of the dragon/devil (who, like the figure in the laments of the Hebrew scriptures, commits blasphemy by accepting worship due God alone [Rev. 13:4]) also seem to presuppose interpretation of the biblical material or related mythical traditions as references to Satan (cf. Yarbro Collins, *Combat Myth*, esp. 79–85). The influence of Isaiah 14 is clearly discernible in the *Life of Adam and Eve (Vita)* 12–16, the composition of which M. D. Johnson dates to sometime between 100 B.C.E. and 200 C.E., "more probably toward the end of the first Christian century" *(OTP* 2:252; cf. 262 n. 12a). On the links between fallen stars and rebel angels in the Enoch material, see Forsyth, *The Old Enemy*, 160–81.

55. On this interpretation of the participle *pesonta*, see Aune, *Prophecy in Early Christianity*, 391 n. 81.

56. The reference to Jesus' being "lifted up" *(hypsōthēnai)* refers most immediately to his death on the cross, but Raymond E. Brown (*The Gospel According to John*, 2 vols., AB 29, 29A [Garden City, N.Y.: Doubleday & Co., 1966], 1·146) argues (in part by means of an analogy with Acts 2:33; 5:31) that in the Gospel of John, " 'being lifted up' refers to one continuous action of ascent: Jesus begins his return to his Father as he approaches death (xiii 1) and completes it only with his ascension (xx 17)."

57. Müller, "Vision und Botschaft," 416–22. On the mythological background to this tradition of a heavenly battle, see Yarbro Collins, *The Combat Myth*, 79–83 and passim; Forsyth, *The Old Enemy*.

58. Ibid., 422. Fitzmyer similarly excludes *a priori* the possibility that 10:18 is a proleptic vision, on the grounds that "the Lucan Jesus is not an apocalypticist of the sort responsible for Rev. 12:9-12" (*Luke* 2:862; cf. 2:860–61).

59. Müller, "Vision und Botschaft," 422. The statement is actually Müller's quotation of Eta Linnemann, "Zeitansage und Zeitvorstellung in der Verkündigung Jesu," in *Jesus Christus in Historie und Theologie: neutestamentliche Festschrift für Hans Conzelmann zum 60. Geburtstag*, ed. Georg Strecker (Tübingen: Mohr, 1975), 249.

60. 11QMelch 13. Reconstructed and translated by Fitzmyer, "Further Light on Melchizedek from Qumran Cave 11," *JBL* 86 (1967): 28. Cf. *Ezekiel the Tragedian* 68–82: in a vision Moses is bade to mount the heavenly throne, at which moment "a multitude of stars fell down" (trans. R. G. Robertson, in *OTP* 2:811–12); Satan does not appear to be in view. The passage is discussed in Meeks, *The Prophet-King*, 147–49. Cf. also *1 Enoch* 69:27–29, a most interesting passage wherein the children of the people rejoice greatly and extol the Lord because there has been revealed to them the name of the Son of Man, who will never pass away or perish from the face of the earth (cf. Luke 10:17,21–22). A proclamation is then made that all evil and all those who have led the world astray will be undone, "for that Son of Man has appeared and has seated himself upon the throne of his glory; and all evil shall disappear from before his face" (trans. E. Isaac, *OTP* 1:49). Here the similitude ends; next Enoch is transported into heaven to become the Son of Man.

61. See Jerome H. Neyrey, *The Passion According to Luke: A Redaction Study of Luke's Soteriology* (New York: Paulist Press, 1985), 12–14, 74–75. On the relationships among Jesus' death, resurrection, and ascension, see Miyoshi, *Anfang*, 19–22.

62. See Luke 9:1-3; 10:3-4; for the "protection" that came with "authority" see 10:19. In having no personal possessions, believers demonstrate that the authority they do have comes from God; cf. Acts 3:3-6, where Peter explicitly contrasts his lack of possessions with his ability to heal; and 8:19-21, where Simon is rebuked for trying to purchase with money the authority *(exousia)* to confer the Holy Spirit.

63. Herein lies the importance of Jesus' prayer for Peter that his faith not fail (22:32). Conzelmann (*Theology*, 16, 80–81) also interpreted the shift in policy with regard to possessions at 22:35-36 as signaling the loss of divine protection, postulating a permanent such loss, so that the Church was from then on the *ecclesia pressa*. The argument to be made here is that the loss was to last only for the duration of the "hour" of the "authority of darkness." Luke T. Johnson (*The Literary Function of Possessions in Luke-Acts*, SBLDS 39 [Missoula, Mont.: Scholars Press, 1977], 163–64) contends that Luke 22:35-36 must be understood in light of the literary pattern of acceptance and rejection by the people. During Jesus' lifetime, the missionaries' lack of possessions "was a sign of the acceptance of their message and themselves"; the words of 22:36 indicate a reversal of the earlier situation. The error in this line of reasoning is the supposition that 22:35-36 pertains to the future acceptance and rejection of missionaries. Rather, the literary context shows that the issue at hand is the *present* and *intensifying* activity and authority of Satan (note the topics in the bracketing passages, 22:31-34, 39–46, 53).

64. Note the military imagery in Luke's allegory of the strong one (11:21-22), where Satan is portrayed as "well-armed" and trusting in "his full armor"; and in *Testament of Benjamin* 7:1, where it is said that Beliar "offers a sword to those who obey him" (cf. also *Acts of Peter* 22). Contrast the emphasis on peace in Luke 10:5-6; cf. also 1QS 2:9, where a curse against the children of Belial includes the malediction, "May there be no peace for you in the mouth of those who hold fast to the fathers"; and Rom. 16:20, where Paul announces that the "God of peace" will "crush Satan under your feet."

65. Minear has argued persuasively that Jesus' words in Luke 22:37 must find immediate fulfillment, but Minear carries his argument a step too far by postulating that the "lawless" with whom Jesus must be "reckoned" are none other than the apostles, who violate Jesus' teachings by having with them a sword ("A Note on Luke xxii 36," *NovT* 7 [1964–65]: 128–34; the argument is adopted by Neyrey, *Passion According to Luke*, 42; and Tannehill, *Narrative Unity*, 267). But this solution is dubious; it reads Jesus' preceding statement as an effort to trip up the apostles. Jesus' symbolic statement is misunderstood, but it is not a deliberate trick.

66. See Neyrey's excellent discussion of Jesus as the "saved savior" in *Passion According to Luke*, 129–55 (Neyrey does not, however, discuss Jesus' salvation as specifically a victory over Satan). In ibid., 149–51, Neyrey discusses Luke's use of Psalm 16 as the cornerstone of the christological proof

from prophecy in Acts 2 and 13, and notes that the content of this important psalm is formally the same as that of Ps. 31:6, which Jesus prays at his death (Luke 23:46). To be considered along with the psalms discussed by Neyrey are at least two other LXX passages wherein Luke found the promise that God would rescue the chosen one in his moment of distress: 2 Sam. 22:6-7 (cited in Acts 2:24), and Ps. 90:15-16 (MT 91:15-16; portions of this psalm appear in Luke 4:10-11 and 10:19, both of which deal with victory over Satan). These LXX passages further stress that the rescue will occur when the afflicted one *calls upon the Lord*—which is what Jesus does on the cross in Luke's account (Luke 23:46).

67. Though a quotation, Acts 2:27 suggests that Luke thought Jesus had descended to Hades; cf. Acts 2:31, and note that 2:24 alludes to Ps. 17:5-6 (LXX) or 114:3 (LXX), both of which describe entrapment in Hades. The idea antedated Luke: see Rom. 10:7. First Pet. 3:19 states that Christ "preached to the spirits in prison"; in *Odes of Solomon* 42:16 the spirits in Sheol beg Christ to "bring us out from the chains of darkness" (trans. James H. Charlesworth, *OTP* 2:771). R. Kratz, *Auferweckung als Befreiung: Eine Studie zur Passions- und Auferstehungstheologie des Matthäus*, Stuttgarter Bibelstudien 65 (Stuttgart: KBW Verlag, 1973) argues that Matthew portrays Jesus' resurrection as rescue or release from the prison of the grave (Matt. 27:62—28:15) in order to demonstrate that the resurrection was the logical and definitive culmination of Jesus' earthly ministry, the essence of which had been the conquering of the reign of death and Satan.

68. Otto Betz (*Der Paraklet: Fürsprecher im häretischen Spätjudentum, im Johannes-Evangelium und in neu gefundenen gnostischen Schriften*, AGSU 2 [Leiden: Brill, 1963], 36–72) argues that the notion of the paraclete, who intercedes before God on others' behalf (e.g., Luke 12:8-9), is rooted in the idea of heavenly conflict between Satan and various protagonists (e.g., Moses, Michael).

69. Based on a comparison with Mark 16:17-18, Rudolph Bultmann (*History of the Synoptic Tradition*, rev. ed. [New York: Harper & Row, 1976], 158) suggested that Luke 10:19 may have originated as a promise made by the exalted Lord to the missionary or to the church at large. The point being made here is related but not identical: Luke himself understood the saying as a promise to take effect at the time when the Lord is exalted. The comparison with Mark 16:17-18 is still relevant: as Miyoshi points out (*Anfang*, 115), the Markan passage and Luke 10:19 may go back to a common tradition in which the exalted Lord speaks to those who will carry out the world mission. Luke would then have incorporated the tradition into Jesus' earthly ministry to foreshadow and to provide a warrant for the Spirit- and authority-endowed world mission portrayed in Acts.

70. Fitzmyer argues (against "many commentators") that the supposed allusion is "farfetched," and does not even concede that "serpents and scorpions" in Luke 10:19 symbolize demonic powers (*Luke* 2:863). But serpents and scorpions were interpreted as Satanic or demonic already in contemporaneous writings (Rev. 9:3,10; 12:7-9 and 20:2; in the *Testaments of the Twelve Patriarchs*, see *Testament of Simon* 6:6; *Testament of Levi* 18:12; *Testament*

of Zebulon 9:8; cf. also *Testament of Job* 43:8). Further, the literary context of Luke 10:19 suggests that the "serpents and scorpions" here ought to be interpreted as demonic (cf. P. Grelot, "Etude critique de Luc 10,19," *Recherches de science religieuse* 69 [1981]: 95–100; also Baumbach, *Verständnis des Bösen,* 180–81). Luke's inexact citation can be explained variously: he may be quoting from memory, using a traditional form of Jesus' saying, or deliberately substituting the names of creatures that he supposed his readers would acknowledge as demonic (cf. Luke 11:11-13; contrast Matt. 7:9-11).

71. In Rabbinic literature, Psalm 91 was thought to guarantee such immunity (see Duling, "Solomon, Exorcism, and the Son of David," *HTR* 68 [1975]: 239). The psalm may already have been so interpreted at Qumran: a small scroll found there contains the remnants of several apocryphal psalms together with Psalm 91 (11QPsAp[a], discussed by J. P. M. van der Ploeg in "Le Psaume XCI dans une recension de Qumrân," *RB* 72 [1965]: 210–17; and "Un petit rouleau de psaumes apocryphes (11QPsAp[a])," in *Tradition und Glaube: Das frühe Christentum in seiner Umwelt,* ed. G. Jeremias et al. [Göttingen: Vandenhoeck & Ruprecht, 1971], 128–39). Though the apocryphal psalms are largely illegible, the remaining traces allude to Solomon (regarded as a great exorcist), demons, and healing. Further, the prose insert in the Dead Sea Psalms Scroll (discussed by James A. Sanders, *The Dead Sea Psalms Scroll* [Ithaca, N.Y.: Cornell Univ. Press, 1967], 134-37) tells that David wrote four songs for "the stricken" *(hpgw'ym)* which Sanders suggests may refer to persons troubled by demons; van der Ploeg ("Un petit rouleau," 129) notes that the root *pg'* also occurs in 11QPsAp[a] col. 4, line 2.

72. Note that also in the *Life of Adam and Eve,* Satan continues to have authority over humans after his fall (reported in *Vita* 13:1—16:3). See further Yarbro Collins, *The Combat Myth,* 82–83.

73. See Robinson, *Problem of History,* 81–90.

74. In "Exodus from Bondage" (see n. 20), I argue that Luke has used the schema as a template for the story of Peter's escape from prison and Herod's fall in Acts 12.

CHAPTER 3

SIMON MAGUS (ACTS 8:4-25)

1. The most important patristic texts are: Justin *1 Apology* 1.26.1-3; 1.56.2; *Dialogue with Trypho* 120; Irenaeus *Against Heresies* 1.23; Hippolytus *Refutation* 6.9-18 (contains excerpts from [or perhaps a commentary upon] the so-called *Megale Apophasis,* a gnostic/philosophical document attributed to Simon but probably composed much later); 6.19-20; and Epiphanius *Panarion* 21.1-4 (contains excerpts from the lost *Syntagma* of Hippolytus). In addition, Simon is the major antagonist in the apocryphal *Acts of Peter* and in the *Clementine Recognitions* and *Homilies.* The texts are discussed thoroughly (albeit from a polemical perspective) by K. Beyschlag, *Simon Magus und die christliche Gnosis,* WUNT 16 (Tübingen: Mohr [Siebeck], 1974), 7–78. For additional patristic references, see R. P. Casey, "Simon Magus," *Beginnings* 5:151 n. 1.

2. This is the point made in Beyschlag's devastating indictment of German research on the origins of gnosticism, in *Simon Magus,* 79–98; cf. the history

of research in Gerd Lüdemann, *Untersuchungen zur simonianischen Gnosis* (Göttingen: Vandenhoeck & Ruprecht, 1975), 9–29. For discussions of the more recent scholarly literature (including Beyschlag and Lüdemann), see Wayne A. Meeks, "Simon Magus in Recent Research," *RSR* 3 (1977): 137–42; and Robert McL. Wilson, "Simon and Gnostic Origins," in *Les Actes des Apôtres: traditions, rédaction, théologie*, ed. J. Kremer (Leuven: University Press, 1979), 485–91.

3. Ernst Haenchen, "Gab es eine vorchristliche Gnosis?" *ZTK* 49 (1952): 316–49; repr. in *Gott und Mensch: Gesammelte Aufsätze* (Tübingen: Mohr [Siebeck], 1965), 265–98 (citations are from the latter); see also Haenchen's subsequent article, "Simon Magus in der Apostelgeschichte," in *Gnosis und Neues Testament*, ed. K. W. Tröger (Gütersloh: Mohn, 1973), 267–79. Haenchen's estimate that Simon had been "demoted" was soon regarded as an assured result by many German scholars (see the long list of such opinions cited in Beyschlag, *Simon Magus*, 90 n. 30; cf. Wilson, "Simon and Gnostic Origins," 491 n. 34).

4. Meeks concludes that "the burden of proof will lie on anyone who wishes to revive the Haenchen hypothesis" ("Recent Research," 141). Wilson approves of Beyschlag's strong caution against anachronism, but would also like to allow for "the trends and tendencies which were undoubtedly already present in the first century, for the development which finally culminated in the classical gnosticism" ("Simon and Gnostic Origins," 490). A recent attempt to establish that the Simonian gnostic system witnessed in the time of Justin may be dated to the time of Luke or his sources is that of Gerd Lüdemann, "The Acts of the Apostles and the Beginnings of Simonian Gnosis," *NTS* 33 (1987): 420–26.

5. Such a self-designation is not, however, impossible; as noted in chap. 1, the term could have positive connotations. Beyschlag argues (in *Simon Magus*, 122–26) that the historical Simon was a *theios anēr;* cf. Morton Smith, "The Account of Simon Magus in Acts 8," in *Harry Austryn Wolfson Jubilee Volume*, English section, vol. 2 (Jerusalem: American Academy for Jewish Research, 1965), 735–49.

6. For an especially successful attempt to use source criticism in discerning Luke's purposes in the Simon Magus account, see C. K. Barrett, "Light on the Holy Spirit from Simon Magus (Acts 8, 4–25)," in *Les Actes de Apôtres*, 281–95, esp. 282–86.

7. Luke's description of the story's location (Acts 8:5: *eis tēn polin tēs Samareias;* with C, D, E, Ψ, and 𝔐 omitting the first article) is problematic, but has little bearing on interpretation; see Lake and Cadbury, *Beginnings*, 4:89; also Barrett, "Light," 285.

8. In Acts 8:6b, *autous* (whose antecedent *hoi ochloi* is also the subject of the governing verb *proseichon*) functions as the subject of the infinitives *akouein* and *blepein* (see BDF §406[3]; cf. Luke 9:34b). It is not obvious whether the implied object of *akouein* is Philip (as the RSV translators have concluded: "when they heard *him* and saw the signs which he did) or "signs" *(sēmeia)*. Luke's mention in v. 7 of the loud cries made by the departing unclean spirits supports the latter option: the people saw *and heard* the signs.

9. Although the dative object of *pisteuein* in Acts 8:12 is "Philip," by means of the immediately subsequent participial phrase (*euaggelizomenō peri tēs basileias*) Luke makes it clear that what the people are giving credence to is Philip's "good news" of the Kingdom and the name of Jesus.

10. The contrast between attention to the wonder-worker and attention to what is preached is very important to Luke: cf. Acts 3:12 and 14:15, where Peter and then Paul (with Barnabas) struggle to shift the people's interest from themselves to their message; and 13:12, where Paul's curse of Bar Jesus provokes not allegiance to Paul but amazement at "the teaching of the Lord." In the Philip/Simon story, the contrast is already embodied in two separate persons (contrast vv. 6 and 11). Cf. Jerome Kodell, " 'The Word of God Grew': The Ecclesial Tendency of *Logos* in Acts 1,7; 12,24; 19,20," *Biblica* 55 (1974): 512.

11. See the passages cited above, chap. 2 n. 46.

12. For example, see Acts 2:22-36; 3:13-26; 8:35; 10:36-43; 13:15, 27-41; 26:22-23; 28:23.

13. See chap. 2 n. 29. On the widespread desire at this time for a Spirit-endowed Messiah, see G. W. H. Lampe, "Holy Spirit in the Writings of St. Luke," 162–63. Specifically, Lampe cites *1 Enoch* 49:3; 62:2; and *Psalms of Solomon* 17:42 and 18:8 (apparently he means 17:37 and 18:7).

14. On the status of the apostles in Acts, see Jacob Jervell, *Luke and the People of God: A New Look at Luke-Acts* (Minneapolis: Augsburg Publishing House, 1972), 75–112.

15. Cf. Heb. 2:14; Rev. 20:10-15. First Cor. 15:24-26, where "death" is named as the last enemy, is also relevant, since the devil was thought to hold the power of death (e.g., Heb. 2:14; Wis. 2:23-24 [death entered the world because of the devil's envy]; cf. 1:13-16; *Barnabas* 18.1 and 20.1).

16. Calling upon the name of the Lord Jesus effects "salvation" (2:21), conceived both spiritually (i.e., the forgiveness of sins: Luke 24:47; Acts 2:38; 10:43; 22:16) and physically (i.e., healings and exorcisms: 3:6,16; 4:7-12, 30; 16:18; cf. 19:13). But spiritual and physical salvation are closely related for Luke, since both involve rescue from the authority of Satan or his demons. "The name" is also spoken of as the object of praise or rebuke (19:17; 26:9), as the cause for which Christians suffer and die (5:41; 9:16; 15:26; 21:13), and as the authority by which they teach (4:17-18; 5:28; 5:40; 9:15; 9:27-28). Cf. George W. MacRae, "Whom Heaven Must Receive Until the Time," *Interp* 27 (1973): 161–62. MacRae observes (162) that also against an Old Testament background "the sense of the reality and power of the name as a presence, especially in worship, is very strong."

17. Concerning Jesus' Nazareth sermon, which combines two Isaian passages featuring the word "release" (61:1; 58:6), Dillon ("Easter Revelation," 253) writes, "This conflation could surely not be read in any 'scroll' of the synagogue collection; it represents a Christian 'splicing' of separate passages to form a doubly emphatic testimony to the messianic 'release' offered by Jesus." The same word *aphesis* means both release from captivity and cancellation of an obligation, punishment, or guilt. Though Luke uses *aphesis* (and *aphiemi*) almost exclusively to refer to forgiveness of sins, it is evident

from such passages as Luke 4:38-39 (discussed above, in chap. 2 n. 15) and 13:16, as well as from the series of healings and exorcisms following (and fulfilling) the Nazareth sermon, that Luke also conceived of these miraculous deeds as a form of "release." See Miller's discussion of release and forgiveness in Luke-Acts, in *Character of the Miracles*, 155–71; see also Sharon H. Ringe, *Jesus, Liberation, and the Biblical Jubilee: Images for Ethics and Christology*, OBT 19 (Philadelphia: Fortress Press, 1985), esp. pp. 65–80.

18. Beyschlag (*Simon Magus*, 99–100) notes that the title became a focal point of the debate over Simon's status as a gnostic. Lake and Cadbury (*Beginnings* 4:91) argued that *tou theou* was added as a gloss (cf. Luke's similar change at 22:69 to Mark 14:62). Beyschlag (*Simon Magus*, 104) points to Acts 3:2, where the articular genitive *(hē thura tou hierou hē legomenē Ōraion)* is likewise an explanatory gloss. The addition of *tou theou* in Acts 8:10 highlights the blasphemous character of Simon's claim.

19. MATTHEW: 13x; MARK: 10x; LUKE: 15x; ACTS: 10x.

20. This is Hull's position in *Hellenistic Magic*, 105–14. Hull consistently reads Lukan references to "power" in terms of the modern anthropological construct of *mana*, and so is unable to perceive that a personal agent is implied by many of the Lukan references. Interpretation along the lines suggested by Hull would seem to be supported especially by Luke 6:19 and 8:46; Luke has taken over the latter reference to power (8:46) from Mark, and may have been prompted by it to insert the similar reference at Luke 6:19 into the earlier summary report (also of Markan derivation). Even in these two passages, however, Luke supposed that the agent behind Jesus' power was none other than God; cf. Luke 5:17, where the anarthrous genitive *kyriou* refers to God; and cf. also Acts 19:11-12.

21. See the preceding note. Other places where Luke stresses that God was the source of Jesus' healing and exorcising power include Luke 8:39 (Luke changes Mark's *ho kyrios* to *ho theos* so as to eliminate ambiguity); 9:43; Acts 2:22; and 10:38. To say that the agent was "God" is for Luke virtually equivalent to saying that it was the "Holy Spirit," as is demonstrated by the prayer and divine response at Acts 4:30-31.

22. See n. 16 above; also Remus, *Pagan Christian Conflict*, 245 nn. 89–90.

23. Suggested by H. Bietenhard, "onoma ktl.," *TDNT* 5 (1967): 277.

24. It would be unreasonable to conclude that because Luke perceived the similarity between the use of names by magicians and the use of Jesus' name by Christians, familiarity with magical practice has somehow "influenced" or "caused" Luke's confidence in the power of Jesus' name. Rather, the same culturally conditioned beliefs about the nature of spiritual beings and the potency of their names (on which see Bietenhard, "onoma ktl.") that made teachings about Jesus' name so persuasive to Luke *also* prompted him to perceive "magicians"—who invoked demonic/diabolical names, or (worse) mistook Jesus' holy name for the name of a common daimon—as a serious threat. In other words, Luke's world view was such that *both* "magical practice" as he understood it *and* the efficacy of Jesus' name were serious matters, but belief in either one did not necessarily "cause" belief in the other (see again the discussion of the difference between "magic" and the "magical

world view," above, pp. 28–29). If one were to seek "influence" or "causation" from any quarter, the most promising target of inquiry would be the Septuagint, where the name of God took on many different functions that can be regarded as precedents for the functions of the name of Jesus in Luke-Acts (see Bietenhard, "onoma ktl.," 252–61).

25. In Luke 22:69, Jesus claims that the Son of Man will be seated at the right hand of the "power *of God*" (contrast Matthew, Mark; see n. 18, above). Here too, then, Jesus and the "power of God" are clearly kept distinct.

26. See above, pp. 40–41. The case of Theudas (Acts 5:36) is particularly relevant, since the wording used to describe his self-aggrandizement *(legōn einai tina heautōn)* is similar to the wording at 8:9.

27. For the association of these three elements (magic, false prophecy, and Satan) in Jewish and Christian thought of Luke's era, see above, pp. 13–17. Cf. *Pseudo-Philo* 34:1-5, the story (unique in extant literature) of Aod the magician, who led the people of Israel astray by "amazing" them with his spectacular magic and persuading them to abandon the law and go after Midianite gods. The passage includes motifs found at Deut. 13:1-5, but (as in the Simon Magus account) the magician is never actually called a "prophet" or "false prophet." The story also exhibits the idea that magic will cease with the advent of the "age without measure" (i.e., the eschatological age).

28. Cf. Jacob Jervell's contention that according to Acts 7 the central thrust of the law is the struggle against idolatry *(The Unknown Paul,* 118–19). In Jervell's view, Luke has Stephen call the Jews "uncircumcised in heart" (7:51) because "they act as Gentiles."

29. Deut. 18:15 is quoted in Acts 7:37, only a few verses earlier (cf. Acts 3:22; also LXX Deut. 13:2-6 [= MT 13:1-5]). Also in Jeremiah the refrain of the people's idolatry and their related preference for false prophets over true ones is loud and insistent (e.g., 7:25-27; 23:25-27; 25:4-7; also see below, chap. 4 n. 18).

30. The omission appears to be tied to Luke's redaction of Jesus' eschatological discourse as a whole (Luke 21:5-36; cf. Mark 13). Luke has omitted or modified those sayings which might suggest that the eschaton was overdue; in John T. Carroll's assessment, "Luke incorporates parousia delay into his eschatological program, but does so in order to persuade his readers that they now live in the time of imminent expectation" *(Response to the End of History: Eschatology and Situation in Luke-Acts,* SBLDS 92 [Atlanta: Scholars Press, 1988], 104; see also pp. 103–117). Luke knows of false prophets who operated well before the end (Bar Jesus and possibly Simon) and may want to avoid suggesting that their appearance was a sign that the end was imminent. The saying at Mark 13:22 might also have been offensive to Luke because it indicated that false prophets could do "signs and wonders"—phenomena which Luke carefully reserves for the Christian leaders (in Luke's view false prophets do, not "signs and wonders," but "magic").

31. See the citations of scholarly literature on these points of resemblance in Beyschlag, *Simon Magus,* 15 n. 18. See also M. Smith, "Account of Simon Magus," 744–49. Smith discusses the false prophet/antichrist material so as to demonstrate the prevalence in the first century of "the notion that a

particular historical individual is a supernatural being" (ibid., 748). Smith
thinks that the wide acceptance of this notion renders plausible Luke's claim
that Simon's followers believed him (in his own lifetime) to be a supernatural
being (749), but Smith does not explicitly reflect upon the extent to which
the false prophet/antichrist expectations may have influenced Luke's own
literary shaping of the narrative about Simon. For general bibliography on
the traditions about eschatological adversaries, see Yarbro Collins, *The Combat
Myth,* 196 n. 65.

32. See Dan. 11:36-37, which is probably the source of the motif of self-
exaltation in the Jewish traditions about eschatological observers (note the
congruence of the Daniel passage with Isaiah 14 and Ezekiel 28). In Revelation
13 the "false prophet" (alias the "beast from the earth"; see Rev. 19:20) also
promotes unrighteous worship, though it is not of itself but of its alter ego,
the "beast from the sea"; in 2 Thessalonians 2, the "man of lawlessness" or
"son of perdition" (who is not explicitly called a false prophet, but who does
deceive people into believing what is false; 2:11) exalts himself above every
so-called god or object of worship and proclaims himself to be God (2:4);
and Hermas notes that a feature distinguishing the true prophet from the
false prophet is that the latter "exalts himself" (*hypsoi heauton; Hermas Mandate*
11.12). Samaria may have had a reputation for spawning false prophets:
Belkira, the unsavory antagonist in the *Martyrdom of Isaiah* (also called the
Ascension of Isaiah; see above, chap. 1 n. 25), hails from Samaria (2:12; 3:1;
cf. John 8:48). M. Smith ("Account of Simon Magus," 746–48) interprets
Ascension of Isaiah 4:2 and 5:9 as well as *Sibylline Oracles* 3:63ff. (which predicts
that "from the men of Sebaste [Samaria] Beliar shall come hereafter. . .") as
references to Simon, whose story, Smith contends, was increasingly fused
with that of Nero. Others argue that *ek Sebastēnōn* in the latter passage designates not one from Samaria but one from the line of the Augusti, specifically
Nero (but with no connection to Simon). For a description of the traditional
positions see John J. Collins, "Introduction to *The Sibylline Oracles,* Book 3,"
OTP 1:360; Collins also refers *Ascension of Isaiah* 4:1 (= 4.2 in Knibb's
translation, *OTP* 2:161) to Nero alone. Beyschlag (*Simon Magus,* 8 n. 4) is
skeptical of efforts to identify the figure of Simon with any of the similar
figures mentioned in Josephus (*Antiquities* 20.7.2), in apocalyptic documents
(incl. the *Sibylline Oracles*), or in the Jewish Haggada.

33. Early commentators who interpreted Jesus' prophecy that "false Christs
and false prophets will arise and show signs and wonders, to lead astray, if
possible, the elect" (Mark 13:22; cf. 13:6; Matt. 24:5, 24; Luke 21:8) as a
reference to Simon Magus include the following (cited in M. Smith, "Account
of Simon Magus," 745 n. 37): Origen *On Matt.* 33 and 41; *On Jer.* 5:3; *On
John* 1:33 (38); Hilary of Poitiers *On Matt.* 24:5; Apollonaris of Laodicea *On
Matt.* 24:5; Jerome *On Matt.* 4:24; Macarius Magnes *Apocriticus* 4.15; *Opus
imperfectum in Matt.* on 24:5.

34. It is widely held that Acts 8:14 marks Luke's transition to a new source;
Barrett ("Light," 283) is probably correct in seeing v. 13 as a Lukan editorial
addition (picking up earlier vocabulary and themes) intending to link the
previously unconnected work of Simon and Philip. Cf. Ernst Haenchen, *The*

Acts of the Apostles: A Commentary (Philadelphia: Westminster Press, 1971), 307; and Hans Conzelmann, *The Acts of the Apostles,* Hermeneia series (Philadelphia: Fortress Press, 1987), 64.

35. Some commentators simply assume that Simon's "false" (from the Christian point of view) interpretation of Philip's actions is historical fact, without giving any attention to the way that the author has led the reader to "read Simon's mind" (e.g., R. P. Casey, "Simon Magus," *Beginnings* 5:151; A. Wikenhauser, *Die Apostelgeschichte,* 2d ed. [Regensburg: Friedrich Pustet, 1951], 79; I. Howard Marshall, *The Acts of the Apostles* [Grand Rapids, Mich.: Wm. B. Eerdmans Press, 1980], 158). Haenchen ("Vorchristliche Gnosis?", 296, and *Acts,* 308) thinks that the motif of Simon's admiration for Christian wonders goes back to an earlier stage of the tradition. Even if based on genuine historical recollection or an earlier source, Luke's heavy-handed editing here (esp. v. 13) ought not to be overlooked.

36. On the "normative" character of the sequence in 2:38, see J. H. E. Hull, *The Holy Spirit in the Acts of the Apostles* (London: Lutterworth, 1967), 95–97.

37. The last suggestion (supported by, e.g., Conzelmann, *Acts of the Apostles,* 65; Wikenhauser, *Apostelgeschichte,* 78; Johnson, *Possessions,* 214) is especially plausible in light of the parallelism between 8:4 and 11:19: in both cases there is a need for sanction by the church in Jerusalem.

38. Barrett, "Light," 287.

39. The passages (cited from ibid., 286–88) are: Plato *Laws* 909A, B; cf. 933A; Philo *Special Laws* 3.100f.; Lucian *Lover of Lies* 15, 16; Celsus, quoted by Origen *Against Celsus* 1.68 (see the whole paragraph); Juvenal *Satire* 6.546; Philostratus *Life of Apollonius* 8.7; cf. 7.39; for additional references in ancient literature see Reiling, *Hermas and Christian Prophecy,* 53–54. Barrett ("Light," 288) also quotes *Acts of Thomas* 20: "We think because of his miracles that he is a *magos.* Yet his compassions and his cures, which are done by him freely (dōrean), and moreover his simplicity and kindness and his faith, declare that he is a righteous man or an apostle of the new God whom he preaches."

40. *The Apostolic Fathers,* LCL 2, trans. K. Lake. See the informative discussion in Reiling, *Hermas and Christian Prophecy,* 53–54.

41. Barrett, "Light," 288.

42. Cf. ibid., 289. Barrett also points to Acts 16, where the owners of the possessed slave girl want profit *(ergasia),* but Paul is indifferent about the financial consequences of his actions; and to 19:19, where a victory over magic is symbolized by the burning of magic books worth a great sum (ibid., 290).

43. "Curse" is here (and subsequently in the study) defined broadly as a spoken wish that evil or injury will befall someone, often but not always accompanied by an explicit appeal to supernatural (whether "divine" or "demonic") power. According to this definition, Acts 8:20; 13:11; and 23:3 qualify as "curses"; Luke 10:11 and 1 Cor. 5:4–5 instruct others to curse evildoers.

44. IMMEDIATE PHYSICAL RUIN: e.g., Deut. 4:26; 7:23; 30:18; Prov. 6:15 (n.b. vv. 12–15). Other relevant LXX uses of *apōleia* include Isa. 33:2

(contrasted with "salvation" [*sōtēria*]); Jer. 51:12 (conjoined with "curse" [*katara*]); and Dan. 2:5 and 3:96 (Theodotionic rescension; both include the phrase *eis apōleian einai;* in the latter the punishment is for blasphemy against God). See also *PGM* IV.1227–64, discussed below, chap. 4 n. 22. DESTRUCTION AT THE JUDGMENT: e.g., 2 Pet. 3:7; Rev. 17:8, 11; see also Matt. 7:13; Rom. 9:22; Phil. 1:28; 3:19. Also noteworthy are 2 Pet. 2:1–3, where the word is used repeatedly in a discussion of false prophets; John 17:12, where the Satan-possessed Judas (13:27) is called "the son of perdition" *(ho huios tēs apōleias);* and 2 Thess. 2:3, where the same designation is used in reference to "the man of lawlessness," the Satanic anti-hero who will exalt himself and proclaim himself to be God, using signs and wonders to fortify his claim.

45. Simon's ostensible repentance, though not mentioned explicitly, is presupposed by his baptism.

46. L. Brun (*Segen und Fluch im Urchristentum* [Oslo: I Kommisjon Hos Jacob Dybwad, 1932], 70) contends that curses in the New Testament are generally expected to take effect at the judgment; see, e.g., Luke 10:10-12.

47. Haenchen (*Acts,* 305) argues that these expressions are not actual Old Testament citations, but merely "metaphors of the state of sin." In argument against this view, it will be shown that the Old Testament texts echoed by the expressions provide relevant commentary on the Simon Magus account, and are passages with which Luke was likely familiar.

48. Luke elsewhere echoes the covenant blessings and curses of Deuteronomy 28–29 in such a way as to suggest that he applied the blessings to those who share in the Christian inheritance, and the curses to those who are "cut off from the people." He alludes to a covenant blessing in describing the blessedness of Mary (Deut. 28:4; Luke 1:42), and a covenant curse in his description of the evil to befall Jerusalem (Deut. 28:64; Luke 21:24). There is also a possible allusion to Deut. 28:28-29 in Paul's description of his blindness at conversion (Acts 22:11), and to Deut. 28:22 in Paul's curse of the high priest (Acts 23:3). As Richard B. Hays has pointed out to me, Paul alludes to the covenant curses in Gal. 3:10 and Rom. 2:9, the latter in the context of condemnation of idolatry. Cf. Heb. 12:15.

49. At Qumran this curse was similarly directed at those who joined themselves to the monastic community while still committing idolatry (see the more extensive discussion in chap. 4).

50. Against Johnson (*Possessions,* 216) and Brown (*Apostasy and Perseverance,* 111), who think that "share *(klēros)* in this word" refers to a part in the apostolic office (cf. 1:17, 26), it must be said that Peter refuses Simon not merely a place among the apostles, but a share in the very rewards of salvation promised to *all* who believe the Word (15:7, 11). Cf. 26:18-20, where those who shall respond to Paul's witness by repenting and turning to God, claiming forgiveness of sins and thereby gaining a "share" or "place" *(klēros)* among the sanctified, are contrasted with those who shall remain under the authority of Satan (cf. also 20:32; Col. 1:12-14). Furthermore, as Wayne Meeks has pointed out to me, in Deut. 12:12 and 14:27, 29, to which Acts 8:21 is an allusion, *klēros* refers to the inheritance of the land, in which

the Levites do not share; against this background *klēros* in Acts 8:21 would again seem to refer to the inheritance of salvation (for "the land" as a typological pattern for the Christian inheritance, see Acts 7:3, 5; cf. also 20:32; and see the discussion in Dahl, *Jesus in the Memory of the Early Church,* 72–76). Johnson and Brown have been understandably influenced by Simon's request for "authority" to bestow the Holy Spirit; i.e., Simon asks to be able to do what the apostles do. But the phrasing of Simon's request is governed more by Luke's aim of making Simon act like Satan (who also coveted divine authority) than by an intention to show that Simon wanted a place in the historical ministry of the apostles.

51. As demonstrated in chap. 2, throughout Jesus' earthly ministry Satan struggled to retain authority. Otto Bauernfeind *(Kommentar und Studien zur Apostelgeschichte* [Tübingen: Mohr (Siebeck) 1980], 125) and others following him have suggested that Simon originally wanted to purchase healing power, and that Luke has changed the request to one for authority; if correct, the editorial change would highlight Luke's ongoing concern with the struggle for authority in which Jesus (or his representatives) and Satan engage. But even if Bauernfeind is mistaken, the parallel between Acts 8:19 and Luke 4:6 is striking, and hardly undermined by the fact that in Acts Simon wishes to confer the Spirit, and not authority per se. Clearly Luke has made the parallel as close as the story line permits. Cf. G. Schneider, *Die Apostelgeschichte,* HTKNT 5, 2 vols. (Freiburg: Herder, 1980–82) 1:493 n. 93.

52. Lake and Cadbury *(Beginnings* 4:92) suggest that the western reading may be original. Certainly the motives for eliminating this notice, which could (as noted above) be taken as an indication of repentance, would have grown along with Simon's notoriety; conversely, the addition of the saying after the legends about Simon had spread is also unlikely.

53. The possible exceptions are Luke 7:38 and 22:62, though the adverb "bitterly" *(pikrōs)* in 22:62 ought to caution against the easy assumption that Luke was here portraying Peter as repentant. In general Luke is fond of the word "weep" *(klaiō),* using it 11x in Luke (vs. 2x in Matthew; 4x in Mark) and 2x in Acts (excluding 8:24).

54. Conzelmann, *Acts of the Apostles,* 66; Brun, *Segen und Fluch,* 101.

55. Bauernfeind *Apostelgeschichte,* 123; and following him G. Klein, "Der Synkretismus als theologisches Problem in der ältesten christlichen Apologetik," *ZTK* 64 (1967): 76.

56. *The Apostolic Fathers,* LCL 2, trans. K. Lake. See also *Hermas Mandate* 12.5.2—6.5. In 12.6.2, the angel tells Hermas that the devil is as "powerless as the sinews of a dead man" when confronted by someone who has turned to the Lord with all his or her heart.

57. Cf. *Testament of Judah* 20:4-5 ("There is no moment in which man's works can be concealed, because they are written on the heart in the Lord's sight. And the spirit of truth testifies to all things and brings all accusations. He who has sinned is consumed in his heart and cannot raise his head to face the judge" [trans. Howard Clark Kee, in *OTP* 1:800]); also *Testament of Benjamin* 5:3.

58. Some servants of Satan (notably Judas; also, Ananias and Sapphira) come to a disastrous end, but this was not necessarily the rule. Acts 19:18-20 and Justin *1 Apology* 14 both indicate that magic was something one could successfully renounce, and *Hermas Mandate* 12.6 argues that it is possible to master the works of the devil, if one turns to the Lord with all one's heart.

59. The texts are *Antiquities* 18.85-87; 20.97-99; 20.167-168 (parallel *War* 2.258-259); 20.168-172 (parallel *War* 2.261-263); 20.188; *War* 6.284-286. For discussions of the passages see esp. P. W. Barnett, "The Jewish Sign Prophets," and Aune, *Prophecy in Early Christianity,* 126–29.

60. Further, Reiling ("The Use of PSEODOPROPHĒTĒS," 154–56) concludes that the supposed association between (false) prophets and pagan divination seen in certain passages of the Septuagint and Philo is totally absent in the writings of Josephus.

61. On this passage (and in general on Josephus's view of magic) see Duling, "The Eleazar Miracle." Duling argues that Josephus was here drawing on traditions about Solomon's magical wisdom (Josephus even compares Solomon to a known magician, Dardanos [ibid., 19]).

62. *Josephus,* LCL 4, trans. H. St. J. Thackeray.

63. Cf. Duling, "The Eleazar Miracle," 11.

64. *GMPT,* xlvii.

65. This focus almost exclusively on the spiritual realm also characterizes the Jewish-Christian *Testament of Solomon* (see Duling's introduction and translation, in *OTP* 1:935-87 also *idem,* "The Testament of Solomon: Retrospect and Prospect," *JSP* 2 [1989]: 87-112). The document describes Solomon's conversation with a series of demons who reveal to him their names, their nefarious deeds, and the names of the angels who are able to thwart their actions.

66. Magic was a dangerous business: the spirits that one utilized to effect magical deeds could turn against one at any moment. Magicians regularly employed amulets to ward off such danger (see Hopfner, *"Mageia,"* cols. 365-67; to illustrate, Hopfner cites *PGM* IV.2506f.: "the goddess is accustomed to make airborne those who perform this rite unprotected by a charm and to hurl them from aloft down to the ground" [lines 2507-2509, trans. E. N. O'Neil, *GMPT* 84]; *PGM* XIII.795–800 is also especially interesting: the practitioner has the god's name as an amulet [phylactery] in his or her heart).

67. Common defenses of Christian miracles vis-à-vis magic were that the Christian miracles had substantial and lasting effect, whereas the effects of magic were fleeting and deceptive; and that Christian miracles were done by a powerful word, whereas magic was effected by manipulations and incantations. For citations of the ancient sources, see Fridrichsen, *The Problem of Miracle,* 87–95; Remus, *Pagan-Christian Conflict,* 52–72. Remus evaluates the criteria, concluding that they did not hold up to scrutiny; what is important for the comparison with Luke is whether or not the criteria were utilized at all.

CHAPTER 4
PAUL AND BAR JESUS (ACTS 13:4-12)

1. Nock writes, "The conclusion to which one is driven is that Luke has some definite tradition which he has incorporated *tant bien que mal.* So lame

a story would not readily have been invented in Luke's time" ("Paul and the Magus," 187–88). For an account of the reactions of some other scholars to the story, see Haenchen, *Acts,* 403.

2. For a discussion of the issues, see Lake and Cadbury, *Beginnings* 4:143–44, n. 8; Haenchen, *Acts,* 398–99 n. 2. See also n. 18 below.

3. The question has long been a topic of discussion; generally scholars have been skeptical. Since Luke regularly uses *pisteuein* to describe conversion (over a dozen times; see esp. 13:48), it is likely that he intended for the remark that Sergius Paulus "believed" also to be taken in this sense. But historically the question is indeterminate.

4. Nock, "Paul and the Magus," 187.

5. Ibid., 188; Kee, *Miracle in the Early Christian World,* 217; Marshall, *Acts,* 216–17.

6. Despite his assessment of the story as poorly contrived, Nock listed three points made by it, which bear repeating: "First, it represented the Roman authorities as very sympathetic at the outset of Paul's active ministry in the Gentile world; secondly, it gave to Paul a *Gottesurteil* comparable with that declared by Peter on Ananias and Sapphira; thirdly, and this was perhaps important, it represented Christianity in very sharp contrast with *magia*" ("Paul and the Magus," 188).

7. This will become Paul's pattern for the balance of his missionary journeys in Acts (13:14, 46; 14:1; [16:13]; 17:1-2, 10; 18:4, 19; 19:8; [20:21]). On Luke's probable reasons for stressing this pattern, see Jervell, *Luke and the People of God,* 41–74, esp. 55, 62–65.

8. Haenchen, *Acts,* 402. It may also be the case that this is the only incident during the first part of the journey about which Luke has any specific information.

9. This is not to say that Luke sees Sergius Paulus as dispensable: it is no accident that this important event is depicted as occurring before someone of such high standing (see n. 6 above). On Luke's portrayal elsewhere in Acts of Paul before important officials, see Abraham J. Malherbe, " 'Not in a Corner': Early Christian Apologetic in Acts 26:26," *Second Century* 5 (1985–86): 193–210.

10. On this expression see Nils A. Dahl, "Der Erstgeborene Satans und der Vater des Teufels (Polyk. 7,1 und Joh 8,44)," in *Apophoreta: Festschrift für Ernst Haenchen,* eds. W. Eltester and F. H. Kettler (Berlin: Töpelmann, 1964), 70–84. Dahl reviews early Christian and Rabbinic occurrences of the expression "first-born of Satan," and determines that it referred to Cain, who according to certain legends had been conceived by Satan. Cain was "sophist and arch-heretic, opponent of the divine truth; the lie is that which he has inherited from his father, the devil" (77). While it is unclear whether Luke had such Cain-legends in mind (Dahl calls attention to Acts 13:10 but does not make a judgment on this point), the possibility is interesting; in any case the relationship between Satan and Bar Jesus is indubitably close.

11. Lake and Cadbury (*Beginnings* 4:146 n. 10) point out the emphatic repetition of *pas* in this and the following phrase. Note also that the only other time Luke uses "enemy" *(echthros)* in the singular, it apparently refers

to Satan (Luke 10:19; cf. Matt. 13:39). As the "enemy of righteousness," Bar Jesus opposes all who would fear God (Acts 10:22, 35) or be obedient to God (Luke 1:17).

12. The term *radiourgia* occurs only here in the New Testament and LXX (*radiourgēma* occurs at Acts 18:14); Barrett ("Light," 289) suggests that the term may connote fraudulent dealing in money matters. The expression *plērēs dolou* occurs in the LXX (Sir. 1:30; 19:26; Jer. 5:27). The first of these references (Sir. 1:30) would have been especially appealing to Luke since it predicts the fall of those who exalt themselves and the revelation of things hidden, both favorite Lukan motifs.

13. Cf. Baumbach, *Verständnis des Bösen*, 168. For examples of Satan's use of human servants, see Luke 22:3; John 13:2, 27; *Martyrdom of Isaiah* 1:8–9; 2:1, 4, 7; 3:11; 5:1, 3, 15; *Jubilees* 48:9-11; *Testament of Naptali* 8:6; CD 5:18-19; *Hermas Mandate* 11.3. For examples of Satan's assumption of human or angelic form, see 2 Cor. 11:3, 14, together with *Life of Adam and Eve* 9–10 (Vita) (= 29:15-17 [Apocalypse]) and the discussion in Dahl, "Erstgeborene Satans," 74; *Testament of Iob* 6:4—7:13 (Satan disguised as a beggar); 17:2 (as king of the Persians); and 23:1-11 (as a bread seller). Regarding Rabbinic traditions about Satan's metamorphosis, see Noack, *Satanás und Soteria*, 20–21.

14. "Paul and the Magus," 182; cf. Klein, "Synkretismus," 61.

15. Klein ("Synkretismus," 61) does not take adequate account of this double occurrence in his attempt to dismiss the title as irrelevant. Klein supposes that since the title *magician* "competes with" that of *false prophet*, both can be safely ignored. But Jewish myths about magicians, analyzed above (chap. 1), suggest that the titles are complementary rather than competing.

16. Regarding the "straight paths *[hodoi]* of the Lord," see Prov. 10:9-10; Hos. 14:9 (LXX v. 10); in both cases there are striking conceptual and verbal overlaps with the Bar Jesus story.

17. Cf. Noack, *Satanás und Soteria*, 109; cf. also Lampe's brief comment that the blinding of Bar Jesus "is like a negative version of a conversion story" ("Miracles in the Acts of the Apostles," *Miracles*, ed. C.F.D. Moule [London: A.R. Mowbray, 1965], 177).

18. Lake and Cadbury, *Beginnings* 4:146 n. 10; Brun, *Segen und Fluch*, 101; R. J. Dillon and Joseph A. Fitzmyer, "Acts of the Apostles," in *The Jerome Biblical Commentary*, ed. Raymond Brown et al., 2 vols. (Englewood Cliffs, N.J.: Prentice Hall, 1968), 2:192. Another relevant passage is Isa. 59:7-10, where similar metaphors describe divine retribution for turning away from God. In "Elymas-Nehelamite-Pethor" (*JBL* 79 [1960]: 297–314), L. Yaure argues that the Bar Jesus incident follows the pattern of Jeremiah's encounter with the dreamer prophets (e.g., Jer. 14:14; 23:25-32; 27:9-10; 29:8-9), especially the incident with Shemaiah the Nehelamite in Jer. 29:29-32 (LXX 36:29-32). Yaure builds his case on his prior argument that "Elymas" is a transliteration of the Aramaic *ḥālōma* referring to persons who interpreted dreams to deliver inspired messages. The etymological suggestion regarding "Elymas" has some merit, and Yaure may be correct that Luke was influenced

by the passages in Jeremiah; influence from the Numbers account of Balaam, which Yaure also suggests, is unlikely.

19. *Dead Sea Scrolls,* trans. Vermes, 63.

20. Cf. *Testament of Levi* 19:1: "Choose for yourselves light or darkness, the Law of the Lord or the works of Beliar" (trans. Howard Clark Kee, *OTP* 1:795).

21. See above, chap. 3, n. 46.

22. Cf. *PGM* IV.1227-64, probably the closest parallel in the magical papyri. This is an exorcistic rite in which the troublesome demon (called "Satan") is condemned to "the black chaos in perdition" *(eis to melan chaos en tais apōleiais).* In its extant form the text has obviously been influenced by Christian practice: the speaker invokes not only the God of Abraham, Isaac, and Jacob, but also "Jesus Chrestos, the Holy Spirit, the Son of the Father, who is above the Seven, who is within the Seven." Here, as in the Bar Jesus incident, the servant of Satan gets his due. But since in this case the servant is a demon, and the formula is pronounced in order to liberate (rather than punish) the human host, the relevance of the text for the present discussion is dubious. The text is more comparable to Luke 8:31, where the demons called "Legion" beg Jesus not to send them "into the abyss" (where evil spirits are confined; Rev. 9:1–11; 20:1-3; contrast Mark 5:10: "out of the country").

23. Trans. W. Schneemelcher (Eng. trans. G. C. Stead), in E. Hennecke, *New Testament Apocrypha,* ed. W. Schneemelcher, 2 vols. (Philadelphia: Westminster Press, 1965), 2:291.

24. In 2 Cor. 11:13-15, Paul refers to the "false apostles" as Satan's "servants" and as "workers of guile" *(ergatai dolioi;* cf. Acts 13:10: Bar Jesus is *plērēs pantos dolou).* Paul asserts that the "end" *(telos)* of these servants of the Prince of Darkness will "correspond to their deeds"—a principle that is also at work in the Bar Jesus episode.

25. The word translated here as "pure" *(haplous)* means "single, simple, straightforward"; or, in reference to persons, "open, frank," or even "simple-minded." It is not well suited to describe the physical health of an eye (but cf. Marshall, *The Gospel of Luke,* 489). The opposition of the word to *ponēros* ("evil, bad"; the word allows a medical interpretation but which can have moral connotations as well) suggests that *haplous* may have been understood to bring out the moral dimension of the saying as a whole. Ferdinand Hahn ("Die Worte vom Licht Lk 11,33-36," in *Orientierung an Jesus: Zur Theologie der Synoptiker* [Freiburg: Herder, 1973], 128) notes that the exhortation in Luke 11:35 (contrast Matt. 6:23b) presupposes a metaphorical meaning for 11:34. Hahn argues cogently that 11:36 (unique to Luke) is an eschatological promise that the one who is now "full of light" will be "illuminated" by the light of Christ when Christ appears at the end (cf. Luke 17:24). This reading of Luke 11:36 adds force (by reverse logic) to the above suggestion that Bar Jesus' present darkness is expected to bring "darkness" at the judgment.

26. Cf. Job 1:22; 2:10; *Testament of Job* 16:1-4; 20:1-3; 25:10; 26:3.

27. Satan also "binds" and "imprisons" (e.g., Luke 13:16), whereas Christ offers release; note that in Isa. 42:6-7, which lies behind Acts 26:18, God commands his servant to *release* persons from prison.

28. From here on (with only a few exceptions: 14:12, 14; 15:25) Paul is always mentioned before Barnabas; contrast esp. 13:1,2,7 with 13:13. Cf. G. Stählin, *Die Apostelgeschichte*, NTD 5, 10th ed. (1st rev. ed.) (Göttingen: Vandenhoeck & Ruprecht, 1962), 177.

29. This was pointed out to me by Abraham J. Malherbe. See Lucian *Timon* 22, and *The Cock* 14; cf. Acts 4:36. On why Paul should have had two names at all (which is different from the question as to why Luke confines the usage of each to different portions of the narrative), see Lake and Cadbury, *Beginnings* 4:145–46 n. 9.

30. The exceptions are at 22:7, 13; and 26:14. But since these are all recollections of an incident that happened prior to the Bar Jesus episode, they actually underscore the deliberateness of Luke's compartmentalized usage of the two names.

31. Cf. F. J. Foakes-Jackson, *The Acts of the Apostles* (New York: Richard R. Smith, 1931), 112–13; Marshall, *Acts*, 220.

32. And to some ancient readers as well: according to Lake and Cadbury (*Beginnings* 4:146 n. 11), "Chrysostom deduces that Paul was anxious to convert Elymas and therefore inflicted on him the blindness which had accompanied his own conversion (Homily xxviii.)." Foakes-Jackson (*Acts*, 112) quotes a similar comment by the Venerable Bede.

33. The temporal designation here *(achri kairou)* occurs only one other time in Luke-Acts, in the problematic Luke 4:13 (discussed above, chap. 2). Klein ("Synkretismus," 66), building on Conzelmann's interpretation of this phrase as the designation for an interim period, claims that Luke "chose the most pregnant phrase available to him" to indicate that the punishment of Bar Jesus was only temporary, and that the way to conversion lay open to him (as to the syncretists that Klein thinks Bar Jesus represents). But Conzelmann's interpretation of the temporal phrase cannot support this weight.

34. SILENCING THE GOSPEL: Acts 4:17-18; 5:40; 13:45, 50; 17:5, 13; 18:6, 12–13; cf. 1 Thess. 2:16. PERSECUTING TRUE PROPHETS: Luke 6:22-23; Acts 7:52; cf. 1 Thess. 2:15 FOLLOWING FALSE PROPHETS, PRACTICING IDOLATRY: Luke 6:26; Acts 7:43, 51b. FAILING TO KEEP THE LAW Acts 7:53.

CHAPTER 5
THE SEVEN SONS OF SCEVA (ACTS 19:8–20)

1. Martin Dibelius, *Studies in the Acts of the Apostles*, ed. Heinrich Greeven (London: SCM Press, 1956), 19, 198 n. 15.

2. E.g., Haenchen, *Acts*, 565, 567; Conzelmann, *Acts of the Apostles*, 163; Schneider, *Apostelgeschichte* 2:267; G. Stählin, *Die Apostelgeschichte*, 257; J. Roloff, *Die Apostelgeschichte*, NTD 5, 17th ed. (Göttingen: Vandenhoeck & Ruprecht, 1981), 284–87.

3. As Deissmann had already noted (*Bible Studies*, 323 n. 5), Luke uses technical magical terms in 19:18-19. The word *praxis* can refer to a magical spell (frequently in *PGM* with this meaning); *perierga* occurs as a euphemism for magical arts (e.g., Plut. *Alexander* 2.5; Philostratus *Life of Apollonius* 4.35; see also J. J. Wettstein, *Novum Testamentum Graecum*, 2 vols. [1752; reprint

Graz, Austria: Akademische Druck, 1962], 2:582); *hai bibloi* (or *ta bibla*, or *bybla*) sometimes refers to books of magical spells (e.g., Lucian *Lover of Lies* 31; *Pseudo-Phocylides* 149; *PGM* XIII. 736-741; cf. Plato *Republic* 364E; Pliny *Natural History* 28.4.14) and as others have recognized, may here be an allusion to the infamous *Ephesia grammata* (on which see Plutarch *Moralia* 706E; E. Kuhnert, *"Ephesia grammata,"* PW 5 [1905]: cols. 2771–73); also Wettstein, *Novum Testamentum Graecum*, 2:582-83. All of the terms can also be used without any reference to magic, but the narrative context, the occurrence of the three expressions together, and the setting of the incident in Ephesus (which had given its name to the *Ephesia grammata*) make the magic-related meanings very probable for the Acts account.

4. Klein, "Synkretismus," 56. Klein is correct that in this passage Luke displays his opposition to the use of Jesus' name by non–Christians. But in trying to show that not only in 19:11-20, but also in Acts 8:6-24 and 13:6-12 Luke's sole concern is to combat "the problem of syncretism" (and that therefore Luke is, indeed, a representative of "early Catholicism"), Klein is pushed to an indefensible position. He contends that Luke carries on no anti-magic polemic at all; the category "magic" is of no interest to Luke (ibid., 56 n. 87; 62; 68; 76 n. 182). The dichotomy Klein presupposes ("either syncretism or magic") is artificial, since magic was itself highly syncretistic.

5. Numerous efforts have been made to account for this apparent historical error; Haenchen (*Acts*, 565) cites several of these (e.g., the seven were imposters, or Sceva was only a member of a high priestly family), but rightly points out that "Luke has not signified any doubt about the authenticity of this high priest." It is likely that by describing the seven as sons of a high priest, Luke wished to put their Jewishness above suspicion: like Bar Jesus, these are children of Abraham, but are doing what Jews ought not to do. On the basis of Apuleius *Metamorphosis* 2.28f, wherein a priest revives a dead person, B. Mastin ("Scaeva the Chief Priest," *JTS* 27 [1976]: 405–12; cf. his "A Note on Acts 19,14," in *Biblica* 59 [1978]: 97–99) suggests that Luke refers to Sceva as an *archiereus* so as to bolster the credentials of the seven; the interpretation has merit, but the parallel on which it is based is gratuitous.

6. The seeming discrepancy has led many to the conclusion that the text is corrupt. According to Haenchen, *Acts*, 564 n. 5, E. Nestle (*Berliner Phil. Wochenschrift* 18 [1898], col. 254) was the first to point out that, in later Greek, *amphoteros* can mean not merely "both" but "all"; Lake and Cadbury (*Beginnings* 4:241–42) cite some objections to this theory, but also point out that Acts 23:8 may be a parallel instance of the idiom. Whether there were seven sons or two is in any case not critical for interpretation of the story; in this study the number "seven" is retained.

7. Manuscript D substitutes the following at v. 14: *en hois kai huioi Skeuas tinos hiereōs ethelēsan to auto poiēsai ethos eichan tous toioutous exorkizein kai eiselthontes pros ton daimonizomenon ērxanto epikaleisthai to onoma legontes paraggellomen soi en Iēsou hon Paulos kēryssei exelthein;* P[38] is similar. Despite a recent attempt to reopen the discussion (W. A. Strange, "The Sons of Sceva and the Text of Acts 19:14," *JTS* 38 [1987]: 97–106), Ernst Haenchen's argument ("Zum Text der Apostelgeschichte," *ZTK* 54 [1957]: 28–29) that

the variant represents a clever attempt by the western editor to resolve several of the passage's exegetical difficulties remains persuasive.

8. According to Dibelius (*Studies,* 19, 198), the sudden mention of the house shows that the beginning of the story had been lost or dropped, but Lake and Cadbury (*Beginnings* 4:242) point out that the belated reference, though awkward, is "quite in the manner of Luke." They compare the references to a "city" in Luke 7:37; 8:27; and 9:5.

9. Eitrem ("Some Notes on the Demonology in the New Testament" *Symbolae osloenses* supplement [Oslo: A. W. Brøgg 1950], 3) perceives the latter difficulty, but unsuccessfully tries to resolve it at the historical rather than the narrative level. Haenchen (*Acts,* 565) thinks that it does not follow that the people should have extolled Jesus' name; therefore Haenchen concludes "that Luke has here made use of material alien to his purpose, which he could not quite mould together in spite of all his vigorous efforts to do so."

10. In defense of this translation, see A.W. Argyle, "Acts xix.20," *ExpTim* 75 (1964): 151. Since *kata kratos* occurs in classical Greek as a standard adverbial phrase (e.g., Thucydides 8.100; Isocrates 4.119) it is also possible to take *tou Kyriou* with what follows ("thus the word of the Lord grew and prevailed *mightily*").

11. This is evident both from the use of the connective particle *te* in v. 11, and also from the use of the imperfect *epoiei,* which refers to God's ongoing miraculous activity during the two–year time span just mentioned (v. 10).

12. On the the possible meanings of the terms *soudaria* and *simikinthia,* see Lake and Cadbury, *Beginnings* 4:237–28 n. 4.

13. Philip was among those who had been forced to leave Jerusalem because of the persecution that arose over Stephen (8:1, 4).

14. See above, 63–65.

15. In interpreting this verse, some commentators focus on what they perceive to be the "mana-like" view of power that underlies the account (see, e.g., Marshall, *Acts,* 310; cf. Kee, *Medicine, Miracle and Magic,* 115). Klein ("Synkretismus," 56) even concludes from such an assessment of v. 11 that Luke is altogether uninterested in showing how Christianity differs from magic, since he accepts magical notions himself. But such reasoning obscures the view of the ancient author. Luke gives no hint that he saw what Paul did as magic, while he gives many hints that he saw what the seven sons did as such. Certainly Luke's world view shared much with the world view of "magicians," including the belief that "power" could be transferred by material means, but the practice of magic is not the same as the world view that renders magic credible (see also above, pp. 27–29, and 142 n. 24).

16. On the Jews and exorcism, see above, chap. 2 n. 31; on Jewish magic in general, see chap. 1 n. 16.

17. Cf. Schneider, *Apostelgeschichte* 2:269; W. Heitmüller, *Im Namen Jesu,* (Göttingen: Vandenhoeck & Ruprecht, 1903), 56; Klein, "Synkretismus," 53–54.

18. No where else does Luke use this verb in connection with Christians' use of Jesus' name. The two occurrences of the verb in Luke (6:13, 14) are in a neutral context.

19. Cf. Plutarch *Moralia* 706E: "For just as magicians direct those possessed by demons to recite and name over to themselves the Ephesian letters . . ." *(hōsper gar hoi magoi tous daimonizomenous keleuousi tas Ephesia grammata pros autous katalegein kai onomazein).*

20. The verb *exorkizō* does occur in Matt. 26:63, in a non-magical context; cf. 1 Thess. 5:27.

21. Cf. Josephus *Antiquites* 8.42–46a, where Solomon is described as the author of *tropoi exorkōseōn;* on this passage see Duling, "The Eleazar Miracle." The word "exorcist" *(exorkistes)* is not listed in Preisendanz's index to the magical papyri, but the verb *exorkizō* does occur very frequently; see, e.g., *PGM* I.225; IV.2060–66: "I adjure *(exorkizō)* [you], dead spirit *(nekydaimon),* by the Destiny of Destinies *(kata tēs Anagkēs tōn Anagkōn),* to come to me, NN, on this day, on this night, and agree to the act of service for me. And if you don't, expect other chastisements" (trans. E. N. O'Neil, *GMPT,* 74); IV.3235; XII.137; XIII.303.

22. Lucian (*Lover of Lies* 16) describes a Syrian from Palestine who frees possessed persons by pronouncing "oaths" *(horkoi);* Josephus (*Antiquities* 8.47) says that Eleazar "adjured" *(horkoun)* the demon never to come back (on this passage, see the preceding note); *horkizein* occurs also in *Testament of Solomon* 5:9; 6:8; 11:6; 18:20, 31, 33; 25:8. *Horkizein* occurs frequently in the magical papyri, usually with an expressed or implied command. Sometimes the verb is followed by a direct object (e.g., IV.345–347: "I adjure all daimons in this place to stand as assistants beside this daimon" [trans. E. N. O'Neil, *GMPT,* 44]; cf. I.305–14; IV.1708–14, 2912); sometimes (as in Acts 19:13) it is followed by a double accusative, with the first accusative referring to the being or object adjured and the second referring to the being or object by whom or by which one swears (i.e., whose authority one invokes to back up the oath; e.g., IV.3065–68, 3068–74, 3075–78); sometimes it is followed by an accusative direct object referring to the being or object adjured and by *kata* + gen. referring to that by whom or which one swears (e.g., IV.396–97, 3019–20).

23. Bauerfeind, *Worte der Dämonen,* 23–26.

24. The word *paraggellein* is used at Luke 8:29; cf. Acts 16:18, and note that in the western text's version of v. 14, the sons command the demon with this word. The word *epitiman* is used at Luke 4:35, 39, 41; 8:24; 9:42, 55; see Kee, "Terminology" (Kee argues that the word "rebuke" is an inadequate translation, but an appropriate alternate translation is difficult to find).

25. A fundamental premise of magic was that a strong sympathetic bond existed between spiritual beings and their true names; by knowing the latter, the magician could coerce the deity to do his or her bidding (see Hopfner, "*Mageia,*" cols. 334–36, 43–44; Bonner, "The Technique of Exorcism," 44; n.b. Mark 5:9 [parallel Luke 8:30]). On the important role played by spirits of the dead *(nekydaimones)* in magic, see Hopfner, "*Mageia,*" cols. 305–6. According to Hopfner (ibid., col. 330), it was commonly supposed that since the violently killed *(biaiothanatoi)* and those who had died young *(aōroi)* had been unable to live out a full life span, they desired to make up what they

had lost or to avenge their untimely deaths. Hence the spirits were roaming (cf. Lucian *Lover of Lies* 29), and could possess persons (thereby extending their own lives after a fashion; see, e.g., Philostratus *Life of Apollonius* 3.38) and also be summoned by those who knew the magical methods to command them. Magical curse tablets were often placed in a spot associated with a violent death, in the belief that the spirit of the dead person would execute the curse. Examples of dependence on *biaiothanatoi* in the magical papyri include *PGM* I.248; II.48, 145 *(biaios)*; IV.1390–1495 (titled a "love spell of attraction performed with the help of heroes or gladiators or those who have died a violent death" [*biaioi;* see esp. lines 1394, 1401; trans. E. N. O'Neil, *GMPT*, 64]); IV.1950.

26. See Mark 9:38-40 (parallel Luke 9:49-50). It is possible that the account originated after Jesus' death and was projected back into his own lifetime, but see the arguments to the contrary in E. Wilhelms, "Der fremde Exorzist: Eine Studie über Mark. 9,38ff," *ST* 3 (1950–51): 168–69. The passage is discussed below, n. 35. In the magical papyri, see *PGM* IV.3019–20: "This is the oath: I adjure you by the God of the Hebrews, Jesus" *(horkizō se kata tou theou tōn Hebraiōn Iēsou).* Cf. IV.1233. According to Eitrem ("Notes," 9), "R. Wünsch probably was right when supplying the name of *Iesous* twice on a leaden tablet from Megara, a *katadesmos (defixio)* which aims at giving the enemy all sorts of physical infirmity" (here referring to R. Wünsch, *Defixionum tabellae Atticae [Corpus Inscriptionarum Graecarum 3.3]* [Berlin: 1873]: 13).

27. The verbs alternate: the demons "know" *(ginōskein)* Jesus and "know" *(epistasthai)* Paul. Haenchen (*Acts,* 564) thinks the meanings are equivalent, and it may be that Luke was merely trying to give his account variety, but the proximity of the verbs makes the switch so striking that one suspects it was deliberate and meaningful. Klein ("Synkretismus," 57–58) observes that Luke elsewhere uses *epistasthai* with reference to a knowledge or familiarity with historical facts or conditions; *ginōskein* is used in a greater variety of contexts. Probably here the demon's "knowledge" of Jesus ought to be understood along the lines of Luke 4:34: the demon knows *(eidenai)* Jesus' identity, i.e., knows him to be "the Holy One of God." By contrast, the demon "is familiar with" the facts about Paul, i.e., knows that he is authorized to use Jesus' name. Cf. Schneider, *Apostelgeschichte* 2:270 (incl. n. 28); Roloff, *Apostelgeschichte,* 286: "The demon 'knows' *('kennt')* Jesus, that is, he acknowledges him in his sovereignty and knows himself to be subject to it; and he 'knows of' *('weiss von')* Paul, that is, he knows that Paul is the only [sic] legitimate representative of the power of Jesus."

28. Compare Luke 4:34 (parallel Mark 1:24), in which prior to its departure a demonic spirit cries out, "What have you to do with us, Jesus of Nazareth? Have you come to destroy us? I know *(oida)* who you are, the Holy One of God." With regard to the Markan version of the pericope, Bauernfeind (*Worte der Dämonen,* 11–18) argued on the basis of parallels from the magical papyri that the demon's claim to "know" Jesus may have been conceived as an attempt to hinder Jesus' action by invoking his true name—i.e., by practicing counter magic on him (cf. the related discussion of Mark 5:7, above, p. 92). Luke has apparently reinterpreted the incident: the demon "knows" Jesus,

and so it obediently leaves the man, "having done him no harm" (the qualifier is Lukan; contrast this with the demon's violence in Acts 19:16). In other words, a demon's "knowledge" of Jesus means that it has no choice but to be docile and obey. Cf. Luke 8:28, 33.

29. On the ever present danger to magicians when utilizing spirits, see chap. 3 n. 66.

30. The word *katakyrieuein* (with several other *kata-* words meaning to "overpower," "oppress," "coerce," etc.) sometimes had diabolic connotations; see esp. Acts 10:38. In the *Mandates* of the *Shepherd of Hermas, katakyrieuein* and *katadynasteuein* frequently refer to the devil's mastery of humans by means of wicked desire (12.2.3; 12.5.1-2); or vice versa, to Christians' mastery of the devil or of the evil desires and deeds that come from him (*Mandate* 5.1.1; 7.2; 9.10; 12.2.5; 12.4.7; 12.6.2; see esp. 12.6.4: "We shall master [*katakyrieuein*] him [i.e., the devil], and have power [*katischyein*] over all his deeds"). In the magical papyri, *katadein* and *katadesmeuein* ("to bind") designate a goal of magical procedures (see, e.g., *PGM* IV.380; V.313, 21, 26; VII.913), as does *katadouloun* (e.g., VII.967; IX.4, 9 [the latter two with *kathypotassein;* cf. Luke 10:17, 20]). Plutarch reports (*Isis and Osiris* 367D) that the Egyptians call Typhon "Seth," "which, being interpreted, means 'overmastering and compelling' *(hoper esti katadynasteuon ē katabiazomenon)'';* Seth-Typhon is invoked a number of times in the magical papyri. Finally, in the *Testament of Solomon,* the term *katargein* very frequently designates the "thwarting" of demons by a superior power (e.g., 2:4; 4:10, 12; 5:9, 13; etc.).

31. Cf. *Jubilees* 10:7-9; also see above, chap. 2, n. 14.

32. See n. 25 above. Because of this ability to compel a response, the gods were thought to hate or fear magicians; in Lucan's gruesome account of the activities of the witch Erictho, for example, it is said that "as soon as they hear her voice uttering a magical prayer, the gods grant her every kind of horror; they are afraid to hear the second spell" (*Pharsalia* 6.507; trans. G. Luck, *Arcana Mundi,* 197).

33. *GMPT,* trans. W. C. Grese, 31.

34. Cf. *PGM* IV.2060-66 (quoted in n. 21 above): the spirit of the dead person is adjured to "come to" the magician to perform an act of service.

35. Jesus' tolerance of the use of his name in Luke 9:49-50 (parallel Mark 9:38-40) seems to conflict with the intolerance implicit in Acts 19:13-16. But several observations suggest that Luke perceived the two situations as entirely different, and so not in contradiction. In taking over the incident from Mark, Luke has: (1) changed John's statement (Mark 9:38) that they "were not following us" *(ouk ēkolouthei hēmin)* to "he does not follow with us" *(ouk akolouthei meth' hēmōn);* (2) in the phrase just quoted, changed the tense of "follow" from imperfect to present; (3) omitted the explanatory statement in Mark 9:39; and (4) changed the pronouns in Mark 9:40 from the first-to the second-person plural. Together these alterations shift the focus of the interchange from the relationship between the one who does not follow *and Jesus* to the relationship between the former *and the apostles.* Luke's wording thus leaves open the possibility that he regarded the one casting out demons as himself a believer, not a part of the apostles' immediate group

but not hostile to it either. Luke may have seen here an allusion to the Eldad and Modad incident in Num. 11:27-29 (see above, chap. 2 nn. 43–44; n.b. also the parallelism between Luke 9:48-49 and 10:16-17). In the Numbers passage, Joshua tells Moses to forbid *(kōlyein)* Eldad and Modad to prophesy, since although they "were among those registered" (v. 26), they had not gone with the others out to the tent. Moses denied Joshua's request, and even approved of Eldad's and Modad's action. Luke may well have reinterpreted the Markan material in light of the Numbers passage, so that "the one who does not follow with us" is regarded as authorized to do what he does, though he follows with a different group. The appointment of the seventy(-two) a few verses later and their remarkable success at casting out demons in Jesus' name then demonstrate the validity of the principle just established, since the seventy(-two) do not "follow with" the apostles, either. For a slightly different treatment (with discussion of secondary literature) see Klein, "Synkretismus," 59–61 n. 107.

36. On the burning of books in antiquity, see A. S. Pease, "Notes on Book-Burning," in *Munera Studiosa,* ed. M. H. Shepherd and S. E. Johnson (Cambridge, Mass.: Episcopal Theological School, 1946), 145–60. Richard Oster *(A Historical Commentary on the Missionary Success Stories in Acts 19:11-40* [Ann Arbor, Mich: University Microfilms, 1974], 62) points out that in nearly all other incidents of book-burning from the Greco-Roman period, the books were forcibly seized, whereas in Acts they are brought forward as "fruits of repentance."

37. Cf. Origen *Against Celsus* 1.60. Origen claimed that at Jesus' birth the power of the demons on which the Magi relied suddenly vanished, and so the magicians' efforts to use their magical arts failed. The magicians went to discover the reason for their impotence: "And they guessed that the man foretold as coming with the star had arrived; and as they had already found that he was superior to all daemons and the beings that usually appeared to them and caused certain magical effects, they wanted to worship him" *(Origen: Contra Celsum* trans. H. Chadwick [Cambridge: Cambridge Univ. Press, 1965], 54; cf. Ignatius *Ephesians* 19.3).

38. Cf. Stählin, *Apostelgeschichte,* 257; Conzelmann, *Theology,* 219, 229. The word *anaggellein* ("report, disclose") does not occur in connection with confession or repentance elsewhere in the New Testament; see ibid., 219. Luke usually uses *exomologein* to refer to moments of praise, and not to repentance, but cf. Mark 1:5 (parallel Matt 3:6), where the people "confess" their sins in connection with John's "baptism of repentance." In *2 Clement* 8.3, *exomologein* is synonymous with *metanoein.*

39. Cf. Acts 5:13-14, where, however, the larger crowd magnifying the apostles (RSV: "holding them in high honor") seems to be distinguished from those who actually converted.

40. See, e.g., Schneider, *Apostelgeschichte* 2:270–71; Bauernfeind, *Apostelgeschichte,* 232; Haenchen, *Acts,* 567; Marshall, *Acts,* 312; Klein, "Synkretismus," 78–79.

41. C. F. D. Moule *(An Idiom Book of New Testament Greek* [Cambridge: Cambridge Univ., 1959], 99) writes, "The ruling consideration in interpreting

participles is that they express something which is dependent on the main verb, or a pendant to it; and one is sometimes given a clue to the interpretation of a participle not by its own tense but by the main verb, or the context in general." Consistent with Moule's observation, in general Luke seems to have chosen the perfect participle of *pisteuein* to indicate merely that the act of "believing" was antecedent to that of action expressed by a principal verb in a past tense (but with no thought of the absolute duration of the interval). In Acts 15:5 the principal verb is *exanestēsan;* 16:34: *parethēken* and *ēgalliasato;* 18:27: *sunebaleto;* 19:18: *ērchonto;* 21:25: *epesteilamen.* Cf. Luke 8:46; Acts 4:34; and 13:12, where the perfect participles of other verbs besides *pisteuein* quite clearly designate action immediately prior to or perhaps (in the case of Luke 8:46) simultaneous with the action designated by the principal verb in a past tense. In Acts 21:20 (where the perfect participle occurs apart from a principal verb in a past tense) it is apparently necessary to show that the persons assembled are not at that moment converting (a meaning which the aorist participle would allow though not require), but rather that they had already believed and yet continued to be zealous for the law. On the interpretation of participles, see also E. De Witt Burton, *Syntax of the Moods and Tenses in New Testament Greek,* 4th ed. (Chicago: Univ. of Chicago Press, 1900), §§154—56.

42. Kodell ("The Word of God Grew") argues persuasively that Luke's odd expression "the word of God (of the Lord) grew" was intended to describe the numerical expansion of the church. Kodell concludes (518–19), "this is not Luke's principal meaning for *ho logos tou theou* and he does not intend by his usage to obscure the more traditional senses of the term. But in the carefully constructed summaries at Acts 6,7; 12,24; 19,20, Luke overworks a traditional Christian term to bind together important theological themes." These themes, Kodell has argued, include especially the OT promises of the growth and expansion of the covenant people of God, and the notion of the "word-as-seed" (from the parable of the sower).

43. This is pointed out by Klein, "Synkretismus," 78 n. 193.

44. Cf. Justin Martyr *1 Apology* 1.14: "We warn you in advance to be careful, lest the demons whom we have attacked should deceive you and prevent your completely grasping and understanding what we say. For they struggle to have you as their slaves and servants, and now by manifestations in dreams, now by magic tricks, they get hold of all who do not struggle to their utmost for their own salvation—as we do who, after being persuaded by the Word *(meta to tō logō peisthēnai),* renounced them and now follow the only unbegotten God through his Son. Those who once rejoiced in fornication now delight in continence alone; those who made use of magic arts *(magikai technai)* have dedicated themselves to the good and unbegotten God." (*Early Christian Fathers,* trans. C. C. Richardson [New York: Macmillan, 1970], 249).

45. See n. 42 above.

46. Cf. Minear, "Dear Theo," 139. The summary reports and the preceding crises include the following: 5:14 follows the apostasy of Ananias and Sapphira; 6:7 follows the dispute between the Hellenists and the Hebrews; 9:31 follows the persecution by Saul, who was overcome by the Lord; 11:21

follows a reference to the persecution that arose over Stephen; 12:24 follows the persecution by Herod; 16:5 follows a reference to Paul's circumcision of Timothy and to the promulgation of the apostolic decree throughout the cities of Asia Minor. (Is this last instance an exception to the pattern? Or is Luke using the reference to church growth to minimize the problem of dissension known to have accompanied these developments?)

47. Recall, however, that in the Simon Magus account Luke does seem to presuppose differences in the accompanying behavior and attitude of the two types of wonder-worker: "magicians" exalt themselves and think that authority can be purchased; Christians bring attention not to themselves but to the word, and recognize that money cannot buy divine authority.

CONCLUSION

1. For evidence that Luke knew of accusations of magic and false prophecy made against Jesus and his followers, see the introduction n. 4.

2. On Luke's understanding of the Samaritans, see Jacob Jervell, *Luke and the People of God: A New Look at Luke-Acts* (Minneapolis: Augsburg Publishing House, 1972), 113–32, esp. 118 ("By placing the Samaritan mission in Chapter 8, that is, prior to the pericope on the Gentiles, Luke shows that the Samaritans were not considered Gentiles"), and 122. As noted above (chap. 3 n. 32), there is evidence for widespread anticipation in the first century of the rise of specifically Samaritan false prophets. Perhaps this expectation was the result of the activity of the historical Simon (as Morton Smith contends), or perhaps it was rather the case that Luke relied on this (independent) expectation to facilitate proper identification of Simon by his readers. In either case, Luke's portrayal of Simon in such stereotyped terms suggests that even if the latter was not a Jew, Luke regarded him as representing the same kind of opposition to God's purposes as was thought to be exemplified by Jewish false prophets.

3. See above, chap. 4 n. 34.

4 Minear, "Dear Theo," 134–35. Minear refers to Frank Kermode, *The Sense of An Ending* (London: Oxford University Press, 1967), chap. 1.

5. This suggestion is consistent with the recent findings on Lukan eschatology of Carroll, *Response to the End of History* (see above, chap. 3 n. 30). Carroll argues that Luke incorporates parousia delay into his account, not to oppose expectation of an imminent End, but to undergird it.

6. See above, chap. 5 nn. 3, 18–22, 30.

7. Cf. Mark 5:1-20; Bonner, "The Technique of Exorcism," 44 n. 45.

8. See chap. 1 n. 30.

9. Cf. Acts 16:16, where Luke exhibits familiarity with "spirits of divination" *(pneuma pythona);* on this expression see Aune, *Prophecy in Early Christianity,* 40; also W. Foerster, "python," *TDNT* 6:917-20. Foerster writes that "Ac. 16:16 tells us that the girl was a soothsayer-ventriloquist and that she thus stood in relation to the demonic."

SCRIPTURE AND ANCIENT SOURCE INDEX

OLD TESTAMENT

161

NEW TESTAMENT

APOCRYPHA AND PSEUDEPIGRAPHA

OTHER ANCIENT JEWISH LITERATURE

EARLY CHRISTIAN LITERATURE

OTHER ANCIENT AUTHORS

Hippocrates
On the Sacred Disease
2.1-5   117 n.6

Isocrates
4.119   154 n.10

Juvenal
Satire
6.546   145 n.39

Lucan
Pharsalia
6.507   157 n.32

Lucian
The Cock
14   152 n.29

Lover of Lies
15   145 n.39
16   145 n.39, 155 n.22
29   155 n.25
31   152-53 n.3

Timon
22   152 n.29

Papyri Graecae Magicae
I.1ff.   120 n.30
I.115   132 n.32
I.225   155 n.21
I.248   156 n.25
I.305-14   155 n.22
II.48   156 n.25
II.145   156 n.25
III.494-501   94
III.494-611   94
III.550   94
IV.345-7   155 n.22
IV.380   157 n.30
IV.396-7   155 n.22
IV.1227-64   132 n.32, 146 n.44,
                         151 n.22
IV.1233   156 n.26
IV.1390-495   156 n.25
IV.1708-14   155 n.22
IV.1950   156 n.25
IV.2060-6   155 n.21, 157 n.34
IV.2506-7   148 n.66
IV.2912   155 n.22
IV.3007-86   132 n.32
IV.3019-20   155 n.22, 156 n.26
IV.3065-8   155 n.22

IV.3068-74   155 n.22
IV.3075-78   155 n.22
V.313   157 n.30
V.321   157 n.30
V.326   157 n.30
VII.913   157 n.30
VII.967   157 n.30
IX.4   157 n.30
IX.9   157 n.30
XIII.736-741   153 n.3
XIII.795-800   148 n.66
LXXXV.1-6   132 n.32

Philostratus
Life of Apollonius
1.2   117 n.7
1.32   117 n.7
3.38   156 n.25
4.35   152 n.3
7.39   145 n.39
8.7   145 n.39

Plato
Laws
10.909B   116 n.1
909A, B   145 n.39
933A   145 n.39

Republic
364E   153 n.3

Pliny
Natural History
28.2.6   117 n.8
28.4.14   153 n.3
30.1   116 n.2
30.1-4   116 n.2
30.2.8-11   117 n.8

Plutarch
Alexander
2.5   152 n.3

Moralia (Isis and Osiris)
367D   157 n.30
Moralia (Table-Talk)
706E   153 n.3, 154–55
                         n.19

Sophocles
Oedipus Tyrannus
387   117 n.6

Thucydides
8.100   154 n.10

INDEX OF MODERN AUTHORS

Wettstein, J. J., 153 n.3
White, L. J., 125 n.102
Wikenhauser, A., 145 n.35, 37
Wilhelms, E., 156 n.26
Wilson, B., 121 n.36
Wilson, R. M., 140 nn.2, 4

Wintermute, O. S., 119 n.26
Wünsch, R., 156 n.26

Yarbro Collins, A., 128 n.8, 135 n.54, 136
    nn.54, 57; 139 n.72, 144 n.31
Yaure, L., 150 n.18

SUBJECT INDEX